EMBODIED AVATARS

SEXUAL CULTURES

GENERAL EDITORS: Ann Pellegrini, Tavia Nyong'o, and Joshua Chambers-Letson

FOUNDING EDITORS: José Esteban Muñoz and Ann Pellegrini

TITLES IN THE SERIES INCLUDE

Cruising Utopia: The Then and There of Queer Futurity
José Esteban Muñoz

Another Country: Queer Anti-Urbanism
Scott Herring

Extravagant Abjection: Blackness, Power, and Sexuality in the African American Literary Imagination
Darieck Scott

Relocations: Queer Suburban Imaginaries
Karen Tongson

Beyond the Nation: Diasporic Filipino Literature and Queer Reading
Martin Joseph Ponce

Single: Arguments for the Uncoupled
Michael Cobb

Brown Boys and Rice Queens: Spellbinding Performance in the Asias
Eng-Beng Lim

Transforming Citizenships: Transgender Articulations of the Law
Isaac West

The Delectable Negro: Human Consumption and Homoeroticism within U.S. Slave Culture
Vincent Woodard, Edited by Justin A. Joyce and Dwight A. McBride

Sexual Futures, Queer Gestures and Other Latina Longings
Juana María Rodríguez

Sensational Flesh: Race, Power, and Masochism
Amber Jamilla Musser

The Exquisite Corpse of Asian America: Biopolitics, Biosociality, and Posthuman Ecologies
Rachel C. Lee

Not Gay: Sex between Straight White Men
Jane Ward

Embodied Avatars: Genealogies of Black Feminist Art and Performance
Uri McMillan

For a complete list of books in the series, see www.nyupress.org.

Embodied Avatars

Genealogies of Black Feminist Art and Performance

Uri McMillan

NEW YORK UNIVERSITY PRESS

New York and London

NEW YORK UNIVERSITY PRESS
New York and London
www.nyupress.org

References to Internet websites (URLs) were accurate at the time of writing.
Neither the author nor New York University Press is responsible for URLs that may have
expired or changed since the manuscript was prepared.

ISBN: 978-1-4798-0211-1 (hardback)
ISBN: 978-1-4798-5247-5 (paperback)

For Library of Congress Cataloging-in-Publication data, please contact the
Library of Congress.

New York University Press books are printed on acid-free paper, and their binding materials
are chosen for strength and durability. We strive to use environmentally responsible suppli-
ers and materials to the greatest extent possible in publishing our books.

Manufactured in the United States of America

10 9 8 7 6 5 4 3 2 1

Also available as an ebook

To Ariel,

My far-flung friends,

and ad infinitum to Simone

CONTENTS

LIST OF ILLUSTRATIONS

ACKNOWLEDGMENTS

Performance art, despite appearances, is never a solo effort. As scholars of performance know, it is activated by the palpable, ecstatic tension between artist and audience, who are challenged and often permanently changed by the transaction, long after the last word has been spoken, the lights have come up, and the performance itself has vanished into molecules of air. Similarly, though the writing of this book has often been a drudgingly solitary affair, one that has frequently required me to go underground for numbingly long stretches of time, it has never been a strictly solo one. It is with boundless gratitude I thank my infectiously enthusiastic networks of mentors, colleagues, friends, and family— biological and otherwise—who often checked on me via phone calls, Facebook, and persistent texts. They graciously listened to me vent in the brief breaks when I emerged for fresh air; encouraged me when I felt defeated by minor (and major) writing setbacks; read and commented on drafts of what now appears in these pages; were patient with my bouts of professorial absentmindedness; and often made me laugh with top-shelf academic shade. It is my hope the words below will suffice in conveying my appreciation.

Thanks to the small but formidable armada that offered sage advice about graduate school, lent me money to take the GRE, left brochures for fellowships on my desk at work, and did what they could to help me land on my feet: professors Lynne Huffer, Betty Joseph, Colleen Lamos, and Robert Patten; Roland Smith and Gloria Bean of the Mellon-Mays Undergraduate Fellowship; and Terry Shepard and Roberta Kelley of the Vice President for Public Affairs Office. Lynne Huffer, in particular, was a generous mentor, a tireless advocate, and a fierce model of how to marry intellectual labor and activist work. She continues to inspire me.

During my graduate studies at Yale University, professors in the American Studies program and the Department of African American Studies trained me in interdisciplinary work, nurtured my budding research interests, and helped shape and develop my ideas into coherence. It is a debt I will never be able to properly repay. The indomitable Alondra Nelson diligently served as my academic advisor my first years of graduate school; I am eternally grateful for the time and patience she took, as an overtaxed junior scholar, in nurturing my incipient and diverse theoretical interests in their earliest incarnations. Matthew Frye Jacobson first taught me the contours of, and rich possibilities inherent in, the discipline of American Studies and has always been willing to offer his support and wise counsel; thank you. Laura Wexler imparted care and rigor in approaching photography and visual culture writ large, especially through her stewardship of the Photographic Memory Workshop; I thank her for intellectual generosity.

This book is deeply shaped by the three juggernauts who each offered copious attention and critical acumen at various points in its development: thank you, Hazel V. Carby for pushing me to articulate what's at stake in this project and imparting the critical import of black cultural studies; Kellie Jones for her tutelage in feminist performance art and black aesthetics; and, finally, to my chair, Joseph Roach, for teaching me how performances reverberate (and matter) long after they're done. I offer this book as a small offering of how much you each have taught me.

My friends in graduate school, scattered across various cohorts and departments, made New Haven a more bearable place during my time there. I appreciate the many conversations had over long leisurely lunches at Lalibella's or a Thai lunch buffet on Chapel Street (in the old days, many an Af-Am'er or AmStud'er survived off those lunches) and those who practiced diasporic dance moves (ahem) at the parties held at 251 Greene Street; and, after I decamped (more like ran) to New York, those who graciously agreed to let me sleep on their couches when I was in town to TA, get library books from Sterling, or meet with members of my committee. Many thanks to Amina El-Annan, Hasani Baharanyi, Kimberly J. Brown, Tiffani Brown, Lucia Cantero, Amanda Ciafone, Kaysha Corinealdi, Stephanie Greenlea, Sarah Haley, Tisha Hooks, Brandi Hughes, Nicole Nicolette Ivy, Chris Johnson, Simeon Man, Courtney J. Martin, Monica Martinez, Carlos Miranda, A. Naomi Paik, Shana Redmond, Petra Richterova, Van Truong, Sam Vong, Calvin Warren, and Suzie Woo. I also acknowledge the women who collectively and tenaciously helped graduate students of color like myself survive, stay, and flourish: Yvette Bernard, Pat Cabral, Liza Cariaga-Lo, Janet Giarratano, and Geneva Melvin.

Special thanks to Lyndon Gill. Meeting in New York, New Haven, and Cambridge, during our respective first years of graduate school, I appreciate him for his friendship, vivacity, Erykah Badu fandom, and for letting me tag along for his fieldwork adventures. I thank him in pushing me in many unforeseen directions, personal and otherwise.

Beyond institutional affiliations, I have had the luck of several mentors who have supported the project at different stages of its development and offered keen professional advice when I have needed it. First among those is Daphne Brooks. She generously read the entire manuscript in its earliest stages, as an outside reader, and offered meticulous, incisive, and vigorous remarks; I thank her for her personal support all these years, creative ways to approach the black performance archive, and recent advice to promptly get a dog. E. Patrick Johnson has been unwavering in his encouragement of my professional and personal growth, since I was a graduate student; thank you. Mark Anthony Neal is always a welcoming presence and has also been a supporter from the beginning; I'm glad to share a press (and an editor) with him now. Finally, I had the fortitude to meet José Esteban Muñoz very early in my graduate career and to take advantage of his intellectual and personal largesse over the years, all of which I am tremendously grateful for; his spirit undeniably imbues these pages.

During my three years in New York, I began writing about contemporary black art, which has shaped a large part of this book's trajectory. I thank the curators at the Studio Museum of Harlem in those days—Naomi Beckwith, Christine Y. Kim, and especially Thomas J. Lax—not simply for repeated opportunities to write about brilliant artists but also for their individual encouragement of my own work over the years.

It is impossible not to invoke my years living in the harsh glittering chaos of New York without honoring Dwayne Nash. I thank him for listening to innumerable drafts written in Butler Library at Columbia University when we lived together; sharing his world, travels, and family with me; and for his continued friendship and love.

I appreciate the efforts of the staff and faculty in Gender Studies and Ethnic Studies, as well as other colleagues, during my tenure as a Mellon post-doctoral fellow at Lewis and Clark College in Portland, Oregon; they include Andrew Bernstein, Isabelle DeMarte, Reiko Hillyer, Nancy Hugg, Tim Mechlinski, and Elliot Young.

I have benefitted from a host of intellectual communities over the years. I thank Alex Cornelius, Besenia Rodriguez, and Kelly Wise of the Institute for the Recruitment of Teachers (IRT) at Philips Academy for their work in getting me (and my peers) into graduate school. Likewise, kudos are due to the tremendous work of the Mellon-Mays Undergraduate Fellowship program, particularly its staff, in aiding the professional success of the professoriate of color; thanks to Emma Taati and Cally Waite. And shout-out to the various friends I have made over the years through both organizations, in particular Vanessa Agard-Jones, Bimbola Akinbola, Janaka Bowman-Lewis, Sabine Cadeau, andré carrington, Julius Fleming, Alisha Gaines, Hanna Garth, Ernest Gibson, Miles Grier, Alexis Gumbs, Jesús Hernández, Jessica Marie Johnson, Treva Lindsey, Stuart Ortiz, Dixa Ramirez, Tyler Jackson Rogers, Jonathan Rosa, Kyera Singleton, Elizabeth Todd-Breland, and Dennis Tyler. The Woodrow Wilson Foundation, Ford Foundation, Beinecke Rare Book and Manuscript Library, Social Science Research Council, and Graduate School of Arts and Sciences all supported my studies while I was at Yale and I am most appreciative. Thank you to the dynamic members of the Black Performance Theory (BPT) working group for their collective vitality and camaraderie and to Tavia Nyong'o for inviting me to become a member. I am grateful to the Woodrow Wilson Foundation for a Career Enhancement Grant for Junior Faculty that enabled me to attend to a year of uninterrupted writing, and my mentor, the dynamo Koritha Mitchell, for her deep commitment to my success during the final push. Finally, in addition to those already named, I thank friends and mentors in the field, including Gershun Avilez, Rizvana Bradley, David Brody, Soyica Diggs Colbert, Roderick Ferguson, Douglass A. Jones Jr., Monica L. Miller, Christine Mok, Joan Morgan, C. Riley Snorton, Jennifer Tyburczy, Shane Vogel, Isaiah Wooden, and Cindy Wu.

I wrote this book while an assistant professor at the University of California, Los Angeles, in the Department of English, the Department of Gender Studies, and the Department of African American Studies; I collectively thank my colleagues in all three for welcoming me into the fold. I owe particular gratitude to my wonderful department chair, Ali Behdad, who, since my arrival, has been a tireless advocate; I thank him for all he has done on my behalf. I also thank Friends of English at UCLA for their generous support. I extend appreciation to the chairs of my joint departments, past and present, for their mutual support and enthusiasm; thank you, Cheryl Harris, Robin D. G. Kelley, Elizabeth Marchant, and Jenny Sharpe. Likewise, Chris Littleton, the vice provost for faculty diversity and development, has been a fervent supporter of my research as well. The English Department staff is indefatigable and has graciously enabled my professional work to run more smoothly; thank you, Janet Bishop, Jeanette Gilkinson, Nicole Liang, Alanna Mori, Caleb "Q" Na, and Bronson Tran. I thank grad student Christina Richieri Griffin, who swiftly pursued research materials for chapter 2 (as well as my Disability Narratives course), and the faculty in Disability Studies—especially Victoria Marks and Helen Deutsch—for providing the necessary funds to hire her as a researcher. My students, from Yale to UCLA, have consistently been an enthusiastic, engaging bunch. Likewise, the sharp-as-tacks graduate students in my fall 2014 Queer of Color Critique seminar remind me of why I went to graduate school in the first place.

Special thanks to Jennifer DeVere Brody and Jacqueline Goldsby who graciously read the entire revised manuscript and offered critical tough love. I have also been fortunate to have a number of excellent readers in addition to several of the people listed above. Kadji Amin, Katie Brewer Ball, Anurima Banerjee, Victor Bascara, Stephanie Batiste, Hershini Bhana, Jayna Brown, Keith Camacho, Sarah Jane Cervenak, Elizabeth Maddock Dillon, Freda Fair, Ramzi Fawaz, Megan Francis, Yogita Goyal, David Hernandez, Grace Hong, Zakiyah Iman Jackson, Rachel Lee, Arthur Little, David Lobenstine, Paige McGinley, Amber Musser, Steven Nelson, Diana Paulin, Roy Pérez, Laurence Ralph, Michael Ralph, Leah Wright Rigueur, Ramón Rivera-Servera, Jennifer Row, Elizabeth Son, Jordan Stein, Kyla Wazana Tompkins, Alexandra Vazquez, Victor Viesca, Richard Yarborough, Damon Young, and Harvey Young have all encountered portions of this text in various stages and offered their enthusiasm and careful advice (which includes, in Alex's words, to "dive into the fog of Fred Moten").

Thanks to the anonymous readers for Duke University Press and New York University Press. I thank my editor at NYU Press, Eric Zinner, for his early enthusiasm for the manuscript and his persistent support through its many developments. Dorothea Halliday, Ciara McLaughlin, and Alicia Nadkarni at NYU Press have also been great to work with. I am honored and humbled to have this book as part of the formidable Sexual Cultures series; thank you to the series editors, past and present: Josh Chambers-Letson, José Esteban Muñoz, Tavia Nyong'o, and Ann Pelligrini. Finally, I thank my NYU Press–mates Robin Bernstein, Dana Luciano, Kyla Wazana Tompkins, and Karen Tongson for being incredibly supportive along the way.

I have presented portions of my research at the following institutions and organizations: the American Studies Association, the American Society for Theatre Research, the Association for Theatre in Higher Education, the Center for Feminist Research at the University of Southern California, the Human Resources Gallery, the Departments of Art and Gender Studies at Lewis and Clark College, the Modern Language Association, the Department of Performance Studies at Northwestern University, Performance Studies International, Pomona College, the Department of English at the University of California at Riverside, the University of Wisconsin at Madison, Wesleyan University, Williamette University, and the American Studies Program and Women's, Gender, and Sexuality Studies Program at Yale University. I am grateful to my hosts, colleagues, and audiences for their attention and engagement in all of these settings.

A genealogy of black performance art across centuries would be vastly incomplete without the many visual proofs of its vitality. For granting reproduction requests, fielding my inquiries, and adjusting resolutions, I graciously thank John P. Bowles; the archivists at the Adrian Piper Research Archive (APRA) in Berlin; Rashida Bumbray; Mel D. Cole; Lisa Darms, Fales Library, New York University; Robert Delap, New-York Historical Society; Daria Dorosh, one of the A.I.R. Gallery's original members, for captions help; Jessica Marie Johnson; Clinton Lam, Center for Digital Humanities, UCLA; Simone Leigh; Julie Lohnes, formerly of the A.I.R. Gallery; Matthew Lyons, The Kitchen, Inc.; JoAnne Mc-Farland, interim director, A.I.R. Gallery; Frank William Miller Jr.; Narcissister; Virginia Mokslaveskas, Getty Research Institute; and Cherise Smith. In addition, I thank the archivists and library staff at the various research collections I obtained materials from, including: the Charles

E. Young Research Library at UCLA; Fales Library, New York University; Camille Billops and James Hatch of the Hatch-Billops Collection; the Museum of Modern Art (MoMA); and the Smithsonian Archives of American Art.

I was very lucky, in moving to Los Angeles, to be welcomed into a broader community of academics who have not only lovingly supported my work, but also my tortoise-slow transition to SoCal life and its attendant pleasures and perils (hello, freeways). *Muchísimas gracias* to Stephanie Batiste, Jayna Brown, Jennifer DeClue, Vanessa Díaz, Jennifer Doyle, Erica Edwards, Aisha Finch, James Ford, Kwanda Ford, Macarena Gómez-Barris, Kai Green, Jack Halberstam, Sarah Haley, Lucas Hildebrand, Grace Hong, Ren-Yo Hwang, Kara Keeling, Shana Redmond, Nayan Shah, Kyla Wazana Tompkins, Karen Tongson, Deb Vargas, and Hentyle Yapp.

I thank Jih-Fei Cheng for his keen sensitivity, his effusive friendship, and sartorial panache (takes one to know one). Carlos Sandoval de León, with his relentless optimism, reminds me to stop, breathe, and enjoy life at critical moments. Megan Ming Francis, an anchor in my life for almost fifteen years now: thank you for your abundant laughter, fierce friendship, (and raucous three-way text conversations with Leah Wright Rigueur). Karen Jaime is my favorite Dominican dandy; I am looking forward to summers in New York and the horizon of friendship #whilst. I am indebted to Simone Leigh, who reminds me not to let my *New Yorker* subscription lapse; I treasure her persistent check-ins; dispatches from far-flung places, from Dakar to Marfa; and always supporting me and the little-book-that-could these past few years. Cassandra Lord, my compatriot in Toronto, is my imaginary big sister; thank you for always being there. I thank the ever-witty Hoang Nguyen (and his counterpart Dredge Kang) for his vibrant presence, laughter, and good taste in food. Bianca Murillo keeps me honest (and productive). Roy Pérez is usually the first person I call when I have a crisis; I thank him for his deep well of compassion and the proper uses of the semicolon. Shanté Paradigm Smalls—thank you for friendship, laughter, and devastating shade.

My parents, Bruce and Shirley McMillan, are undoubtedly perplexed by how two chemistry majors bore a super-humanities freak such as myself (the clotheshorse part, however, they get). I thank them and my younger siblings—Ian, Kai, and Ariel—for going along for the ride, even when it hasn't always been clear where I am going. My maternal grandmother, Blessing Adelaide Shockley Anderson, passed away while I was in graduate school, but would undoubtedly be proud of this book. Meanwhile, my firecracker goddaughter Shania is indeed a performance artist if there ever was one; I appreciate her love as well as that of Berneda Brothers and Brenda Nash.

Last, but certainly not least, thanks to Danny Andrews, who one evening shrewdly reimagined this book for me and made me believe in its fecund possibilities. Across multiple time zones, from Los Angeles to Washington, D.C., and now Abu Dhabi, I thank him for believing in me when I often did not, his patience, his eagerness, and above all, his friendship.

Introduction

Performing Objects

Let's begin with an elegant avatar. A black woman wears a tiara, elbow-length white gloves, and a dress made entirely of white gloves. A sash across her bodice says "bourgeoise." A white object with a knotted handle rests on the floor, but beyond that, the almost uniformly blank background of the photograph in which this woman appears gives no indication of where she is, what she is doing, or why she is wearing this elaborate outfit, which seems suited for a pageant. And perhaps most ambiguous is her expression: lipstick-lined mouth agape, bulging throat muscles suggesting she is in mid-yell, eyes intense and glowing. Her refined and opulent attire appears at odds with the fierce, ecstatic look on her face, the disjuncture indicating that this outfit may indeed be a costume. Yet, without any particulars, one thing is clear: this woman seems to be thoroughly enjoying herself.

This image captures Mlle. Bourgeoise Noire, in the midst of one of her unruly and provocative performances. Ms. Noire is the avatar of conceptual artist Lorraine O'Grady. The playful purpose of this disruptive agit-prop persona—"French for Miss Black Middle-Class," as O'Grady describes her—is to interrupt art gallery openings. Ms. Noire, according to her fantastically hyperbolic autobiography, "won her first title in 1955," and after decades of "maintaining a lady-like silence," on the occasion of the "Silver Jubilee of her coronation in Cayenne," she deigned to celebrate by "invading the New York art world."[1]

The debut of O'Grady's irate debutante came at the opening-night benefit for the *Outlaw Aesthetics* show on June 5, 1980, at Just Above Midtown, the first gallery in New York dedicated to regularly exhibiting the work of cutting-edge artists of color, especially black artists.[2] O'Grady utilized her rebellious doppelganger as a conduit through which to express her disdain toward the overly safe work of fellow black artists she had seen at the opening of the *Afro-American Abstraction* show at P.S.1 four months earlier. That disdain followed her initial joy at the masses in attendance—the "galleries and corridors were filled with black people who all looked like me, people who were interested in advanced art, whose faces reflected a kind of awareness that excited me"—which soon shifted to utter despondency. "By the time I left, I was disappointed because I felt that the art on exhibit, as opposed to the people, had been too cautious—that it had been art with white gloves on." Eager to respond, albeit artistically, to the artists in the P.S.1 show, O'Grady had an epiphany when walking across an "incredibly filthy and druggy" pregentrified Union Square: a vision of herself "completely covered in white gloves. That's how my persona Mlle. Bourgeoise Noire was born."³

At Just Above Midtown, O'Grady staged her incendiary black performance art. Dressed in the elaborate gown, made with 180 pairs of white gloves, O'Grady whipped herself with a white cat-o'-nine-tails spiked with white chrysanthemums, and shouted at bemused gallery denizens turned spectators:

> THAT'S ENOUGH!
> No more boot-licking . .
> No more ass-kissing . . .
> No more buttering-up . . .
> No more posturing
> of super-ass . . . imilates . . .
> BLACK ART MUST TAKE MORE RISKS!!!

O'Grady's confrontational character—staged again in September 1981 at the New Museum exhibition *Personae*, a show of nine performance artists—became a potent physical critique, particularly of contemporary black artists' assimilationist aspirations to enter the mainstream and, as this performed poem implies, overwhelmingly white art market.⁴ The seemingly innocuous accouterments of this performed being, particularly the taut and pristine white gloves, became theatrical props symbolic of the aesthetic suffocation that black artists, and their "well behaved abstract art," voluntarily submitted to. O'Grady's satirical self-inflicted whipping was intended as a wake-up call to black artists, while her irate embodied double temporarily transformed the neutral white cube of the gallery into a black box—a kinetic theatrical experience. O'Grady exploited the great possibility of the avatar to transform herself into an art object. Wielding her body as a tabula rasa, O'Grady's eccentric performance art hinted at the corporeal risks black artists could take: not the abandonment of representational art, but rather an amalgamation of self, a fashioning of oneself as both the subject and object of art.

* * *

The term "performance art" usually refers to art that incorporates the "body as an object" to subvert cultural norms and explore social issues; a time-based medium, performance art's most potent, electrifying, and lasting challenge is its radical evaporation of the distinction between art object and artist, blurring the lines "between action, performance, and a work of art."[5] By focusing on performance art staged by black women, *Embodied Avatars* fiercely rebukes two standard art world assumptions: the perceived incommensurability of "black" and "avant-garde," and the marginalization of black female artists within our conceptions of feminist art.[6] As I explain below, I have positioned black women performers at its center for two reasons: both to trouble the focus on white female subjectivity that serves as an unofficial norm and to recognize that the initial prejudice the black art world cognoscenti expressed toward performance art was tied to the gender of its practitioners. I examine a set of performance works, starting in the early nineteenth century and stretching to the early twenty-first century. Across four case studies, I analyze a wide breadth of cultural materials—including freak show paraphernalia, slave narratives, and engravings in the nineteenth century; artists' writings, photographs, and video art in the twentieth century—to expand the scope of materials counted under the aegis of "performance art." I extend the historical timeline, in the conclusion, to consider bravura performances exacted in contemporary art, popular culture, and new media in the twenty-first century. In doing so, I construct a robust multicentury and multigenerational network of black performance art.[7]

The Eurocentric narrativization of performance art elides the presence of black artists as historical coconspirators. *Embodied Avatars* moves beyond these racially determined omissions to reveal how black performance art challenges the assumptions underlying what and whose work has traditionally counted as "performance art." The standard narrative, dominated by white male artists, and since the 1970s, by mostly white and American feminist artists, begins in early-twentieth-century Europe. If we trace performance art's origins to the influence of Italian Futurist manifestos and variety theater in the early twentieth century, we find a common cause: to unsettle painting's place as the dominant artistic medium and infuse art with a vitality that directly engaged (and often confronted) audiences.[8] Eventually, performance art surfaces in the United States in forms that further upend dominant artistic paradigms, for instance, the ordinary sounds recorded by musician John Cage starting in the late 1930s and the everyday movements of dancer Merce Cunningham in the early 1950s. Feminist performance art, at its zenith in the 1970s, adopted performance art's axiom of the body-in-motion as the objet d'art, but recalibrated it to address the specific concerns and life experiences of women, albeit mostly white women.[9]

More recently, scholars like Coco Fusco and Amelia Jones have both sought to eschew traditional historical renderings of performance art, grounding it in the ethnographic displays of non-European races, for instance, or the collapse of "distances between artist and artwork, artist and spectator" that arise from artists, especially feminist artists, enacting themselves "*as representation*."[10] They have even argued that the genre needs a new name. While I agree with the impetus behind their renamings, I find it useful to retain the term *performance art*—rather than *the other history of intercultural performance* (Fusco) or *body art* (Jones)—precisely to apply pressure on the assumed meanings of the term. How do we know what we know about performance art, particularly in *who* makes it and *what* counts as such? Part of this rhetorical move is to, again, question received histories of performance art. I am not, however, advocating a simple additive—a sprinkling, if you will—of black women into already existing discourses of feminist performance art and the larger category of performance art. Instead, by beginning this study in the touring antebellum spectacle of Joice Heth, the so-called "ancient negress," I construct a dynamic matrix of black performance art that begins prior to the mythic origins of performance art *and* expands its environs to include cunning acts of self-exhibition, and dangerous subterfuge, staged by black historical actors in the nineteenth century.

I focus, specifically, on black women in this book—as opposed to black performance artists, male and female alike—for two primary reasons, beyond their fascinating narratives. My intent is partly to counter *context* the stubborn focus on white female bodies that, too often, is the unacknowledged norm in feminist theories of the body. The writings of the late Toni Cade Bambara and Marxist feminist Hazel Carby in the 1970s and early 1980s are early forebears that articulated the importance of a feminist practice attuned to the specificities of black women's bodies and experiences. The former insisted that black women are subject to multiple dominant forces, not just whiteness and racism, but also "America or imperialism, depending on your viewpoint or your terror," while the latter cogently warned white feminists against writing black feminists' history, or "herstory," for them. In a discussion of slavery and embodiment, however, Bibi Bakare-Yusuf directly interrogates this persistent elision, when she writes, "I am talking about the body that is marked by racial, sexual, and class configurations. It is this body, this fleshy materiality, that seems to disappear from much of the current proliferations of discourses on the body."[11] Black women's performance work has deftly and unapologetically embraced the feminist axiom "the personal is political." This theme loudly resonates in, for instance, Howardena Pindell's exploration of family ancestry and satirical castigation of white feminists in her 1980 video art piece *Free, White, and 21*, discussed in chapter 4. These performances have also tangled with deep histories of objectification, particularly the memory of chattel slavery. And in some performances these twin imperatives occur simultaneously. Meanwhile, though men *do* appear as collaborators in the first half of the book— whether willingly (in the case of fugitive slave Ellen Craft's husband, William) or not (in the case of circus impresario P. T. Barnum)—I again turn my attention to how black women performers in the nineteenth century were interpreted against a different set of often gendered and racialized discourses, be it the cult of true womanhood or the visual iconographies used to substantiate biological racism. In sum, the ensemble of artful performances I analyze here illustrates both the aesthetic risks taken by performers not always recognized as such (or even as artists, *risks &* for that matter) as well as the literal danger, in some cases, of assuming *dangers* faux identities in the public sphere.

My focus on black women performers, moreover, acknowledges a perhaps inconvenient but nonetheless important truth: not only have the traditional gatekeepers of the art world been biased against performance art, but the black art community (itself subject to plenty of gatekeeping) historically has been biased against performance art as well. And that bias, at least initially, was tied to gender. The black art world's suspicion of performance art (and video art) in the early 1980s was partly due to its status as a noncommodity and a form not easily digested by middle- and upper-class audiences (black and white alike); yet, as Lowery Stokes Sims suggests, the resistance within the black art world was not only class based, but also implicitly gendered. In her words, if the "older guard of painters, sculptors, printmakers, and photographers" were leery of performance art as an ephemeral medium, the "overwhelmingly male focus of black American art" was slow to "accommodate an expressive form that is dominated by women."[12] Nevertheless, black women artists continued to adopt performance art for specific ends, be it autobiographical expression, or to bridge the gap between black communities and artistic experimentation, or as a manifestation of the long-useful strategy of "acting out." The efficacy and urgency of performance art practiced by black women artists continues today. As we will see below, the black women performers in this book repeatedly wield performance art—and their "ambiguous status" as both real persons and "theatrical representation[s]"—as an elastic means to create new racial and gender epistemologies.[13]

Yet the exclusion of black women artists from membership in the American avant-garde has resulted in a fraught relationship with it. For many twentieth-century artists, performance has served as a catalyst, a method of moving forward when they have reached impasses in their work. Hence, for those who populate the history of the avant-garde, those who lead the breaks with each successive field, "performance has been at the forefront of such an activity: an avant-avant garde."[14] Inclusion in the American avant-garde, though, has been selective, resulting in a lopsided distribution of the cultural prestige that attends it, frequently involving the exclusion of certain groups of artists, notably women and black Americans.[15] While artists in the vanguard have often been interested in a democratization of the avant-garde, the expansion of its membership has primarily been along lines of class, seldom gender, and hardly ever race and ethnicity.[16] "The avant-garde has nothing to do with black people," a member of the New York–based Heresies Feminist Collective famously told fellow member Lorraine O'Grady.[17] For the performers in this book, both black *and* women, this quagmire becomes even more pronounced. Though they (and their work) share qualities often attributed to the avant-garde—cutting edge, marginal, seamless moves across disciplines—their relationship to it is deeply vexed. This tension surfaces in the second half of the book, in particular, in the discussion of artists Adrian Piper and Howardena Pindell, who are explicitly *not* a part of esteemed groups of artists (sometimes white, other times black) perceived as avant-garde. Piper and Pindell both desired inclusion at different times, yet often found themselves at odds with these groups. In fact, as we will see, both struggled to be recognized simply as bona fide "artists." The historical constraints of the American avant-garde, furthermore, means the nineteenth-century figures in this book are not technically part of the avant-garde either, though I argue they staged daring performances that broke new ground in various ways. The black women performers in *Embodied Avatars*, despite this erasure, execute skilled and soignée performance art that intersects with Conceptualism, freak show dramaturgy, and the 170-year history of photography.

Objecthood

My central contention in this book is that objecthood provides a means for black subjects to become art objects. Wielding their bodies as pliable matter, the black women performers discussed herein repeatedly become objects, often in the form of simulated beings, or what I term "avatars." I call this process *performing objecthood*. Becoming objects, in what follows, proves to be a powerful tool for performing one's body, a "stylized repetition of acts" that rescripts how black female bodies move and are perceived by others.[18] Put differently, performing objecthood becomes an adroit method of circumventing prescribed limitations on black women in the public sphere while staging art and alterity in unforeseen places. Objecthood's putty-like attributes are manipulated by conceptual artist Adrian Piper in the early 1970s in her philosophical experiments in self-estrangement. Likewise, her contemporary Howardena Pindell deploys objecthood to perform multiple avatars of herself in the provocative *Free, White, and 21.* Meanwhile, in the mid-1830s, elderly and partially paralyzed Joice Heth uses objecthood to dramatically transform herself into a maternal icon of American national memory. And, a little over a decade later, fugitive slave Ellen Craft employs its slippery properties to enact a daring escape (for her and her husband, William) in the guise of a disabled white gentleman. Tracing this practice of self-objectification—one that provides the possibility for (though never the guarantee of) an emancipated subjectivity—I am concerned with the personal and artistic risks incumbent in becoming and/or performing as an object. Put simply, what are the pleasures and perils of objecthood?

Objecthood—a charged concept in postcolonial studies, black feminism, and art history—is reconfigured here as a specific strategy of black women performers. In dialogue with postcolonial treatises on the nefarious effects of colonization,[19] Hortense Spillers' theorization of black subjectivity in the New World, and Michael Fried's spirited polemic on the overt theatricality of minimalist art, my notion of performing objecthood indexes what Saidiya V. Hartman has described as the challenges in "rethinking the relation of performance and agency" in black history. Put another way, blackness and performance have, historically, existed via a violent tethering, built upon often theatrical spectacles of torment that reinforced relationships defined by dominance.[20] The muddying of the line between free will and force makes it particularly difficult to discern agency, commonly understood as the intentional choices made by humans alone or in collaboration with others.[21] Consequently, black performance art's usage of the black body as its artistic medium is especially loaded when confronting a historical legacy of objectification and the generations of slaves who did not legally own the bodies they acted with.[22] Spillers extends a similar logic to chattel slavery and the violent denial of personhood, especially to black women. She demarcates a difference between the *body* and the *flesh.* The former is the apotheosis of a liberated subject-position, while the latter is a total objectification, an "absence *from* a subject position," a forceful reduction of the body "to a thing, becoming *being for* the captor." For black women, this denial of will (coupled with other violations) is often so severe that it excludes them completely from female subjectivity.[23] Spillers strongly suggests that to be reduced to an object (or thing) is the ultimate debasement, a denial of subjectivity. Thus, to exist as an object is to be located toward the very bottom of the "great chain of being," with humans poised at the top and inanimate objects and nonhuman animals located at the bottom. This paradoxical blending—of human, object, animal—produces what Mel Y. Chen calls an "abject object": "a subject aware of its abjection; a clashing embodiment of dignity as well as of shame."[24] Blackness itself, in this narrative, is delineated and defined by such abjection, a history of grappling with defeat and terror.[25]

In this book, I argue for rescrambling the dichotomy between objectified bodies or embodied subjects by reimagining objecthood as a performance-based method that disrupts presumptive knowledges of black subjectivity.[26] What happens, I ask, if we reimagine black objecthood as a way toward agency rather than its antithesis, as a strategy rather than simply a primal site of injury? Far from avoiding the high stakes delineated above, I contend that precisely because of them, objecthood is a concept that offers us a powerful lens to think through art, performance, and black female embodiment. In its counterintuitive logics, performing objecthood is akin to what Darieck Scott calls an "embodied alienation."[27] Scott's term gestures toward the surprising powers, and even pleasures, possible in blackness-as-abjection. Taking up a different archive, and focusing more precisely on black women and their archival traces, I propose that forms of subjectivity and agency are always present, however minuscule they may be, in the often complex and rigorous performances of objecthood I trace in this book.

Objecthood, as practiced here by black women performers, is not the negation of art—as Michael Fried decries—but rather a method of suturing art *and* performance together. In his notorious essay "Art and Objecthood," published in *Artforum* in 1967, Fried wrote of his dismay at sculptures by artists Donald Judd and Robert Morris (among others) that had a peculiar, aggressive relationship with viewers. As opposed to passive paintings on a wall, these works seemed to make spectators subject to their presence. These objects' dubious theatricality, he argued, nullified their status as "art." In these pages, I celebrate objecthood's ostensible staginess and the ability of these art objects to get in the spectator's way—like the "silent presence of another *person*."[28] The very qualities that Fried treats with alarm I treat with amazement, the hallmarks of how figures like Adrian Piper and Ellen Craft, separated

[margin handwritten notes: performance-based method; objecthood as a means of agency / strategy] by over a century, both adroitly navigate slippages between subject and object and, in doing so, reveal that the borders between subjectivity and objecthood are not nearly as distinct as we pretend they are . . . and never have been.

Akin to anthropologist Bruno Latour's "hybrids," the black female objects I discuss violate the "distinct ontological zones" between human and object. Meanwhile, the sense of the uncanny provoked by some of these more nefarious objects, as Bill Brown observes in a discussion of black collectibles, is precisely because they uncomfortably remind us that "our history is one in which humans were reduced to things (however incomplete that reduction)." Indeed, he argues, this subject/object uncertainty is one of slavery's most sordid leitmotifs, its ultimate moral crime. Yet, while I concur with this logic, I depart from Brown's exclusive focus on the eerie material objects that contain this repressed history of "ontological confusion," focusing instead on the performers whose bodies bore those slippages.[29] Thus, I investigate the elastic recurrence of this dialectic in black performance art, specifically the savvy performances of objecthood staged by the cultural subjects in this book. Put simply, theories of object life[30] become deeply fortified when black women's performance work is recognized as a key player, rather than an aberration, in interrogating the dense imbrications of beings, objects, and matter.

What I call *prosthetic performance* serves as an instance of how objecthood, far from acting alone, instead often acts in collaboration with inanimate props that are transformed into active agents. I develop this term in my discussion of fugitive slave Ellen Craft, whose impersonation of a disabled white male slaveholder enabled her and her husband, William, acting as this gentleman's valet, to escape from slavery in 1849. It includes both her feigned behaviors as well as the quotidian items, such as two poultices, that facilitated her multiple role-reversals. Her clever use of one of these poultices, and a sling, to hide her right hand not only enhanced the myth of her white male avatar's disability, but also allowed the illiterate Craft to avoid being called upon to sign in at hotels or to register "him" (or "his slave") with white officers en route. Seemingly inert matter, Craft's sling can be reinterpreted as an "actuant," to use Latour's term: a source of action that makes things happen. In Craft's case, the sling's strange abilities to repeatedly incite white spectators to act on Craft and *its* behalf "rewrite[s] the default grammar of agency" to include both embodied acts as well as inanimate things.[31]

In what follows, prosthetic performance is one example of the unique object lessons these black women performers implore us to heed. It is my contention that the various artistic and social concerns of these performers repeatedly coalesce around a single strategy: the use of avatars.

Avatars

This hybrid group of black women performers, as we shall see, repeatedly performed objecthood by deploying the tactics and aesthetics of the avatar. The concept of the avatar has a distinct genealogy. "Avatar," a term from Hindu mythology, is derived from the Sanskrit word *avatara.* Combining the prefix *ava* ("down") with the base of *tara* ("a passing over"), its translation of "downcoming" denotes the descent of a deity to earth in order to be reincarnated in a human form. Entering the English language at the end of the eighteenth century, its meanings grew less spiritual and more rhetorical and allegorical. In 1985, the word "avatar" was first applied to virtual persona.[32] As a result, it has acquired a much more banal, technological meaning, specifically to denote a graphic representation of a person—a human-like figure, usually—controlled by a person via a computer. Today, it is most often used to refer to the computer-generated figures that abound in video games. James Cameron's 2009 film *Avatar* has brought the obsession with these alternate selves—long the purview of geeks and techies and gamers—into the global zeitgeist. Meanwhile, avatars increasingly act, as B. Coleman argues, as "reliable proxies for mediated face-to-face engagements" in a "wider array of media forms and platforms," including text messaging (SMS) and social media like Facebook.[33] As we increasingly communicate via our various screens, she suggests that avatars act as extensions of our agency, while also revealing a persistent slippage between real and virtual worlds, a phenomenon she calls "x-reality." Avatars, in short, act as mediums—between the spiritual and earthly as well as the abstract *medium* and the real—and the uses of those mediums, as well as their attendant meanings, continue to morph.

While befuddling, the dual connotations of "avatar"—of a spiritual reincarnation and an alternate self—are in fact quite revealing for our purposes. I rerender "avatar" in the service of black performance art to gesture toward some of the oldest (and newest) forms of impersonation staged by black women *and* the conversion of these self-effacing performances into literary, visual, and digital remains.

I employ what I call *avatar production* as an analytic for understanding the cogent and brave performances of alterity these women enact. As Hazel V. Carby and Carla Peterson have noted, black women have historically been excluded from forms of artistic production (writing and oratory, for example), if not from the category "woman" itself.[34] Black women performers have long utilized the tools of performance to assert claims to social space; these artistic strategies were "forms of mobility" that "were key in claiming subjecthood."[35] Avatars, as alternate beings given human-like agency, are akin to the second selves the black women performers in this book create, inhabit, and perform. I use the concept of avatar production to foreground how these women engage in spectacular, shocking, and even unlawful role-plays. The deployment of avatars in these performances, however, extends beyond mere mimesis; instead, these avatars are a means of highlighting (and stretching) the subordinate roles available to black women. Thus, I conceive of avatars functioning, to borrow the words of Sianne Ngai, as particularly unique "ways of inhabiting a social role that actually distort its boundaries." The efficacy of these avatars, in other words, is their agile ability to comment back on identity itself, to subvert the taken-for-granted rules for properly embodying a black female body. The performances I delineate here push us, then, to consider the morphing of social roles, "from that which purely confines or constricts to the site at which new possibilities for human agency might be explored."[36]

Furthermore, I utilize avatar production to reveal how these performers transmute their simulated identities into transhistorical figurations. Put differently, avatar production describes how these rogue corporeal stagings are "reincarnated" into other mediums, transcending the original place of their conception. Objecthood, as noted earlier, made it possible for these performers to become objets d'art. In doing so, these cultural subjects, in the words of Stuart Hall, "used the body—as if it was, and it often was, the only cultural capital we had. We have worked on ourselves as the canvases of representation."[37] The concept of avatar production, similarly, limns how experiments in ontological play create haunting res-

[margin notes: avatar production to performance of alterity; mobility towards subjecthood; subversion of embodiment]

onances in word and image. Thus, I utilize it to analyze the reanimation of these disguises and fraudulent identities in faux biographies, video art, printed newsletters, and by the book's conclusion, digital media like Tumblr and YouTube. In this manner, this book is not only about avatars that are embodied, but also those that become *dis*embodied, as these synthetic selves are distended across disparate representational forms.

I argue that avatar production is a unique and particularly useful prism through which to view and interpret these dazzling performances. This frame, of course, is my own. After all, none of the performers in this book explicitly call their constructed characters "avatars." Nor do they term their intricate labor in fabricating and animating these secondary selves via performance "avatar production." And yet, I suggest, these performances all share qualities remarkably analogous to both older and more contemporary understandings of avatars. For example, the supernatural and transcendent properties of avatars—able to seemingly supersede normal progressions of time—are present in Joice Heth's performed hoax as a living (yet impossibly old) embodiment of national history. They are also present in artist Adrian Piper's description of the Mythic Being as "timeless," with a personal history existing "prior to the history of the world."[38] Meanwhile, the idea of the avatar as a flexible representational stand-in is visible in the multiple supporting roles Howardena Pindell alternates between in her plaintive and confrontational *Free, White, and 21*. Finally, the reappearance of Ellen Craft's white male slaveholder likeness in print and portraiture is a literal illustration of how avatars are projected into other representational forms.

I also make use of avatars' shape-shifting qualities to index the slipperiness of time itself. While this book unfolds in a historically chronological form, beginning in the nineteenth century and ending in the twenty-first, it does not aspire toward linear temporalities. Indeed, its pointed *moves*—leapfrogging over short and long temporal spans—disrupt any semblance of taut historical causation or a sequential passage of time. Instead, I argue, time (like avatars themselves) recurs, reverberates, and exceeds artificial distinctions between the past and the present. Time is *polytemporal*;[39] what has come before is not contained in the past, but is continually erupting.

Mammy memory, a concept I develop in this book, begins to delineate this ontological and temporal slippage, capturing both the hazy mergers between self and other endemic to avatars and the entanglement of the *then* in *now*.[40] I make use of mammy memory, specifically, to describe how Joice Heth's impersonations as George Washington's feeble nurse-maid indexes the very real historical practice of black wet nurses caring for white infants. I also deploy it to reveal the more ephemeral and inchoate: the affective surplus produced by nineteenth-century white spectators as they reexperienced this ostensibly tender cross-racial kinship—and romantic vision of an American past—through Heth's performances. Her fraudulent exhibits routinely tripped up the logic of linear time; indeed, through her virtually immobile proxy, the past and present seemed to touch. This fluidity of time, where history refuses to stay dead or seemingly finished, is inherent to the category of reenact-ments themselves. In them, "the past is the stuff of the future, laid out like game show prizes for potential (re) encounter."[41] Heth's *performance* of history (scripted by P .T. Barnum) suggests a break from a narration of history "as presenting the past 'as it really was'" and instead introduces the possibility of getting it wrong, of a historical memory "ridden with glitches and mistakes."[42] And this temporal ambiguity, as we will soon see, is amplified not only by the *multiple* elderly black female avatars that perform mammy memory in the mid-nineteenth century, but also by the confusion over the "real" Joice Heth. This uncertainty, over the limits between the role of "Joice Heth, George Washington's nursemaid" and the black female slave portraying her, continues to plague the archive. This indeterminancy, though, is the quintessence of avatars, producing a "zone of relationality" where "the categories of self and other are rendered undecidable."[43] In short, mammy memory is illustrative of how the maverick black women performers in this book, from Joice Heth to Nicki Minaj, repeatedly manipulate avatar production as a strategy to transubstantiate themselves into porous beings with the capacity to mutate across time.

Malleable Bodies, Flexible Methodologies

This book's emphasis on the critical moments where black performance art, objecthood, and avatars meet challenges foundational (and often fetishized) notions of "truth" and accuracy that are thought to reside in more typical forms of evidence. After all, if performance itself is by definition elusive, how does one then analyze these proxy characters, whose protean qualities and unmooring from temporal constraints make them further resistant to capture? The study of these nimble performers, their savvy bodily acts, and their reanimation in literary, visual, and digital mediums does not require us to forsake empirical tools of analysis, but does require us to use them differently.

Performance's ephemerality, at first glance, seems fundamentally at odds with the production of knowledge. Put differently, how do we study that which "becomes itself through disappearance," as Peggy Phelan so famously put it?[44] Several scholars have sought to debunk this idea, suggesting that performance is not inherently loss. They have proposed queering evidence by suturing it to ephemera, argued that performance is intrinsically linked to memory and history, or insisted that performance remains and becomes itself not through disappearance but through its "messy and eruptive re-appearance."[45] In this way, performances are not simply the residue of past events but closer to, in Joseph Roach's words, "restored behaviors that function as vehicles of cultural transmission."[46] Performances are indeed captured and stored, albeit in unusual ways. This seemingly contradictory linkage, "the *conjunction* of reproduction and disappearance," as Fred Moten explains, is "performance's condition of possibility, its ontology, and its mode of production."[47] The clasping of performance to liveness, to the *here* and *now*, is particularly pronounced in conceptualizations of performance art; yet that idea and its attendant belief—that one has to witness performance art directly in order to fully understand it—has been rebuked as well.[48] Amelia Jones has questioned, for instance, whether her writing about Carolee Schneemann's *Interior Scroll* would have been more "truthful" if she had observed Schneemann pulling the scroll out of her vaginal canal firsthand. If bodily proximity, she argues, does not guarantee full knowledge of the subject, neither does the documentation (photographs, writings, etc.) that scholars like myself analyze and that performance art is dependent on to become an object of analysis in culture writ large.[49]

I utilize the porosity of performance studies, a self-professed "provisional coalescence on the move," to similarly construct a dynamic and flexible methodological apparatus capable of mutating across time and shifting across disciplines.[50] Consequently, I perform in this book a "more panoramic reading" of black performance art, placing objects of analysis together that previously would be kept apart.[51] I purposely position black women's audacious (and at times, coerced) self-displays in the antebellum era alongside increasingly self-conscious works of contemporary visual and conceptual art in a single, if necessarily discontinuous, study. In doing so, Nicki Minaj's exuberant manipulations of grotesque aesthetics in the twenty-first century and Joice Heth's staging as a spectacularly aged negress in the nineteenth century are squarely situated within each other's environs and, in the conclusion, discussed *together* via their sonic outbursts. The different political stakes of these performances do not always lead to their easy alignment, even within time periods; this seeming discordancy, however, is exactly my aim: to suggest, in other words, how black women performers have repeatedly seized upon performance, objecthood, and avatars as instruments to gain agency—with varying degrees of success—precisely because of the pesky persistence of oppressive social forces encouraging their use.

Mirroring the intrepid moves of these fleet-footed performers (and their avatars), I deploy an amalgamation of methods and interpretative frames suitable to the sinuous paths these performances take. Adrian Piper's kinetic experiments in self-estrangement (see chapter 3) are a prime example; in tracing and unspooling them, I necessarily move through conceptual art, black dance, photography, and theories of racial formation, not to mention Piper's own voluminous writings. After all, as scholars *and* artists, both Piper and Howardena Pindell have been explicit about the need for their art to be properly considered, i.e., that the art objects take precedence over their personal biographies and the theory that aids, Darby English notes, "in making such art visible *as criticism.*"[52] I heed their calls by taking their art (and them, as artists) seriously on the rigorous terms they offer. But I also purposely analyze their art outside of strictly art-historical contexts in efforts to expand the range of interpretations applied to this work while, simultaneously, highlighting what black performance art can *do*. In short, a vigorous and interdisciplinary black arts criticism is one of this book's raisons d'être. For antebellum figures Joice Heth and Ellen Craft, I employ a similar approach, applying a concatenation of disciplinary gazes to them and their rogue acts, including disability studies, visual culture studies, psychoanalysis, and African American literary theory. Still, my use of performance studies as my primary frame is intentional, to anchor performance theory in discourses of blackness, particularly to illuminate how, in Stephanie Batiste's words, "black performers made meaning within often problematic representational structures."[53]

Overview

The efforts that percolate in *Embodied Avatars* do not represent the entirety of black performance art nor that staged specifically by black women; there are certainly other nervy acts that fit within the genre. Yet the six cultural subjects discussed here were chosen for their aesthetic affinities and what they reveal about the interwoven workings of black performance art, objecthood, and avatar production at seemingly disparate moments. Each chapter assiduously attends to the historical, cultural, and artistic regiments these performers operated in and that influenced, if not shaped, their performances of alterity. To build a fulcrum for this investigation into the stakes of avatar production, the possibilities of objecthood, and the problem of agency, I begin my study with the phenomenon of Joice Heth, the "ancient negress."

Chapter 1, "Mammy Memory: The Curious Case of Joice Heth, the Ancient Negress," focuses on resituating Heth's brief but iconic impersonations, as George Washington's nursemaid in 1830s America, as performance art. I begin to do so by tracing what I earlier termed mammy memory, an affective charge suturing race, childhood, and nostalgia, both in photographic depictions of the black wet nurse and that figure's seeming recurrence in two additional black female avatars enacted in this time period: "Joice Heth's Grandmother" and "Mother Boston." Paired with her performances of disability, I ruminate on these sundry attempts to script the partially paralyzed Heth as both a cultural and biological anomaly as well as an embodied portal to a mythic and majestic American past. I then shift gears to the brief rumor of Heth as an inert automaton ventriloquized by Barnum, using Sianne Ngai's concept of "racial animatedness" to delimit the complex interplay between race and the mechanical. Coupled with Barnum's visual and literary reanimations of Heth, I detail the seduction of this ontological mystery: is Joice Heth a human or a machine? These incidents lead us to a final discussion of her ostensible resistance, a brief vocal interjection that I call a *sonic of dissent*. My focus on Heth's sonic of dissent, while *not* an explicit

(handwritten margin note)
(a)
embodied
memory
(b) legacies
of brutal
objecthood

attempt to solve the quandary regarding her agency, has a dual aim: (1) to privilege embodied memory over the textual and visual distortion of Barnum (and others), and (2) to engage with the disturbing legacies of brute objecthood and fabulation[54] that are central components of black performance art's haunting historical backdrop.

I continue reinterpreting otherwise banal nineteenth-century behaviors and fierce acts of bravery as forms of black performance art in chapter 2, "Passing Performances: Ellen Craft's Fugitive Selves," shifting to an examination of Craft's passing performances; her radical actions succeeded in freeing Craft and her husband, William, from chattel slavery in rural Georgia, and eventually transforming them into veteran performers in the United States and British Isles. I lay bare the sundry sartorial and synthetic props of Craft's handicapped white male avatar, "Mr. William Johnson." I reveal how her aforementioned *prosthetic performances*—fusing clothing-based items to faux acts of disability—succeeded in eliciting sympathy (and prompting action) from white spectators. I also briefly turn to Craft's cousins, Frank and Mary, to emphasize their shared use of performance-based methods in their equally perilous collaborative escape. I then lead us across the Atlantic Ocean as I move from Craft's improvised escape acts to her otherwise banal peregrinations at the Great Exhibition in London in 1851 and her staging of her white mulatta body as a disruptive agent. I end with a discussion of the engraving of Craft in her partial escape costume that appeared in the *London Illustrated News* the same year (and later as the frontispiece to *Running a Thousand Miles to Freedom*), urging a reading of it as a unique depiction, neither of her nor of her white male avatar, but rather *both* simultaneously.

We then travel back to the United States—and leap across a century—as I move from 1850s Britain to 1970s New York. The purpose of this strategic maneuver is twofold: (1) to construct a more far-reaching view of black women's performance work, as I shift from politically resistant self-displays in the shadow of chattel slavery to self-conscious performance art that circulated in New York's fine art world, and (2) to highlight how, in spite of these temporal divergences, traces of coercion and subjugation haunt more recent black female performance art. Chapter 3, "Plastic Possibilities: Adrian Piper's Adamant Self-Alienation," focuses on conceptual artist Piper's dense explorations of objecthood and her bold experiments with disorientation, self-estrangement, and becoming a confrontational art object. Utilizing Daphne Brooks's concept of "afro-alienation," I argue that Piper's complex praxis of self-observation and an aggressive nonidentification with her audience is suggestive of a strategic self-alienation employed by black historical actors, albeit in the halcyon days of 1970s performance art. Building on conceptual art's emphasis on ideas and process, and Minimalism's antipathy toward formal art objects, Piper deftly manipulates her body as artwork and as a catalytic agent for audiences. I illustrate this in my initial discussion, mapping her unique traversal from Minimalism to Conceptualism to performance art, to reveal her agile attempts at aesthetic mobility. Following this, I briefly ponder Piper's relationship to incipient notions of "feminist art" and "black art," meditating on her seeming absence from both. I then focus on two sets of Piper's lesser-known performances—the *Aretha Franklin Catalysis* (1972) and *The Spectator Series* (1973)—revealing how she probes objecthood via black dance in the former while engaging with the disguise of a mysterious witness in the latter. Both lead us to *The Mythic Being* performances (1973–75), in which she dressed as a third-world male avatar in blaxploitation-esque attire, before ceasing street performances and shifting to a strictly visual icon. I dissect the various artistic strategies and ideological aims of *The Mythic Being* performances as well as the posters and advertisements featuring the avatar; both, I assert, are in the service of deconstructing the visual field that racial formation (and racism) maneuver in. Finally, I address Piper's very public withdrawal of her work from the 2013 exhibition *Radical Presence* at New York's Grey Art Gallery, arguing that the tactical removal of her work is in closer dialogue with her larger corpus than we may initially think.

Chapter 4, "Is This Performance about You?: The Art, Activism, and Black Feminist Critique of Howardena Pindell," centers on Piper's historical contemporary, abstract painter Howardena Pindell, as we shift from Piper and her inscrutable black male avatar in the streets of New York City to Pindell and her white feminist impersonation on film. Specifically, this chapter focuses on her controversial *Free, White, and 21* (1980), a video art piece in which Pindell—playing all parts—staged a dialogue between plaintive reincarnations of herself and a caricature of a white feminist who callously debunks the veracity of her experiences. I interpret the video as creating a black feminist counterpublic that is not simply about critique, but also racism-as-trauma; furthermore, I detail its performative engagements with cross-racial embodiment and avatar-play. Yet in efforts to contextualize both the video's content and Pindell's career, the chapter begins with an examination of the various political and artistic communities she participated in, or was denied access to, in the late 1960s and 1970s. In doing so, I aim to render visible not only the manifold tensions that arose from the merging of art and politics in this period, but more explicitly the difficulties in being a black woman artist excluded from avant-garde circles (both black *and* white), partly for making abstract work that was deemed not sufficiently "black." In the last part of the chapter, I detail Pindell's vociferous rebuke of "art world racism" through her involvement in PESTS, an anonymous arts organization that, the evidence suggests, grew out of her activism. I turn to PESTS's remains—a flyer, poster replicas, and two obscure newsletters— that serve as public engagements with the invisibility, exclusion, and tokenism faced by artists of color. As such, I contend, these visual paraphernalia enable the possibility of counterpublics as well.

The conclusion, "'I've Been Performing My Whole Life,'" serves both as a summation of the book's arguments and an extension of its recurring trio—objecthood, black performance art, and avatar production— into the twenty-first century. Mimicking the architecture of the chapters, I end the book with yet another unlikely historical pair: pop and hip-hop dynamo Nicki Minaj and sculptor Simone Leigh. I zero in on Minaj's canny manipulation of her voice in her zesty cameo on Kanye West's single "Monster"; her thrilling scream in that song recalls Heth's earlier outburst, and the women's shared wielding of *grotesque aesthetics*. Building off of Kobena Mercer's scholarship, I restage and develop this term through Minaj's artifice-laced performance in the music video accompaniment to West's single, a particularly fraught piece that was swiftly banned upon its release. I follow this discussion with Leigh's video art opus *Breakdown*, in which an archetypal black woman (performed by opera singer Alicia Hall Moran) performs a stunning mental breakdown. I dissect this artwork's avatar-play via its skilled execution of failure, its suggestion of the roles diasporic black women perform for the duration of their lives. This provocative pair, bridging high art and popular culture, is enhanced through brief appearances by other contemporary subjects (and their avatars)—including visual and performance artist Narcissister, digital creation Kismet Nuñez, and musician Janelle Monáe.

What emerges is a fantastic cacophony—of voices both raucous and dirge-like—that confirms the urgency of black female avatars in performance art, new media, and black musical cultures of the twenty-first century. The artful performances of objecthood and avatar-play I amass here are a capacious worlding;[55] they hint at new possibilities for self-making in the African diaspora amid the imbroglio of history, as well as an expansive vision of the incredible risk and rewards of art making—a demanding black art that is made, and as Lorraine O'Grady suggests, must be received by taking the white gloves off.

learn & transmit knowledge through
embodied action, cultural agency

episteme

conserving memories & transmission of social knowledge

  constative vs. performative : another instance

1

Mammy Memory

The Curious Case of Joice Heth, the Ancient Negress

The world is studded with Joice Heths, with a difference and
unending variety of names.
—*Chicago Daily Tribune*, July 29, 1878

Let's begin with a ghost and a museum placard. One frigid winter evening,
while a graduate student living in Harlem, I took a bus (or was it the C
train?) to the Upper West Side to attend the monumental and much-hyped
exhibition *Slavery in New York*. It was here—amid the stunning textual
and visual proofs of an indelible black presence lurking in the catacombs
of the metropolis—that I first encountered Joice Heth's haunting presence.
She was a mere sentence, on an easily overlooked white note, the size of
an index card, tacked on a wall. It may not have been a full statement,
maybe an errant sentence fragment, a cluster of descriptors, or simply
"Joice Heth." Regardless, Heth's name was an utter mystery to me. I hastily
wrote her strange-looking moniker down in what was probably a barely
used Muji notebook. Years and innumerable drafts later, the obscure performances of this mysterious cultural actor ignite our explorations.

Joice Heth is a fragile footnote in history whose name is scattered
across historical newspapers and faux autobiographies like forgotten
seeds. As we will soon see, her spectacles of the body have long been forgotten, but in the mid-1830s were iconic. They were also highly protean,
traveling erratic paths across print and visual media and increasingly
peculiar, if not bizarre, modes of objecthood. Yet despite their pointed
refusal to settle into anything resembling a linear, coherent narrative,
these corporeal stagings are indeed <u>traceable</u>. These slippery embod- *trace*
ied acts serve as the first notes in the orchestral score of black female
performers and their accompanying avatars that animate, compose, and
enliven the pages that follow.

In the shadows of 1830s America lurked the dubious and touring spectacle of a putative ancient negress, staged as "Joice Heth, George Washington's nursemaid." Prior to her mythic scripting, Joice Heth was an elderly black slave purportedly discovered in Kentucky and brought for display to Philadelphia's Masonic Hall. Phineas T. Barnum—a then twenty-five-year-old white man who would eventually become the circus impresario of Barnum & Bailey fame—purchased the rights to exhibit Heth for a thousand dollars.[1] Quickly realizing the potential for profit, Barnum first exhibited her inside Niblo's Garden in August 1835. A large "pleasure garden" limited to white patrons and taking up an entire block at Broadway and Prince Street in downtown Manhattan, Niblo's included service by a retinue of black waiters, a theater, and access to a saloon featuring contortionists and opera singers, all for the fifty-cent price of admission.[2] For an additional twenty-five cents (twelve and a half cents for children), visitors could walk into one of the separate viewing areas and view the magical living personage of Joice Heth, deceased president George Washington's putative 161-year-old black wet nurse. After this illustrious debut, Heth, a veritable *"living skeleton,"* was repeatedly displayed in New York and soon traveled to other major northeastern cities, including New Haven, Boston, and Providence. These tightly choreographed shows began with a reciting of Joice Heth's ostensible history, while Heth herself rested on a bed covered "in fine blankets," and the subsequent reading of a bill of sale, that confirmed transfer of her ownership from George Washington's father, Augustine, to Elizabeth Atwood, a neighbor and family friend.[3] Questions were then put to Heth by "Barnum and managers," followed by the inquiries of audience members to Heth and her managers, before she "regaled her auditors with several of her choice hymns."[4]

A week after her death, on February 19, 1836, Heth staged her last and perhaps best-attended costume drama: in the amphitheater of the City Saloon on Broadway, anatomist Dr. David L. Rogers executed a public and well-publicized post mortem dissection of Heth's ossified heart before fifteen hundred spectators, declaring her to be eighty years of age. Both alive and dead, a venerable American icon and a dubious black hoax, "Joice Heth, George Washington's nursemaid" was an avatar that sustained the interest of theatrical, visual, and later literary audiences in spite of, if not *because* of, her ontological ambiguity. Nev-

avatar: ontological ambiguity

GREAT ATTRACTION
At the Masonic Hall!
UNPARALLELED LONGEVITY.
[FOR TWO DAYS ONLY.]
JOICE HETH,
NURSE TO
Gen. George Washington,

(The father of our country,) who has arrived at the astonishing age of **161** years! will be seen in the large room at the Masonic Hall, opposite the Franklin House, for TWO DAYS ONLY, as she is on her way to Boston, where she must be early next week.

JOICE HETH is unquestionably the most astonishing and interesting curiosity in the World! She was the slave of Augustine Washington, (the father of Gen. Washington,) and was the first person who put clothes on the unconscious infant who in after days led our heroic fathers on to glory, to victory, and to freedom. To use her own language when speaking of the illustrious Father of his country, "she raised him." JOICE HETH was born in the Island of Madagascar, on the Coast of Africa, in the year 1674 and has consequently now arrived at the astonishing

Age of 161 Years !

She weighs but forty-six pounds, and yet is very cheerful and interesting. She retains her faculties in an unparrelleled degree, converses freely, sings numerous hymns, relates many interesting anecdotes of Gen. Washington, the red coats, &c. and often laughs heartily at her own remarks, or those of the spectators. Her health is perfectly good, and her appearance very neat. She was baptized in the Potomac river and received into the Baptist Church 116 years ago, and takes great pleasure in conversing with Ministers and religious persons. The appearance of this marvellous relic of antiquity strikes the beholder with amazement, and convinces him that his eyes are resting on the oldest specimen of mortality they ever before beheld. Original, authentic and indisputable documents prove that however incredulous the fact may appear, JOICE HETH is in every respect the person she is represented.

The most eminent physicians and intelligent men both in New York and Philadelphia, have examined this *living skeleton* and the documents accompanying her, and all *invariably* pronounce her to be as represented 161 *years of age!* Indeed it is impossible for any person, however incredulous, to visit her without astonishment and the most perfect satisfaction that she is as old as represented.

☞ A female is in continual attendance, and will give every attention to the ladies who visit this relic of by gone ages.

She was visited at Niblo's Garden, New York, by *ten thousand persons* in two weeks.——Hours of exhibition from 9 A. M. to 1 P. M. and from 4 to 10 P. M.—Admittance 25 cents—Children 12½ cents.

Figure 1.1. "Great Attraction at the Masonic Hall!" 1835. Broadside; 25 x 15 cm. © Collection of the New-York Historical Society.

ertheless, as one doubtful reporter noted, despite his ambivalence as to "whether or not she be the original Joice Heth," the sheer spectacle of witnessing her strikingly decayed body "amply compensates the time and cost of a visit."[5]

spectacle

While we cannot erase the tragic circumstances of Heth's life (and afterlife), we *can* reimagine the way we discuss these corporeal illusions and impersonations. Sandwiched historically between Sarah Baartman's invasive self-exhibitions in London and Paris two decades earlier and the nefarious beginnings of J. Marion Sims's medical experimentation on black women in the United States a decade later, Heth's elusive somatic acts intimate the all-too-familiar and "recurring theme in the 'body dramas' that Black women experience. Being black and female is characterized by the private being made public," writes Beverly Guy-Shetfall. Their bodies, unlike most bodies, are "not off-limits, untouchable, or unseeable."[6] Impossible to ignore, this history of black women's bodies-made-abject continues to resonate. However, by utilizing performance art as a framing mechanism, I resituate Heth—as a purportedly ancient female witness to history—within another tradition, one that takes as a given the portrayal of _multiple subjectivities_ and the emphasis on the body itself as _a proverbial canvas_. I seek to place more attention on the ontological work she performed and suggest that she is an important (though generally overlooked) cultural actor. Yet, I also rerender her explicitly as a performance artist. This purposeful move positions Heth's performances as forebears to the more recent corporeal play and aesthetic provocations we will witness in the second half of this book with figures like conceptual artist Adrian Piper and pop star Nicki Minaj. In short, via this reimagining and recontextualization, Joice Heth surfaces in the "scenarios," or "meaning-making paradigms," that follow as less a dire example of black objecthood's disturbing legacy and more an astute actress and key antecedent to the twentieth century's artful and often-cerebral black performance art.[7]

Mammy Memory

Joice Heth's power lies in the specificity of her role: she embodied the archetypal black nursemaid. The evocative abilities of her (fictitious) role underscore the potent sentimental link between childhood, race, and nostalgia; I call this affective charge _mammy memory_. I use this idiom to delineate and coax together a very real historical occupation and a less tangible array of feelings. Put another way, mammy memory indexes the _historical practice of black wet nurses caring for their master's white children_ (or their "charges," as these infants are often labeled in nineteenth-century photographs) and the more tentative and inchoate _emotions of white spectators_ who reexperienced this domestic vision through Heth's performances. As an affect, mammy memory resembled a nascent "structure of feeling." It was a social "pre-formation" whose routine recollection of cherished childhood memories (and George

Washington's specifically) via a black female proxy hovered "at the very edge of semantic availability."[8]

Mammy memory, to emphasize the point, was neither fixed nor fully realized, but rather elusive and phantom-like. It was, in Raymond Williams's parlance, a "kind of feeling and thinking [. . .] each in an embryonic phase before it can become fully articulate and defined exchange."[9] Yet, despite its seemingly undetectable markings, its vestiges reveal themselves, in what immediately follows, in the visual archive and the exhibitions of other ancient black female witnesses, as well as—eventually—the spectral-like presence of Joice Heth herself. To gesture toward the latter, while Heth was an embodied portal to an already distant past, the ersatz memories she claimed to possess were particularly maternal. The unique kinship between Heth and Washington was exploited in the quotation repeatedly attributed to her in publicity materials—"I raised him!"—as well as the rituals she repeatedly performed for audiences, such as her singing of hymns she claimed to have taught Washington as a child.[10] The normalcy of this incessant restaging of an intimate transracial encounter between a white toddler and his eternal black mammy is indicative of how childhood innocence, itself raced as white, extended toward Heth. The "propinquity between the sentimental white child" and "the enslaved adult," writes Robin Bernstein, enabled the transference of the "white child's aura of innocence" to the "African American character." As the problematic dynamics of Heth's performances suggest, the effect of such a romantic gesture was a magnification of her role as a nurturing caretaker, while her abject status as a partially paralyzed slave was simultaneously shifted out of focus. Underneath its tender veneer, then, mammy memory was a form of what Bernstein calls "racial memory."[11] As such, it secured a remarkable set of binaries in place: white versus black, citizen versus slave, able-bodied versus disabled, and the young male child accompanied by his seeming opposite—his adult female caretaker. Mammy memory, I am suggesting, warrants our attention, for below the surface of its potentially saccharine affection toward black wet nurses and presumed innocuous tone lurk complex identifications and sinister racial undertones.[12]

From a psychoanalytic perspective, the audience's repeated cross-identification with a racial "other" highlights Joice Heth's role as a potential stand-in for a lost love-object. Identification, in Diana Fuss's words, names the "embarrassingly ordinary" process by which "surrogate others" are installed to fill the void left by the departed object of affection.[13] Mammy memory, similarly, gestures to Heth's psychic work as a type of flesh-and-blood substitution for vanished mammy figures and a haunting replacement for George Washington himself. Her performances, in that sense, provoked their own unique death encounters. Moreover, if we consider the metaphors of pregnancy and consumption endemic to psychoanalysis,[14] we are confronted with a startling image: the strange incorporation of Heth inside these audiences' (and later, P. T. Barnum's) psyches, their peculiar and collective ingestion of an icon of black motherhood. The spectator's seemingly benign attachment to Heth, however, was complicated by the fact that she also circulated as a convenient racial foil, whose wizened corpselike black body aided in buttressing white American identity. This paradoxical dynamic in the racial formation of whiteness—attachment to the racial other via denial of them—is emblematic of what Anne Anlin Cheng calls the "melancholic bind between incorporation and rejection" that non-whites have, historically, been forced to negotiate in American society.[15] If these contradictory impulses signal identification's ambivalent "double current," they also signal Heth's simultaneous uses as a beloved object of affection and, conversely, an embodiment of racial monstrosity.[16]

The photographic sphere is one site where we can perceive echoes of this ideological underbelly of mammy memory. Its nefarious logic persists, specifically, in the innumerable nineteenth-century images of black wet nurses with their white charges that continue to circulate. The usually nameless black mammy figure, in these black-and-white pairings, served a very specific function: since "small children would not sit still for the long exposures required by early photography," she held the child steady, and, therefore, guaranteed the success of the portrait.[17] In spite of this merely utilitarian function, though, the mammy's presence directs us to how the "photograph as a sentimental family memento may have also performed a racial function."[18] Specifically, these images reproduced the ideology of whiteness by a process of what Harryette Mullen terms "enhance by contrast," the whiteness of the child bringing into sharp relief the blackness of the caretaker.[19] These photographs,

moreover, evinced a vexing, but commonplace, antebellum social reality: the white infant's dependence on the black female servant, who
would eventually be subject to the authority of that same child, once he
or she became an adult.[20]

All of these pernicious dynamics were at work in a carte-de-visite
dated approximately 1850, attributed to the Poole Art Company of
Nashville, Tennessee. The elegantly dressed black wet nurse's role as
a supportive prop for the white child is evident in her barely discernible hands, her left disappearing behind the child's left shoulder—
presumably holding her (or possibly him) firmly in place—while her
right hand is partially visible behind the child's right arm, seen gripping
the side of the high chair. The flowing white christening gown of the
child bleeds almost seamlessly into the skirt of the nurse and is virtually
indistinguishable from the child's skin itself. Unblemished fabric blurs
into infantile skin, casting the lower half of the portrait in an angelic
(and unequivocally *white*) glow. The nurse's blackness is in stark contrast
to the whiteness of her cherubic charge. Yet that blackness is rendered
even *more* distinct by the dark color of the long-sleeved buttoned garment she wears. Ironically, the anonymous nurse is framed in the center
of the picture, directly peering back at us with pensive eyes, though it
is the subjectivity of the distracted toddler, rather than her own, that
is supposed to be privileged in the mise-en-scène. After all, due to the
cost of early photographs, as Laura Wexler observes, "the white family
was virtually the only context in which the 'nursemaid' would have a
portrait made." In their active scripting, visual portraits like this were
not transparent records, or an "inert collage of the ways things were," but
rather illustrative of photography's power to "make certain things invisible just as surely as it has made other things appear."[21] As such, in their
ideological "upside-down reality,"[22] these relics are visual rejoinders to
the residues of mammy memory I locate momentarily in the field of
performance, illustrative of a cultural nostalgia that was rooted in racial
domination.

Essentially ephemeral, mammy memory resists efforts to definitively
locate it just as it challenges the very notion of evidence itself. It is only
fitting, then, that we trace its peculiar resurfacings in the most enigmatic and evasive of cultural forms: performance. As I noted earlier,
Joice Heth was not the only elderly black female witness exhibited in the

Figure 1.2. "Three quarter length double portrait;
black woman formally attired; dark top, white skirt,
stands behind small white child seated in high chair
in white christening gown," ca. 1850. Carte-de-visite.
Poole Art Company, Nashville, Tenn., and Randolph
Linsly Simpson. Courtesy of the Beinecke Rare Book
and Manuscript Library, Yale University.

mid-nineteenth century. Alongside Heth, two other characters—"Joice
Heth's Grandmother" and "Mother Boston"—evince the serial seduc-
tions of mammy memory. Their presence in the historical record is extremely fleeting—both vanish into archival silence soon after their brief
mentions—but they direct us, nonetheless, to the importance of an al-

ternative approach to proof. Evidence itself has to be queered, unmooring it from concrete facts and instead, as José Muñoz suggests, suturing it to the concept of ephemera, or the "trace, the remains, the things that are left, hanging in the air like a rumor."[23] Despite their disappearing acts, these performances indeed have an afterlife.

In March 1837, a little over a year after Heth's death and public dissection, the first of these dubious characters appeared, a mysterious figure named "Joice Heth's Grandmother." "Another old negress has been discovered in Virginia," a newspaper in Portland, Maine, reported, "and is to be taken about for exhibition, as the grandmother of Joice Heth."[24] In spite of Heth's all-too-recent exposure as a fraud, another newspaper account suggested a belief in the veracity of the exhibit, stating "she really might be" the grandmother of Joice Heth, "without being older than Joice pretended to be."[25] Ironically, this reporter cast Joice Heth as the imposter versus her putatively "real" grandmother, even though the latter's very title seemed exceptionally hyperbolic, considering Heth was already supposed to be over a century old. This implausibility was not lost on one reporter, as demonstrated by his joke printed three days later: "By an article on our outer form it will be seen that another humbug has been got in the shape of an old negress, purporting to be the grandmother of Joice Heth. If it be true that she is really the grandmother of old Joice, who was said to be 160 years of age, what an awfully old black wench, she must be, eh!"

This same reporter's exasperation at the "gullibility of mankind . . . worse than all the perpetual motions, leather whales and manufactured mermaids and sea serpents that were ever exhibited" suggests that his true horror was not how easily the public could be duped, but rather the seeming desire for a black female witness to history in the first place.[26] Still, this facsimile of an ancient negress evaporates from the historical record after this succinct mention, leaving several questions unanswered. Who, for instance, "discovered" this performer? Where was she exhibited? Akin to most freak show performers, there are no identifiable answers or narrative closures to guide us toward clarity, only conjectures, pregnant pauses, and the abyss of the unknown. However, what we *can* perceive, to borrow from Diana Taylor, is yet another "scenario" of mammy memory, a dramatization of memory—national or otherwise—staged by an elderly black woman. As a compelling, if not peculiar staging, this scenario was never enacted for the first time. Rather, it was a "portable framework," flexible enough for multiple repeats and different "endings." It made evident what was "already there: the ghosts, the images, the stereotypes."[27] In that regard, Joice Heth and these other ancient negresses were striking effigies. As Joseph Roach writes, "Such effigies are made by performances. They consist of a set of actions that hold open a place in memory into which many different people may step according to circumstances and occasions."[28] In short, these exhibits were black maternal dramas of memory. Even when ridiculed, as with the aforementioned reporter's crude humor, they indicate a potential clamor for the seemingly incommensurate: collective national memory through the surrogate of an ostensibly ancient black woman.

If the performances of "Joice Heth's Grandmother" hint at this dynamic, the emergence of a second performer—named "Mother Boston"—makes explicit these curious stagings of American memory. In 1855, close to two decades after Heth's death, Mother Boston was exhibited inside the Bateman Show, a "colored baby show" organized by local shoemaker Josiah Bateman. Baby shows, brief and controversial cultural rituals in the mid-nineteenth century, involved the judged display of white (and eventually black) babies, accompanied by their mothers or nurses. Mothers who participated in these vulgar spectacles of maternity were deemed insensitive because "In putting themselves and their offspring on display, mothers renounced fundamental canons of domesticity. They made public what should be private and they suggested that their children were, like cattle or the objects Barnum displayed in his museum, commodities."[29] Coincidentally, the Bateman show was competing with P. T. Barnum's own black baby show occurring in Boston simultaneously, suggesting the latter's keen and continued interest in spectacles of racial embodiment post-Heth. It is in this context, amid the display of undoubtedly the youngest of black performers, that perhaps the *oldest* stole the show, as explained by the Boston correspondent for the *Anti-Slavery Standard*:

> But the main feature of the Bateman Show was a rare specimen of old age, in a venerable colored woman, commonly known as Mother Boston, who is believed to be no less than a hundred and eight years old. There was

some suspicion that there might be a spice of humbug about this feature of the exhibition, and men mindful of Joice Heth were slow to believe that the specimen was really what it was ticketed to be. But I am assured by unquestionable authority, that there is no reason for doubting the authenticity of her story. As she has always lived in Boston or its vicinity, the chain of recollection and tradition is unbroken, and the evidence would be sufficient to establish the fact in a court of justice, were it important. No one could look at her, and doubt that she was astonishingly old. She is extremely bowed by the weight of her limbs, but her appearance is by no means repulsive; her face is not corrugated with wrinkles as is common in old age but is comparatively plump and smooth, her eyes bright, and her hearing perfect. She walks to church every Sunday, and was baptized (surely at the eleventh hour of her days work) only last year. One could not help thinking how much history was included in the span of her life. What strange events have happened, how many famous men who have filled all mouths with wonder or with praise have begun and ended their career since she was born![30]

This detailed account of ancient negress–ness illuminates the special role of abject and elderly black women, and the redemptive possibilities of their mythical and profoundly maternal ties to the nation.

The merging of adoration and scientific-like inquiry in the very first sentence describing Mother Boston warrants attention. The ambiguity—she is at once a "venerable" subject and a "rare" object or "specimen"—serves to delineate how the awe that ancient negresses inspired was tempered by their value as embodied, and hence biological, signs of racial difference in commercial exhibitions. This pernicious practice encompasses not only Mother Boston's as well as Joice Heth's exhibits, but also freak show performances by raced, and especially black, historical actors writ large.[31] Similarly, the language of the law is utilized here in anticipating, and swiftly countering, claims of corporeal fraudulence. An "unquestionable authority" vouched for Mother Boston's identity, the "evidence" of which was substantial enough to ostensibly pass cross-examination in a "court of justice," but just who was this anonymous figure whose authority was above reproach? And what claims did he (or maybe she) have on the "truth" of this black maternal icon staging a possibly fallacious body-drama of memory?

While these questions are never answered, the article suggests, none-theless, that Mother Boston's physicality, or rather the sheer sight of it, was sufficient proof: "no one could look at her, and doubt she was as-tonishingly old." Lacking more information, Mother Boston's identity, and veracity as an embodied relic of the nation, remains a conundrum. Yet if Joice Heth or any of the other provocateurs in this study are any example, the elastic and protean properties of black performers' bodies were perhaps the least static and reliable of proofs. This is hinted at in the description of Mother Boston, whose relatively youthful facial ap-pearance, "not corrugated with wrinkles" as expected, seems to belie her unusual old age. Nevertheless, the voluntary display of her aged body, all the more remarkable as a counterpoint to the panoply of infants it was shown among, enabled the profusion of a form of national memory. After all, as evinced by the reporter's parting exclamatory comments, in viewing Mother Boston, "one could not help thinking" of a long and tumultuous history conveniently contained inside the portable frame of a performing black matriarch.

This primal scene of simultaneous black infancy and old age—staged, judged, and viewed before rapt spectators—brings us full circle, further revealing the intertwining of race, national memory, and maternity-by-proxy implicit in discrete performances of mammy memory. This trio share in role-playing as black mothers of the nation. Their fecund potential to embody historical change, as if they collectively gave birth to an unruly toddler named America, is signaled by their sobriquets: the "mother" in Mother Boston, "grandmother" in Joice Heth's Grand-mother, and finally "nursemaid" in Joice Heth, George Washington's nursemaid. Black performance art, as staged here, was in the service of national memory; as objects, these elderly black women performed as embodied vessels of history, signs of generational shifts. Deploying maternal yet mythic identities, these were not mere roles, but fanciful avatars that rescripted these performers' bodies and perception by oth-ers; they became iconic emblems of American identity itself. Mammy memory highlights how black performance art, objecthood, and avatar production converge in these antebellum performances, albeit in strange fashion. It provides a frame, though an elusive one, as I begin tracing the mechanics inherent in the bodily phantasmagoria performed by Joice Heth in the site where it all began: the freak show.

How to Do Things with Freaks: Staging Blackness, and Other Myths

Perhaps no one understood the enormous dramatic and financial potential of Joice Heth, qua "the pretended negro nurse of George Washington," better than astute fabulist and future businessman P. T. Barnum.[32] Prior to her brief iconographic career, Heth was an unknown slave, not yet the national phenomenon she would become after Barnum "discovered" her. In 1841, five years after Heth's death, Barnum published a series of articles in the newspaper *The Atlas* under the alias Barnaby Diddleum about his early reminiscences and adventures in hokum. Joice Heth, or "the negro wench" he built his "principal hopes of fortune" upon, was described in detail as a "remarkably old looking animal [. . .] so wrinkled and shriveled and drawn-up by disease that her appearance indicated great longevity" or extreme old age.[33] In a later biography, Barnum went further, carefully delineating Heth's multiple bodily anomalies, such as her lack of teeth, her eyes that were so "deeply sunken in" that "the eyeballs had seemed to have disappeared altogether," her immobile left arm positioned stiffly "across her breast," and her remarkable fingernails measuring "four inches in length" that "extended above her wrist."[34] Yet, in *The Atlas*, Barnum tempered his responses to Heth's striking corpus with a more benign rendering of her as the "nurse of the immortal George Washington," "petted" by the patriot as a slave in the Washington household "for more than a century." The "fame" of the latter, he mused, would "herald old Joyce above all negro wenches ever exhibited, and I was right."[35] While elements of these and other ruminations were fictionalized, and undoubtedly written for readers' maximum enjoyment, they nonetheless offer glimpses, however tentative, of the machinery behind these exhibits. As Barnum's partially concealed confessions suggest, a concatenation of clever props, disguises, and carefully rehearsed framings transformed Joice Heth from a geriatric slave of little distinction to, as one observer of her noted, an "extraordinary specimen of humanity" regarded by innumerable witnesses "with something bordering on awe and veneration."[36]

The aesthetic structure of freak shows, a legitimate theatrical form by the mid-nineteenth century, harnessed the acute curiosity of spectators and framed exceptional bodies, like Heth's, as legible objects of percep-

[margin notes: freak show - site for visual consumption of corporeal difference]

tual consumption. While the often forced display of *lusus naturae*, or "freaks of nature," had occurred since medieval times, the exhibition of these atypical persons took on a distinct valence in the nineteenth century, when the freak show became the primary venue through which to view corporeal difference.[37] Once confined to independent exhibits of human oddities, freak shows became a burgeoning commercial enterprise. The proliferation of circuses and dime museums, the culmination of which was the debut of Barnum's own American Museum in New York City in 1841, was "institutionalized as part of an increasingly complex urbanizing America."[38] These arenas housed cultural rituals structured around what Rosemarie Garland Thomson calls "freak discourse," an interpretative practice that "seized upon any deviation from the typical, embellishing and intensifying it to produce" dramatic spectacles that rendered "every somatic feature" as "laden with significance before the gaping spectator."[39] As such, freak shows were carefully designed dramaturgical enactments that provided a specific interpretive frame, which delineated those on display as spectacularly odd, unabashedly strange, and ripe for analysis.

[margin notes: conventions - pseudo science - dialectique - medicaliza tion]

The dramatic conventions of the freak show were often merged with pseudo-scientific discourse, creating an additional didactic imperative to *read* the racialized bodies of so-called "freaks," especially black ones, as corporeal evidence of medical abnormality. In Harriet A. Washington's description, the "boundary separating popular display from medical display was a porous one, a permeable membrane with copious migration in both directions" as African American performers, in particular, were used to bolster not only freak discourse, but also often-bogus and racially inflected theories of humankind's evolutionary origins.[40] The publication of Darwin's *Origin of Species* in 1859, alleging the existence of a "missing link" between ape and man, and the concomitant performances of black performer William Henry Johnson *as* the missing link evince these very tethered bonds, the latter making a career out of embodying the fallacious musings of the former.[41]

Yet if Darwin and Johnson, respectively, epitomize the most notorious nineteenth-century scientist and the most beloved black circus performer, less visible cultural actors and even more perplexing pseudo-scientific theories existed earlier. Medical treatises published well before Heth's performances proposed particularly imaginative hy-

potheses in regard to the mysterious origins and causes of blackness.
These curious conjectures deemed blackness, for instance, as a "universal freckle" or a peculiar form of leprosy called "negritude" that was in-
explicably cured by, among other things, the juice of unripe peaches.[42]
Meanwhile, the racial inflections inherent in the rare phenomenon of
extreme old age, or "longevity," were referenced in an anonymous letter
published in a medical journal in 1842 that alleged that "pure Africans"
had the highest levels of longevity, one position in an ongoing debate
that Heth's performances were cleverly situated in.[43] And, in addition
to Heth and Johnson, there were numerous other performers, racialized and often disabled, who masqueraded as ostensible proofs of racial
and bodily deviation. These included "white negro" Henry Moss, conjoined African American twins Millie and Christine McKoy, and Afong
Moy, a Chinese woman with extremely small feet exhibited around the
same time as Heth.[44] Their performances, while heavily dependent on
spectacle, had implicit ideological impulses. "These exhibits and the
resulting photographs," Nicholas Mirzoeff writes, not only "created and
sustained a desire to understand people in terms of a racialized hierar-
chy" but also provided white spectators with the explicit ability to make
these distinctions, a "mark of citizenship and reason that the object of
display inevitably lacked."[45] Freak show theatrics, in other words, built
an "us" versus "them" division around not just race but also nation.
Put differently, these ritualized stagings of corporeal otherness delimit
how freak shows, in a virtually seamless cohabitation with pseudo-
Darwinian evolutionary discourses, defined undesirable racial subjects
as foreign and biologically degenerate curiosities, if not outliers, in the
mythic nation.

Joice Heth's performances fused both of these discursive frameworks,
cleverly suturing the dramaturgical techniques of the freak show with
the structured granting to audiences of a "medical gaze."[46] The success
and legibility of freak shows being interpreted as such depended, in
Rosemarie Garland Thomson's typology, on the implementation of four
narrative components(1) the "oral spiel" by the "showman or 'professor,'"
(2) "fabricated or fantastic textual accounts" such as "long pamphlets
and broadside or newspaper advertisements," (3) the "costuming, cho-
reography, performance, and the spatial relation to the audience" inherent in staging, and (4) a "visual image of staged freakishness."[47] Heth's

meticulously designed theatrical scenarios contained elements of these four attributes, evident in both the publicity for and the rigid scripting of these mobile exhibits. For the former, Barnum adroitly wielded "illuminated transparencies," a "very attractive" visual technology "new in the city of New-York," to incur audience fervor for Heth's exhibitions. Constructed by W.J. and Hannington, these colorful "two feet by three" transparencies—"placed on a hollow frame and lighted from the inside"—featured the phrase JOICE HETH 161 YEARS OLD in simple "white letters."[48]

In addition, Barnum commissioned an extremely crude woodcut of Heth that was reproduced in "huge banners" and the newspaper advertisements announcing her appearances.[49] In this murky rendering, made four years before the advent of photography, a barely discernable Heth wore a bonnet with the talon-like fingers of her left hand extended outward in the gesture of an anticipatory handshake, underneath the bold phrase "THE GREATEST NATIONAL AND NATURAL CURIOSITY IN THE WORLD." Coinciding with a radical shift in the format of New York newspapers—from "staid six penny commercial journals" to cheaper "penny papers" "sold directly by street hawkers" and small enough to be stuffed in pockets—we can imagine the travels of Heth's ubiquitous and mechanically reproduced visage, peeking out of the jackets of countless citizens in the urban metropolis.[50]

In addition to the group viewing and the question-and-answer sessions, the twenty-five-cent price of admission also granted adult white spectators permission to become pseudo-scientists.[51] Specifically, while "plied with small and comforting drinks and a pipe," Heth's deteriorating body was made available to witnesses for examination of discernable clues of her extreme old age.[52] The imagined medical expertise thus encouraged was implicit in the strangely formal assertions made by some spectators, such as the one who noted the "most remarkable circumstance" that Heth's pulse was "full, strong, and perfectly regular, and near 80 in a minute without the slightest ossification of the artery."[53] Still another participant eschewed scientific evidence altogether, insisting that Heth's wizened body alone was sufficient proof of its uniqueness:

> Before having seen this woman, a person may be inclined to be incredulous as to the story of her very great age—He may think of demanding

documentary evidence in proof—By the first look at the original before him will banish all scepticism on the subject, and on examination, he will find evidence stamped upon it by the hand of nature, too plain and forcible to require corroboration.[54]

Such descriptions, rich in legalese and medicalese, suggest the slippage between freak show conventions and medical science discourses. But as important, how easily the dramatic spectacle of the freak show, and the fantastic, seemingly unbelievable claims of those on display, could morph into biological believability. According to the latter witness, the truth of Heth's status as an ancient negress was visible to the naked eye (conspicuous proof so "plain and forcible" upon "the first look") by way of her physical body's very decrepitness, seemingly "stamped" by the "hand of nature." In a remarkable parallel to fugitive slave Ellen Craft, Heth's deceiving body-in-performance replaced the documentation normally needed to authenticate the truths of black subjects in the nineteenth century. As we will see, the frontispiece of Craft in disguise for *Running a Thousand Miles to Freedom* became an unusual stand-in for the abolitionist letters typically required to assert the veracity of former slaves' testimony. Heth's decimated and monstrous bodily morphology—at least for this witness—similarly superseded the textual props designed to support its ontological truthfulness. The irony, of course, was that Heth's supposedly stable aged body was perhaps the *most* ultimately misleading marker of quantifiable proof. Heth was not the "original" she was perceived as, nor were the other ancient negresses who would follow her. Rather, her performance as the proverbial nursemaid of the nation was a deliberate imitation of a preexisting cultural role. And it was undeniably successful—earning Barnum an estimated $50,000 return on an initial $1,000 investment in less than a year—at least in part because it seemed to fulfill an unconscious longing of her audiences for this mammy role.[55]

Joice Heth's role-playing may be considered a form of what Diana Fuss calls "miming masquerade": her identification with Washington was as illusory as the supposed clues seen so plainly on her body.[56] Her performance partly—and importantly—undid scientific racism's sinister impulse to make raced bodies evince themselves as proof of their inferiority; instead, Heth's slippery avatar illustrates the performativity of na-

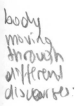
body
moving
through
different
disguises

ture itself, demonstrating how her body's protean and excess meanings (its blackness, its disability, its age) could trick even the most discerning of spectators. Her unwieldy corporeality became a tacit form of proof, even though the truth she exhibited was a complete fiction. The display of the ancient negress, in other words, was a repeated act of subterfuge, which sutured the bombastic theatrical tactics of freak shows with the fraudulent assertion that these performers were biological aberrations. The result? An imagined avatar was transformed into a legible and plausible cultural object.

Textual Impersonations

Joice Heth's faux memoir, a truly unique historical document, suggests the starring role fantasy occupied in these performances, its elastic contours stretched to bulwark far-fetched tales of Heth's ostensible origins and more. Published in 1835 in New York and purchasable for six cents, the twelve-page narrative of Heth's life entitled *The Life of Joice Heth, the Nurse of George Washington (The Father of Our Country,) Now Living at the Astonishing Age of 161 Years, and Weighs only 46 Pounds* is one of the few—perhaps the only—remnants of her performances that has survived intact. Peering inside, readers would find several signed testimonials, excerpts from newspaper notices of Heth's appearances, and a concocted set of fascinating—if not wholly invented—stories of her life. One of the most bizarre was the claim that she was born in 1674 on the island of Madagascar, an origin narrative that was distinctly didactic. This outlandish assertion scripted Heth as a foreign presence in the metropolis, transported from the farthest reaches of the "dark continent," while also augmenting the already temporal distance between her and her spectators. Moreover, the details of the aforementioned (and also fake) bill of sale, a "certified copy" of which was prominently "exhibited" during Heth's appearances, were also included in the fraudulent memoir and reprinted in promotional materials. This textual overlapping evinces the memoir and the bill of sale's entanglements with each other as fantastic texts, each presented so as to reinforce the other's mimicry of an evidentiary document.

Even more notable was P. T. Barnum and his associates' keen and sinister manipulation of abolitionist sentiment in Heth's alleged life story.

THE LIFE

OF

JOICE HETH,

THE NURSE OF

GEN. GEORGE WASHINGTON,

(The Father of our Country,)

NOW LIVING AT THE ASTONISHING

Age of 161 Years,

AND

WEIGHS ONLY 46 POUNDS.

Price Six Cents.

New-York:
PRINTED FOR THE PUBLISHER.
1835.

Figure 1.3. *The Life of Joice Heth*, 1835. Pamphlet biography (New York: Printed for the publisher). 12 pages; 20 cm. © Collection of the New-York Historical Society.

Toward the end of the pamphlet, the anonymous writer—revealed later in *The Life of P.T. Barnum* as lawyer and coconspirator Levi Lyman—declared that he had but "one single motive" in this "brief sketch of the life and character of Joice Heth" and that was "charity towards the descendants of this living monument of antiquity." Specifically, Heth's five living great-grandchildren, ostensibly owned by a master in Kentucky, were promised freedom with the money earned from both sales of "this work" and proceeds from the "exhibition, after deducting expenses." As if this hyperbole was not sufficient, the pamphlet went further, declaring that two of Heth's descendants were "uncommonly intelligent and active, quick to learn, and great favorites of their master" and were inculcated with the Scriptures "of which they were fond to learn," so they could "become fully qualified to teach their poor unfortunate race the way to future happiness." Hence, "the writer of this little work would feel amply compensated for all his labor" in aiding these "unfortunate beings" in obtaining the "blessings derived from knowledge of the gospel."[57] These flagrantly false sentiments make transparent Barnum's assiduous scripting of Heth for maximum audience exposure (and profits) and his willingness to push past limits of decorum to do so. By recasting the fabricated biography as a material object in allegiance with the abolitionist movement, analogous to a slave narrative, Barnum seemed to push the audience's veneration for Heth to the edge, to move beyond the bounds of the freak show and into the more respectable realm of what we might call abolitionist theater. This sector was similar to freak shows in its dependence on the self-staging of black subjects, except the venues were lecture stands and the performers were demonstrating their humanity and dexterity with oration and the written word, rather than solely their spectacularity. The memoir, then, executed multiple moves, camouflaging its own construction while attempting to stabilize the paradoxical claims about the racial aberration from a faraway land whose status as a slave was unclear and her pious and atypically smart descendants in need of charity.

I foreground the sly literary enactments of dubious materials like the memoir and bill of sale to call attention to the close imbrication of textuality and performance that only increase across this book's investigations. More than a century apart, both fugitive slave Ellen Craft (chapter 2) and conceptual artist Adrian Piper (chapter 3) redeploy their avatars via the written word, transferring and preserving their performances in a different medium. Writing enables an afterlife for Heth's vanishing acts similar to those of Piper and Craft, though the faux memoir—and the bill of sale especially—are particularly unwieldy. Not only were they less reliable, but also in their explicit erasure of Heth's voice, both actual and literary, they were distinctly alien in their relationship to her. Rather, they were material objects whose explicit design for audiences, skeptics and believers, makes them strangely akin to what Robin Bernstein has called "scriptive things." The act of "reading material things as scripts" according to Bernstein, calls our attention to how seemingly inert objects can incite behaviors and "prompts" from their users. Thus, the bill of sale and memoir are important not only for what they said, but also for what they gave permission to audiences to *do*. They buttressed all the meanings, for good or ill, that audiences projected onto Heth's body, including, perhaps most importantly, mammy memory itself. These responses are, of course, unquantifiable. Yet, despite this, the "issuing of a culturally specific invitation, is itself a historical event—one that can be recovered and then analyzed as a fresh source of evidence."[58] Likewise, the bill of sale and faux memoir, as textual impersonations intrinsic to Heth's performances, are important historical documents as well, even as they obscure the lines between exaggerated truths and outright falsehoods, making them exceptionally difficult to grasp.

Thus, while these narrative ploys complicate my own necessary reliance on them in the scant historical record documenting Heth's perfidious shows, they should not be jettisoned altogether. These slippery documents were themselves engaged in role-play, their trickiness and disguising of their very construction mimicking the literary aesthetic of P. T. Barnum's autobiographies. This disorienting style, where "every true story is rendered false by a succeeding explanation," as Barnum scholar Terrance Whalen writes, produces reader "vertigo," muddying the seemingly salient delineation between truth and lies.[59] Consequently, expectations of "merely evidencing" will never suffice in the analysis of these protean representations.[60] Rather, these sources require a divergent approach, a methodological *mis*alignment, that engages with the very processes of myth making and concealment they participated in. I am advocating, then, a more ambiguous interpretive method that, in lieu of traditional practices of history, seeks to, in Tavia Nyong'o's words, "examine such anomalies for the historical truths that become visible in the negative space around them, training our attention precisely upon that which an empiricist gaze will overlook."[61] In doing so, the illusion of veracity in the bill of sale and fake memoir does not impede our progress, but rather propels us further into the multiple ideological motives governing these performances. As such, these texts were prosthetics, necessary replacements for the missing "truth" and "evidence" needed to stabilize both Heth's fabricated ancientness and her overt ties to America's founding father. The bill of sale's dubious materiality—"sallow in appearance" and "folded for such a great length of time that the folds were worn nearly through, and in some parts entirely so"—reveal this process, its wear and tear feigned for audiences.[62] Both texts partook in acts of "surrogation," in other words, though the authenticity and personal histories they sought to perform were seemingly nonexistent.[63]

Performances of Disability

Joice Heth's deceitful exhibitions were also performances of disability. She was reportedly blind and unable to straighten "her lower limbs" or move her "left arm that lay across her breast," the latter two infirmities presumably the product of an earlier stroke.[64] "She usually lies upon a bed when exhibiting, and travels in the same manner," a newspaper in Massachusetts noted, but the bed was no mere prop; Heth's near-immobility made it an essential component of these dramatic acts.[65] I purposely call these performances of disability, rather than impairment, because the repeated viewing of Heth's disfigured and handicapped body by able-bodied white citizens helped make her defects seem emblematic of the larger social category of disability.[66] This is especially important because she was not alone in this endeavor. As Rachel Adams has noted, many of the cultural actors performing in freak shows in the nineteenth and early twentieth centuries were what we would term today disabled persons, all instrumental to the freak show's promise of a "panoramic view of the most sensational forms of alterity at any given historical moment."[67] Black performers in particular, before and after Heth, offered similar striking performances of corporeal and racial otherness in the freak show realm. If Henry Moss and conjoined twins Millie and Christine McKoy's aforementioned self-exhibitions attest to the popularity of such somatic spectacles, so too do the numerous exhibitions of nameless microcephiliacs whose visual depictions indicated, as Mel Y. Chen emphasizes, the taut connections between race, disability, animality, intelligence, and ostensible freakishness.[68]

Joice Heth's performances were especially unusual, however, both for their intense duration and their absence of barriers. Barnum began by exhibiting her six days a week, fourteen hours a day, from 8 a.m. to 10 p.m.; a few days in, he reduced his star's availability (due to her fatigue)

to two four-hour blocks, 9 a.m.–1 p.m. and 6 p.m.–10 p.m.[69] Atypically
for a freak show, there was no rope or other demarcated boundary between audiences and performer to hyperbolize Heth's supposed strange-
ness; audiences were able to freely touch her, whether that involved
taking her pulse, as with the aforementioned spectator, or the more per-
functory desire to shake her hand. The brute and incessant objectification of Heth—coupled with her inability to freely move, or even to see
the spectators as they watched and touched her—exemplifies forms of
black female performance in the antebellum era that were done under
duress.[70] While the indistinct boundaries between Heth's potential free
will (however picayune it might be) and her volition under Barnum
will remain forever smudged, the too-easy transformation of her handicapped body into the vehicle for a scripted stage performance remains
particularly disquieting.

Joice Heth was not alone in mixing disability and black performance;
as I discuss in the next chapter, Ellen Craft created fake bodily ailments
for her white male avatar—his poultices and other elements of what I
term *prosthetic performance* drew attention away from Craft's dangerous
dual disguises of race and gender. In Craft's case, disability was her key
role, the impersonation that often enabled her fraudulent maleness, and
especially her fraudulent whiteness, to go undetected—precisely because
her faux infirmities were so visible and so easily induced sympathy from
nineteenth-century white witnesses. In contradistinction, Heth's very
real ailments offered her neither freedom nor mobility, traits possessed
by her audiences. Her physical defects were conveniently cast—like actors in a play—as bodily proof of her extreme old age. And where her
body failed to supply enough uncontestable evidence of its own, Barnum intervened: in a passage written under a nom de guerre, he admits
that "I made her look a great deal older. I extracted her teeth, which
caused her cheeks to sink in, and then I stated that she was the nurse of
the immortal George Washington."[71] The alarmingly casual reference
to his orthodontic procedure is suggestive of the lengths Barnum was
willing to go to in order to convince paying viewers of Heth's extraordinary lifespan. In this passage, the mention of Barnum's removal of her
teeth is fleeting, with no discussion of specifics or acknowledgement of
the operation's effect on an already partially paralyzed and blind Heth.
More important was that this additional bodily deformity—an *enhance-*

ment, in Barnum's eyes—was explicitly linked to the narrative of George Washington. The removal of Heth's teeth and the tethering of her to Washington seem the foundational pairing that inspired this deceptive performance in the first place. It starts to become evident that her disabled body, while not always the explicit focus of these performances, was the urtext that held it all together. While her somatic depravities inspired repugnance among several white spectators, her seemingly impossible body was what framed her performance as "real."

As Lennard J. Davis writes, the body is "never a single physical thing so much as a series of attitudes toward it."[72] Cultural beliefs toward abnormal bodies like Heth's versus normalized ones were rationalized by such bogus disciplines as phrenology and teratology. The latter, introduced in 1832 by a French zoologist, was the "science of monstrosity" itself, etymologically derived from the Greek word for "monster," transforming the sideshow freak into "the pathological specimen of the terata."[73] In contrast, the mock science of phrenology, which depended on the measure of human heads and was often used to link Africanized bodies to apes in the chain of human development, utilized none other than George Washington himself as the opposite extreme. In the 1820s, as cultural historian Benjamin Reiss notes, Washington's head began to be identified by artists and phrenologists as a "model of proportion and overall strength of character," and by the 1840s was interpreted as the "phrenological—and classical—ideal of harmony." Perhaps it is no coincidence, then, that Washington's esteemed profile was also among the first images of an American leader to be widely reproduced. By 1860, he could be found on everything from medallions to mantelpieces.[74] Washington's visual representations serve as an ideological counterpoint to Heth's: her abject blackness and physical monstrosity only emphasize his recurrent framing as a national icon and exemplar of evolutionary perfection. Purity, in other words, was being ideologically constructed to script a national narrative, a "pure past" that George Washington embodied.[75] This process was already underway in 1835, the year Heth's exhibits began, as news surfaced that someone was raising money to build a memorial for the "mythic Father of the Nation."[76] Barnum's tethering of Heth to the nation's ideal figure demonstrated his astuteness in selling a theatrical phenomenon to American audiences who "desired a living link to their revolutionary past."[77] And, by association, Heth's protean physicality, which so inspired reactions of repulsion and perplexity from spectators, became sign and symbol of Washington, American heritage, and even time itself. "Aunt Joice" was no ordinary handicapped female slave, but at once an "extraordinary negro woman," a "renowned relic of the olden time," and as one newspaper declared, an awe-inspiring "impersonation of Time."[78] Cultural attitudes toward the bodies of Joice Heth and George Washington, then, make evident how these seemingly diametrically opposed icons were manipulated into a queer union, transforming a freak show into an occasion to collectively remember, and an elderly black woman into America's proverbial wet nurse.

Animate Automatons, Wicked Illustrations

Yet, if Joice Heth was so utterly fantastic, was she even real? Her wandering exhibit took a momentarily zany detour in New England, when her very authenticity as a human being, far from a fait accompli, became openly contested. In the winter of 1835, Heth was accused of being a double imposter—not just a fraudulent actress with no actual connections to George Washington, but also a simulacrum of a human. According [*human simulacrum*] to *The Life of P. T. Barnum Written by Himself,* the anonymous accuser's unusual claims surfaced while Barnum was exhibiting Heth in Boston in a "small-ballroom of the Concert Hall, at the corner of Court and Hanover Streets." In an interesting twist, another exhibit—Johann Nepomuk Maelzel's "equally celebrated 'automaton chess-player'"—was being shown simultaneously when the story first appeared. In Barnum's words,

> When the audiences began to decrease in numbers, a short communication appeared in one of the newspapers, signed "*A Visitor,*" in which the writer claimed to have made an important discovery. He stated that Joice Heth, as at present exhibited, was a humbug, whereas if the simple truth was told in regard to the exhibition, it was really vastly curious and interesting. "The fact is," said the communication, "Joice Heth is not a [*automaton*] human being. What purports to be a remarkably old woman is simply a curiously constructed automaton, made up of whalebone, india-rubber, and numberless strings ingeniously put together, and made to move at the slightest touch, according to the will of the operator. The exhibitor is a ventriloquist, and all the conversations apparently held with the ancient

lady are purely imaginary, so far as she is concerned, for the answers and incidents purporting to be given and related by her, are merely the ventriloquial voice of the exhibitor."[79]

Unsurprisingly, this shocking accusation of staging was, in all likelihood, staged. *The Sunday Morning News,* a newspaper in New York, printed a similar article, by way of news from a mysterious female correspondent in New Haven, Connecticut, simply named "The Lady on Temple Street." Yet, as cultural historian Benjamin Reiss notes, Levi Lyman—Barnum's ever-clever lawyer-turned-associate, who was also responsible for Heth's ersatz biography—probably planted the original story. Moreover, he argues, Barnum's assertion was partly false: the accusation was made not in Boston, but rather in New Haven when Lyman was in charge of exhibiting Heth.[80] This admixture of originals and facsimiles, a recurring theme throughout this chapter, occasions a seemingly unanswerable question: are there any originals in these performances? The question seems relevant as we consider that the printed accusation—that Heth was an inert mechanism willed to life by Barnum, a literal puppet on a set of "numberless strings"—revived interest in Heth, as audiences now sought to determine if this "curiously constructed automaton" was, in fact, a human or a hollow double, a mere frame that Barnum's trained voice reverberated through, like an instrument.

While automatons existed for centuries prior to Joice Heth's performances, as popular entertainment in the late 1830s and 1840s shifted toward blackface minstrelsy, their metallic gears, as we will see, were *blackened.* The first forms of automatons or "proto-automata"—talking Egyptian statues, featuring jointed arms and trumpets concealed in their hollows—alluded to the taut relationship between astronomical clockwork and biological automata. This peculiar marriage of man and machine was furthered by philosopher Albertus Magnus's construction in the Middle Ages of a "mechanical man" out of metal, wax, glass, and leather and the creation of the first android, a "mechanical figure which simulated a living human, or animal, operating with apparently responsive action" by Hans Bullman of Nuremberg.[81] A sudden appearance of black automatons in the United States, meanwhile, was undeniably connected to the emergence of blackface minstrelsy as an increasingly beloved racialized expressive form. In 1835, the same year of Heth's first exhibits, T. D. Rice—famous for his debut with the song and dance "Jump Jim Crow" on the Bowery three years earlier—performed in his *Bone Squash Diavolo*, also in New York.[82] Rice's "Ethiopian operas" were early prototypes for later blackface minstrel shows that, according to George Templeton Strong, were by 1840 a "runaway craze" and, a mere four years later, a bona fide "epidemic."[83] Yet, in 1843, seven years after Heth's death, this rapture for blackface minstrelsy collided into the mechanical when Peale's Museum featured "live minstrel entertainment" in the form of "Negro" singing and dancing performed by clockwork automatons."[84]

This fascinating footnote in history broadly, and black performance specifically, is perplexing. How did these automated persons simulate "black" movements? Did their jerky appendages, for instance, mimic angularity, one of the so-called "characteristics of Negro expressions" Zora Neale Hurston so expertly satirized almost a century later? After all, Hurston writes, it is "the lack of symmetry that makes Negro dancing so difficult to learn. The abrupt and unexpected changes."[85] In this odd convergence of race and the mechanical, we return to Joice Heth. Her supposed resemblance to an automaton encouraged a unique and spectacular mystery: just who, or *what*, was animating this black object? Black objecthood shifts here as already-abject Heth was imaginatively reduced further: into a mere doll-like object. Audiences were, thus, able to revel in this fantasy of a human-like contraption masquerading as grotesque Heth. This staged scenario reveals the almost gleefully scripted slippages between "inert matter and vital life" that represent the more nefarious extremes of black performance art.[86]

Sianne Ngai uses the term "racial animatedness" to describe similar scenarios, especially the troubling historical conflation of "exaggerated emotional expressiveness" with "racial or ethnic otherness."[87] "Animatedness" refers to one of the most rudimentary of emotional states: simply, "being moved." Yet, when positioned on raced bodies, especially African Americans, animatedness morphs into a "surprising interplay between the passionate and the mechanical." The body of the now "over-emotional racialized subject" becomes a prototype, an "instrument, porous and pliable, for the vocalization of others." This uniquely racialized ventriloquism is especially disquieting considering the legacies of

objecthood into a reduction : doll

animatedness: being moved, passion & mechanics

historical practices, like freak shows themselves, which privileged "objectification, exaggerated corporeality or physical pliancy, and the body-made spectacle."[88]

Interestingly, the excessive emotive responses inherent to "racial animatedness" were present in Barnum's delineation of Joice Heth's religious fervor. Despite her numerous corporeal ailments, Heth's body was unusually responsive to musical cadences. "Joice Heth was very fond of church-music," Barnum noted in his autobiography, "to which she would beat time by waving her long withered arm." If this rare display was not remarkable enough, Barnum described an "occasion in New York" in which an "aged Baptist minister stood by her side as she was singing one of her favorite hymns, and he joined her, and lined each verse." Heth, in turn, was "much pleased by this circumstance, and sang with renewed animation." This improvisatory vocal exchange continued, with the minister beginning a hymn and Heth immediately joining in to sing it with him. So comprehensive was her knowledge of hymns, that not only did Barnum hear "several hymns entirely new to me," but the minister himself "in one or two instances refreshed his memory when he found himself at a loss to recall the exact language of the verses."[89]

Here, Heth's animatedness was doubly inflected by her bodily *and* vocal expressivity: the "long withered arm" that noted time of its own accord and the effervescent voice that intoned with "renewed animation." Yet when juxtaposed against Heth's virtual immobility, against her elderly body that had been forced to appear even more aged, this vigorousness was jarring. How could such an extremely disabled and ancient woman possess such great energy? This disjuncture seems to have anticipated the accusations of ventriloquism that came later. Heth's emaciated corpus, in other words, belied her ability to move so vigorously, while her appearance already strained audiences' definition of the human. The accusation that she was a machine, mere India rubber and whalebone, therefore, was indeed bizarre and silly but in line with the already extraordinary meanings attached to her. And within the freak show's emphasis on corporeal spectacle, this supplementary interpretation of Heth was especially tempting. By rendering her as a mechanical contraption, the already indistinct limits between subjectivity and objecthood could be imaginatively dissolved even further. She could be regarded as a puppet, devoid of agency entirely. In this imaginative act of completely severing will from Heth, audiences did not avoid the disturbing aspects of her self-objectification; rather, they blithely participated in it.

Joice Heth as automaton offers a particularly bizarre lens onto objecthood and its limits. On the one hand, her performance as George Washington's nursemaid was linked to national anxieties about history and time. On the other hand, the claims that she was an automaton hint at other equally powerful misgivings about the limits of the human, the repression of which made chattel slavery possible. Paradoxically, Heth's decayed bodily morphology was elastic enough to buttress both descriptions and their attendant discourses. Her enactment of an ancient negress, and her new role as an automaton, were both avatars linked to her slippery human form. Similar to the other cultural actors in this book, Joice Heth was a performer maneuvering a tricky ontology, between subject and embodied object. Yet, in the accusation of Heth-as-automaton, we perceive a strikingly brute form of objecthood. While fugitive slave Ellen Craft and conceptual artist Adrian Piper, for instance, transformed themselves into perceptible objets d'art, neither was accused of approximating the most base and inert of objects: a ventriloquized device approaching the dull splendor of a machine. Heth's portrayal of an "animate automaton" cogently reminds us of the mechanical-like calibrations inherent in performing objecthood.[90] Her performances, moreover, were also closer to prototypical theatrical experiences, as spectators purchased tickets to view Heth under the makeshift proscenium arch of the freak show. In short, Joice Heth is simultaneously the most performative and the most acutely an object of all the performers I discuss in these pages; as a result, she stretches the limits of objecthood in disturbing directions.

One other incident of befuddlement produced by Heth's ambiguous ontology is of use here. Returning to Barnum's lively narration, in Boston, "an ex-member of Congress [. . .] a gentleman highly esteemed" along with his wife, two children, and "aged mother" attended Heth's exhibition. As the family "approached the bed where Heth was resting, the visitors respectfully gave way to them." Yet, while the former congressman conversed with Barnum, his elderly mother engaged in an examination of her own, "closely scrutinizing Aunt Joice" to determine *its* authenticity as a wondrous apparatus simulating a human. An intrigu-

ing dialogue ensued between Levi Lyman, Heth's aforementioned han-
dler, and the curious elderly woman, ostensibly overheard by Barnum
and detailed for readers:

> Presently, the old lady spoke up in an audible tone, and with much ap-
> parent satisfaction, "There, it is alive after all!" I caught the remark in-
> stantly, and was glad to perceive that her son did not hear it [. . .] I
> listened anxiously to their conversation. "Why do you think it is alive?"
> asked Lyman quietly. "Because its pulse beats as regularly as mine does,"
> responded the old lady. "Oh that is the most simple portion of the
> machinery," said Lyman. "We make that operate on the principle of a
> pendulum to a clock." "Is it possible?" said the old lady, who was now
> evidently satisfied that Joice was an automaton. Then turning to her son,
> she said: "George, this thing is not alive at all. It is all a machine." "Why,
> mother," said the son with evident embarrassment, "what are you talk-
> ing about?" A half-suppressed giggle ran throughout the room, and the
> gentleman and his family soon withdrew. Lyman maintained the utmost
> gravity of countenance, and the keenest observer would have failed to
> detect in his visage any evidence of his having played off a joke upon the
> unsophisticated old lady.[91]

This anecdote, restaged for Barnum's readers twenty years later, reveals
something about the audiences and operations of these performances.
The striking cross-section of ages in the ex-congressman's family, for
instance, suggests the wide import of Heth's bodily phantasmagoria—
seemingly perfect for a family outing, even a respectable upper-class
one—while also implying the far reach of Barnum's publicity. In addition,
this event also demonstrates how slyly Barnum and Lyman folded the
fable of Heth-as-automaton into the already rehearsed elements of the
freak show. The aged white woman's desire to measure Heth's pulse draws
on the blatant scripting of the latter as a remarkable biological aberration.
The difference, of course, is that same pulse's steadiness was retooled as
startling evidence of the virtuosity of this black automaton, its amazing
ability to so closely mimic a human heartbeat. And in this literary reenactment, Heth's ontological slippage is repurposed yet again as the crux of
a joke played on an innocent spectator, unable to definitively determine
who, or *what*, was animating the mysterious form before her.

Figure 1.4. "Joice Heth." Engraving. P. T. Barnum, *The Life of P. T. Barnum Written by Himself* (1855; Urbana and Chicago: University of Illinois Press, 2000), 158.

There is more: this scene is accompanied in Barnum's autobiography by actual animation, via a black-and-white illustration; the literary, performative, and now visual all comingle. In the lightly drawn engraving, signed "Whitney & Jocelyn, SC" at the bottom, stand five adult white spectators (three women and two men) encircling a raised platform, where Heth, seen in profile, sits with her hands clasped and resting on her knees. Presumably, the elegantly dressed man in the top hat on the far left is the ex-congressman, the Lilliputian legs of one of his children to the immediate left and his elderly mother, in glasses and a bonnet similar to Heth's, to the right. Meanwhile, the man on the far right, in a tailored jacket with tails with one hand on his hip and the other extended toward Heth, is assumedly Levi Lyman. While the representation of Heth here does not match the grotesquerie of the woodcut made fifteen years earlier, she appears equally inscrutable—her face mysterious and unreadable, its blackness delimited by extra shading. If the overall cultural meaning conveyed by the image, or what Roland Barthes termed the *studium*, was the startling intimacy with which audiences viewed Heth, the *punctum*—the "accident" or "cast of dice" that "will disturb the *studium*"—was the empty chair in the foreground.[92] Tacitly, the chair suggests that the former congressman's mother (or someone else, for that matter) could stand on it as a means to gain an even better view of the woman—or thing—seated on the bed-cum-platform before them. Perhaps readers of Barnum's autobiography are that someone else? The lonely chair, pointed toward Heth, seems a sensuous temptation, an invitation for curious readers to step inside the text and determine for themselves if Heth was real or a device animated by outside hands. This tableau, then, was not mere textual ornamentation, but rather didactic and theatrical. The ambiguous engraving, in other words, attempted to instruct readers in how to interpret and remember Joice Heth post mortem, while acting as a conduit linking the literary and performative, infusing the ephemerality of performance with the permanence of ink.

Barnum, true to form, had one additional trick up his sleeve: in the last remaining visual representation of Joice Heth, he wildly embraced animation's ductility for sinister purposes, wielding it to circumvent the limits of realism, if not decorum. Barnum, in a prolific turn, published in 1856 another autobiography, a year after his first, only this one was authored under the nom de plume "Petite Bunkum, the Yankee Showman." In an arresting convergence with Heth, Barnum seized on the ability of an avatar to partly camouflage his identity. In typical Barnum fashion, however, this willful self-cloaking was too facile, so he created a literary simulacrum of Heth as well, an avatar named "Judy Heath." In his fanciful description of her, Barnum deftly folded in a remnant of the automaton myth with this evocative portrait:

Let me try to describe her personal appearance. Fancy a skin of India-rubber stretched on bones; jaws without teeth, eyes that looked on vacancy, wool as white as snow; a nose and chin in close proximity; her complexion black as jet, her whole form lean and skinny. There you have Judy Heath.[93]

In this suggestive rendering, redolent of Barnum's dexterity as a showman, he provided literary spectators with stark contrasts (snow-white hair/jet-black skin), strange antinomies (jaws without teeth, eyes that could not see), and a stroke of the fantastic (India rubber as skin). Yet, as in his first autobiography, Barnum did not rely on this string of adjectives alone to convey the spectacle of witnessing Joice Heth. Instead, he inserted what is the third and final visual approximation of Heth that has survived, though this one far outstrips the faux realism of the previous two in its outrageousness. Above the caption "Judy Heath, dressed up to receive company," is an extremely crude representation of a short animalistic being with a beak-like mouth, dressed in a top hat and military-style garb, holding a rifle. While, at first glance, the visual elements seem incongruous, they are in line with Barnum's later discussion of Heth's supposed recalcitrance. He recalls, for instance, how a drunken Heth "bestowed upon me the compliment of a black eye, by a blow of her crutch," after he refused to bring her "another half pint" of rum, and the soldierly dress and rifle's presence in the engraving seem intended to mock her inebriated intransigence.[94] While I will discuss a similar incident of Heth's insurrection momentarily, I am interested here in her vicious transmogrification into a vulgar literary creature. Her subjection in real time ceased after her death and the orchestrated public dissection that followed. Barnum, however, seems not to have been done with her memory and the possibilities to radically reshape and alter it, as these engravings and literary enactments reveal. These efforts to manipulate Heth are as indelible as the printed letters and swirls of ink that hold versions of her, or rather the many Joice Heths, captive. Yet the outlines of this literary and visual portraiture illustrated her evasions of devious desires, two decades later, to still render her docile.

These strange scenes, and increasingly unsettling images, ultimately manifest Barnum's attempted ventriloquism of the past itself. Ironically, despite her near paralysis, Joice Heth exuded surpluses, both in written descriptions of her racial animatedness and in the visual renderings of her body. If the former denote her affective excess, even at the hand of

Judy Heath, dressed up to receive company.

Figure 1.5. "Judy Heath." Engraving. Petite Bunkum [P. T. Barnum], *The Autobiography of Petite Bunkum, the Yankee Showman* (New York: A. Ranney, 1856), 24.

others, the latter gesture toward the visual delineations of Heth that fail to fully capture her elusive presence in the archive. Heth's slipperiness, however, did not prevent Barnum from attempting to edit, exaggerate, and rewrite her memory and the past she appeared in. Returning to the event that opened this section, it was not just Heth, but rather the sordid past itself that was made to "move at the slightest touch, according to the will of the operator."

Barnum's keen puppetry of historical time, already salient in Heth's mimesis of an ancient nursemaid, implies his understanding that the past possessed, to quote José Esteban Muñoz, a "performative nature, which is to say that rather than being static and fixed, the past does things."[95] Barnum's memorialization of Heth was highly atypical. It was not a solemn gesture that sought to "tidy up disorderly histories" or read "a continuous narrative into one full of ruptures and contradictions," in the words of Judith Halberstam.[96] Rather, this continual reanimation of Joice Heth delighted in inconsistencies, half-truths, gaps, willful omissions, and visual warpings and distortions.

"Dey Make Me Say Dat All the Time": Joice Heth's Sonic of Dissent

Hearing, too, is central to witnessing. Heard images haunt
the mind as much as visual ones.
—Elizabeth Alexander, "'Can You Be BLACK and Look at
This?': Reading the Rodney King Video(s)"

If we could attune our ears to the echoes of history, what would the strains of Joice Heth in the archive *sound* like? I now turn toward the frequencies of the aural, a reminder that, though we are spectators twice removed—once by the passage of time, and again by our necessary reliance on the testimony of others—we are not only posthumous viewers of Heth's orchestrated exhibits, but also listeners. And, as Elizabeth Alexander intimates, we are witnesses as well. This move toward sound may seem sudden and abrupt, yet we have been digesting the resonances of Heth's speech acts, however brief, all along. From the exclamatory "I raised him!" to the animated and perhaps sonorous tones of her singing from the previous discussion, I follow the continuum of Heth's vocal interjection toward their most acute end: her possible resistance.

Something was indeed amiss the day an anonymous spectator observed a shocking aside at one of Joice Heth's performances, captured in the pages of an edited medical journal. Published in *The Scalpel*, a twenty-five-cent magazine "adapted to popular and professional reading" (per its subtitle), the report was written in a tone that was far from objective, seeming to delight in its crude descriptions of Heth. Similar to Barnum's increasingly bizarre characterizations, the anonymous writer's delineation of her as a "smoke dried wench" or simulacrum of a "large monkey" made plain his disgust and amusement.[97] Still, according to the report, Heth's apparent exhaustion provoked an unusual, if brief, deviation from her usually well-rehearsed repertoire:

> One day, however, a Yankee friend, who was cognizant of the whole scheme, observing her with a little less steam on than was desirable to keep her in training, asked her in presence of her keeper, if she remembered Massa George, meaning her alleged industrious owner. A ray of anger shot from the old woman's hitherto closed eyes, as she replied. "No! debil take 'em all; don't know notin bout him! Dey make me say dat all the time: gimme drink!" The ladies stared, and Joice speedily got her drink, with a soothing reproof for her impiety.[98]

This outrageous outburst, a series of exclamations punctuated by a demand, was a fierce rebuke to her routinized role-play as a relic of national memory. An aside can be easily dismissed, but as Alexandra Vazquez suggests, it can have a powerful pedagogical function.[99] Likewise, for the remainder of this section, I will dwell on this momentary deviation—relishing "in the break"—to consider the broader implications of Heth's outcry.

What emerges from this irate and profane aside are a sound and embodied form of knowledge I am terming a *sonic of dissent*. Heth's indignant reply troubles, in other words, the slick schematics of her bodily exhibits. It is an interregnum that forcibly pauses the "linear logic(s) of narrative construction" predicated on the cooperation of her performing body, and particularly her speech.[100] Heth's indisputably black voice, as the dialect-like syntax of the quotation suggests, uses her distinct register as a weapon to interrupt the manufactured histories her audiences were persuaded to believe in, a process that the partially disabled and virtually enslaved Heth was otherwise unable to impede. Strikingly, Frederick Douglass describes in his autobiography witnessing how his Aunt Hester also used a sonic of dissent, albeit horrific screams, to contest a beating by her master. Philosopher Fred Moten calls the sound of Hester's shrieks a "phonography," drawing our attention to the "freedom drive" her anguished cries animated.[101] The violent abuse of Aunt Hester, and her propulsive shouts, are analogous to Heth's brief angry aside and its suggestions of her forced compliance. Heth's furiously improvised utterances also articulate a freedom drive—in this case, the bold articulation of her subjectivity in the midst of a carefully orchestrated mise-en-scène.

The remarkable surfacing of Heth's exuberant and sacrilegious vocal interjection, an escape from the propriety of Barnum's staging, swings the focus away from how she was handled (and depicted) and toward the way that she handled (and depicted) herself. Put differently, much ink has been spilled on the themes of agency, coercion, and consent in Heth's performances and in freak show performance writ large. However, given the absence, palpable and glaring, of these black performer's own accounts, ascertaining evidence of their agency becomes exceptionally difficult, if not impossible, requiring different modes of perception and analysis.[102] This interpretative challenge is compounded when trying to extricate any sort of truth from the often sinister motivations and purposeful distortion of others, as we saw in the previous discussion of P. T. Barnum's increasingly hyperbolic imaginings of Heth. In contrast, a focus on Heth's speech shifts attention toward the meanings transmitted in embodied forms of knowledge, so often obscured in favor of the supposedly more stable textual documents of the archive. Heth's defiant aural exclamation (and perhaps pleasurable fantasy) that the devil dispose of her white female spectators, is a hint of an alternative rendering to the benevolent narrative she was conscripted to engage in. In that regard, her outburst signaled her "counter-memories" that told of the "disparities between history as it is discursively transmitted and memory as it is publicly enacted by the bodies that bear its consequences," in Joseph Roach's terms.[103] As the passage evinces, the spilling out of Heth's temporary vocal insurrection despite continued efforts to suppress it, or at least—as her swift procurement of alcohol implied—control and mitigate it, speaks to the sheer force of her sonic of dissent.

However, I do not want to underemphasize the perhaps violent means of cajoling Heth's participation. The *Scalpel* article makes more explicit the efforts to forcibly produce her performing body; the writer remarked, for instance, that "Heth was usually remarkably tractable," receiving her "religious education" from a lawyer "perfectly cognizant of the power of whiskey and tobacco in producing compliance with the wishes of a legal advisor." He continued, noting that Heth was polite in her rehearsed responses to audiences, "unless the words whiskey or tobacco fell upon her ear, when she would generally give an expressive grunt of assent."[104] These comments are dubious, to say the least, clearly invested in deemphasizing Heth's possible torture in favor of the literary spectacle of an inebriated Heth who willingly performed to procure salves for her addictions. The predicament of the question of free will and consent is made plain here; in other terms, the difficulty in "rethinking the relation of performance and agency," as Saidiya V. Hartman puts it, is great because the "spectacle of black contentment" in these tricky archival sources is so pervasive.[105] Heth's willful acts of black corporeal deceit (or not) are part and parcel of what Coco Fusco exposes as a long history of intercultural performances,[106] the larger dramatic and historical landscape that Heth's stagings are undoubtedly framed by.

I return to objecthood, its perils and its pleasures, to emphasize the brute labor—affective and otherwise—that Joice Heth was contracted to engage in, making the rare surviving fragments of her voice all the more remarkable. Her bodily enactments triggered various modes of objecthood, as I detailed in the accusation of her as a black automaton, and the accompanying rumor that a disembodied and ventriloquized voice echoed through it. Here, objecthood indicates the implicit force used to render Heth a proper (that is, well-behaved) aesthetic object for the perception of others, most especially as a stable bodily conduit for the uninterrupted flow of mammy memory for her white spectators. The ontological onus that her role as Washington's "ancient negress" necessitated, reducing her to a decrepit body explicitly designed for the nostalgic pleasure of others, made plain objecthood's exploitive properties. Moreover, Heth's objecthood highlighted, in Lauren Berlant and Elizabeth Freeman's words, the "historic burden black women" in representational practices "have borne to represent embodiment, desire" and, in this case, the fortification of white American identity in the nineteenth century.[107] Historians Eric Lott and Brian Currid have written about how forms of expressive blackness operate as conduits for iterations of white identity formation.[108] Heth's iconic role performed similar cultural work; her exclamations can be interpreted as a momentary rupture in the quotidian and all-too-normalized mechanics of this disturbing process. She was an object made docile and kept "in training" like a disciplined pet—the worst workings of black objecthood. But she also illustrates that black performers, and disabled performers, could indeed perceive, witness, and even speak back, in the midst of their objectification.

Continuing the quirky logic of objecthood, I suggest reconceiving of Heth's multiple identifications and ontological hoaxes as subtle forms of antebellum performance art; in doing so, these bodily and narrative instabilities are not slippery lacunae, but part of the performances them- [*not slippery, but performances*] selves. After all, in Heth's case, facts are as performative as "being" itself. Rather than insisting on the phantasm of a singular corporeality, Heth's contingent identities—nursemaid, automaton, and medical curio—are numerous. Similar to black conjoined twins Millie and Christine McKoy's confounding subjectivity, Heth's odd occupation of the pronouns "she" and "it" signaled the ability of these protean historical figures, as Daphne A. Brooks describes, to "push the limits of what and how 'Black' and corporeal authenticity might be redefined and reimagined in the nineteenth century."[109] Pushing further, if the ontology of performance itself is predicated on loss—a representation that lacks reproduction, as Peggy Phelan has argued[110]—the irrevocable silence I face in reconstructing Heth's aural textures is a given of performance's vanishing acts. Granted, Heth's silence in the archives is distressing. Yet, rather than lament this absence, we can see performance as a point of departure that forces scholars like myself to use different techniques, to explore Heth's stagings more creatively. Avatar production is one such method; it enables us to perceive how Heth's black maternal dramas of memory [*what the performance traces*] extend beyond the moment of performance and become mythic (and often distorted) representations. Thus, while her fragmented materiality has indeed disappeared, reframing these bodily acts as early iterations of black performance converts this seeming loss into a vantage point.

Finally, my aim in focusing on Joice Heth's off-script blasphemy is twofold: first, to counteract the mastery of narrative ploys privileging [*① counter*] the voices of others at the clear expense (and erasure) of Heth's; second, [*complete erasure/objectification*] to explore the limits of my own abilities, as a scholar, to analyze a set of performances that eludes my grasp. Testimonies to Heth's performances, as the aforementioned medical journal illustrates, threaten to reinscribe [*② limits of performance*] the spectacle of her bodily impostures, blithely remaking her into an eternal object of audience amusement. Barnum's multiple contradictory accounts of his torture of Heth by the removal of her teeth as well as her drunken resistance, meanwhile, do exactly what they intend: they not only transform any transparent truths about his (and her) roles in these performances into a perplexing hall of mirrors, but also center *his* versions of their mechanizations and their legacy for us, as contemporary readers. If, as Benjamin Reiss suggests, Heth is lost to history "once through slavery and once through imposture," the seemingly purposeful literary omissions and visual distortions I have delineated throughout this chapter are a third layer of obfuscation.[111]

Furthermore, I am cognizant that my own biased desire to locate scintillas of Heth's subversion from the paucity of information that has survived may situate resistance where there is in fact none at all. I am trying to save her, to quote Saidiya V. Hartman's words in another context, "not from death but also from oblivion."[112] Perhaps, to evoke Toni Morrison's *Beloved*, this is a story not to pass on. But I persist in preserving these aural disturbances as vital remains of Heth's elastic corporeal theater, even if I have to speculate as to their tonal registers. Though elusive, they are as much a part of what Daphne A. Brooks calls "Black(ened) cultural marginalia in the archives" as the performances themselves.[113] Joice Heth's sonic of dissent is an echo in the genealogies of black performance, its faint reverberations demonstrative of how embodied memory far outlives the mortal participants in the staging of history.

Coda: Disappearing Acts

But everything must have an end including ancient negresses.
—P. T. Barnum

Perhaps the biggest disappearing act was the elision of Joice Heth's complex performance art, the specter of these fascinating "body-dramas," to use Beverly Guy-Shetfall's term, lurking in the musty penumbras of American history.[114] And who Joice Heth was outside of her mythical avatars—if that was even her real name—continues to remain sealed, like the contents of a secret envelope or a hidden tomb. I have reexamined these submerged and devious corporeal art forms, extricating them from their too-facile categorization as side-show freakery or—to return to the beginnings of this chapter—as a mere sentence on a placard, and instead positioned them as a critical node in an unfolding constellation of dexterous, artistic, improvisational, and often dense black performance work. Like fugitive slave Ellen Craft's performances that follow, Heth's bodily exhibitions were intricate, if not idiosyncratic, suturing disability to race, freak shows to mammy memory, and resistance to the decibels of a vocal echo across centuries.

There is not one Joice Heth, but many. The continued reemergence of this icon—the ancient black female witness to history—in black theater, hip-hop, and contemporary politics illustrates the persistence of this particular rendering of an archetypal American past.[115] The black maternal avatar did not disappear, but rather is continually reenacted. And the presence of these reincarnations—with their intertwining of past and present—induces, in Rebecca Schneider's words, the "quasi and queasy sensation of cross-temporal slippage."[116] We perceive the unremitted desire for a black expressive and maternal embodiment of American history, but also the consequences of that collective fervor for an embodied link to the past. As the curious phenomenon of Joice Heth makes abundantly clear, black performers can—and did—perform exuberant fictions for a ravenous public who often chose to ignore the ontological labor of those on display. Black maternal avatars, the many Joice Heths, are performance artists who enable us to become observers watching a show, and that show is history itself.

sonic of dissent in an echo in performance

2

Passing Performances

Ellen Craft's Fugitive Selves

The history of blackness is testament to the fact that objects
can and do resist.
—Fred Moten, *In the Break*

I begin this chapter with the barely audible tones of a daring (and collaborative) secret escape. In December 1848, two slaves, William and Ellen
Craft—married but living on two different plantations in Georgia—fled
from slavery together. The secret of their success? Artful embodiment.
In William's words,

> We were married, and prayed and toiled on till December 1848, at which
> time (as I have stated) a plan suggested itself that proved quite successful,
> and in eight days after it was first thought of we were free from the horrible
> trammels of slavery, and glorifying God who had brought us safely out of
> a land of bondage. Knowing that slaveholders have the privilege of taking
> their slaves to any part of the country they think proper, it occurred to me
> that, as my wife was nearly white, I might get her to disguise herself as an
> invalid gentleman, and assume to be my master, while I could attend as his
> slave, and that in this manner we might effect our escape.

William notes that, upon first mentioning this plan to Ellen, "she shrank
from the idea" out of fear that it would be "almost impossible for her to
assume that disguise, and travel a distance of 1,000 miles across the slave
States." Yet, the narrative suggests, after Ellen pondered her possible life
under the legal system of slavery—which did not recognize her as anything other than "mere chattel"—she decided that William's idea, while
dangerous, was worth an attempt. In her words: "Therefore, if you will
purchase the disguise, I will try to carry out the plan."[1]

Subsequently, William and Ellen worked together to covertly acquire and collate the various sartorial mechanisms needed for her disguise as an upper-class white gentleman. William purchased multiple articles of men's clothing "piece by piece" in "different parts of the town," which Ellen then stored in a chest of drawers until the night before the escape. Likewise, the timing of the Craft's escape near Christmas gave the Crafts an opportunity to obtain alibis. Specifically, the custom of some of "the best slaveholders" was to occasionally grant "their favourite slaves a few days' holiday at Christmas time." Hence, Ellen obtained an individual pass from "her mistress, while William obtained one from the cabinet maker for whom he worked. While neither Ellen nor William were able to read their respective passes, the documents were fundamental to the perilous four-day staging that was about to occur—without them, the Crafts would have been left with little time, if any, between their escape, their respective master's discovery of their absence, and recognition of their plan.

The Crafts had additional practical and logistical concerns that needed to be solved by additional layers of disguise and impersonation. Specifically, two predicaments needed immediate solutions: how to hide Ellen's feminine face, but also, more importantly, how Ellen, unable to read and write, would sign her, or rather Mr. William Johnson's, signature. This last act was important, since as William notes, "it was customary for travellers to register their names in the visitors' book at hotels, as well as in the clearance or Custom-house book at Charleston, South Carolina." In an act of imaginative agency, Ellen devised a solution: she designed a poultice to bind her right hand up in to feign injury—and hence the inability to write—so she could "with propriety ask the officers to register my name for me."[2] Ellen's pretense that she knew how to write but was temporarily unable to do so, or what the late critic Lindon Barrett termed her "pantomime of literacy,"[3] was complemented by a second poultice that Ellen designed to go into "a white handkerchief to be worn under the chin, up the cheeks, and to tie over the head" that disguised both her facial expressions as well as her "beardless chin." The objective of these tactics, of Ellen "being muffled in the poultices," as William states, in addition to her later pretending on the train to be deaf, was to avoid the conversation of which "most Yankee travellers are passionately fond."

"Mr. William Johnson" emerged as a live, flesh-and-blood man when Ellen Craft left her plantation on the morning of December 21, 1848, in

PASSING PERFORMANCES | 67

the guise of a white male slaveholder, parted ways with her husband, and attempted to successfully purchase train tickets, for *himself* and "his" slave. William describes this scene in their escape narrative:

> We shook hands, said farewell, and started in different directions for the railway station. I took the nearest possible way to the train, for fear I should be recognized by some one, and got into the negro car in which I knew I should have to ride; but my *master* (as I will now call my wife) took a longer way round, and only arrived there with the bulk of the passengers. He obtained a ticket for himself and one for his slave to Savannah, the first port, which was about two hundred miles off. My master then had the luggage stowed away, and stepped into one of the best carriages.

On Christmas Day, after four dangerous days, the Crafts reached Philadelphia, successfully crossing the threshold between the captivity of the South and the promise of freedom and liberty guaranteed in the North. Once the Crafts were reunited and eventually situated at a boardinghouse kept by an abolitionist—ironically, recommended to William by a "coloured gentleman" on the train "if I wished to run away from my master"—Ellen Craft "threw off the disguise and assumed her own apparel." Eventually, the Crafts took up residence in Boston, where they remained for two years, William working as a "cabinet-maker and furniture broker" and Ellen as a seamstress.[4] Fellow fugitive slave William Wells Brown introduced them into the New England abolitionist lecture circuit in January 1849, less than a month after their escape.[5] While Brown had lectured for more than three years with the Western New York Anti-Slavery Society, from 1843 until 1847, the Crafts were not initially prepared for their new careers. As biographer Dorothy Sterling suggests, their lack of knowledge in regard to the abolitionist movement meant "they had not anticipated a role in it."[6] Yet they quickly adapted, appearing in over sixty towns with Brown by May 1849 and refining a carefully orchestrated program.[7] "The alliance between Brown and the Crafts," historian R.J.M. Blackett writes, "later became one of the most renowned and influential abolitionist combinations in both America and Britain."[8] Hence, the Crafts rapidly and remarkably transformed themselves from escaped chattel into veteran performers on the abolitionist lecture circuit.

Unfortunately, their residence in Boston was short-lived. The passage of the Fugitive Slave Law in 1850, along with multiple devious efforts by Ellen's former master to recapture her, compelled the Crafts to flee to Liverpool by way of Nova Scotia. In England, William Craft soon resumed speaking with William Wells Brown, albeit in conjunction with a better funded and more prestigious abolitionist movement.[9] Ellen, once recovered from illness due to travel and stress, resumed her participation as well, aiding in increasingly outspoken stagings of antislavery dissent. The Crafts utilized their time in England to become polished and poised performers. Popular in the press, the Crafts also wielded the lecture stand as a means through which to self-publicize themselves. British newspapers, in turn, proclaimed audiences' ardor for the Crafts; a report in 1851, for instance, declared that "William and Ellen Craft are also exciting much sympathy and attention in England."[10] Both their subsequent enrollment in Lady Byron's industrial school in Surrey for formal education and their self-penned letter to the press confirming their whereabouts were reported widely in newspapers, both in England and America.[11] The Crafts raised four children in England, before returning to the United States in August 1869. They later settled in Georgia, where they eventually purchased a plantation and opened the Woodville Cooperative Farm School, which by 1875, according to Blackett, was the "finest [school] for whites or blacks in the entire county."[12]

The Crafts' escape narrative, *Running a Thousand Miles to Freedom: The Escape of William and Ellen Craft from Slavery*—from which much of the above is excerpted—*was* originally published in London in 1860. The book reveals how the Crafts' performance, both in its three-dimensional reality and its restaging in the two-dimensional landscape of the literary, borrowed from a playbook that had yet to be invented: their escape was a set of "actions, interactions, and relationships"—in other words, a lot like performance art.[13] Together, via repeated iterations in varied and often verboten social spheres, this pair constructed a shadow body—a white, male avatar—for Ellen Craft: a disabled upper-class planter named William Johnson.

* * *

Following their lead, I will trace a dual set of peregrinations—the wanderings of fugitive slave extraordinaire Ellen Craft *and* her ghost persona, Mr. William Johnson—in disparate geographical locales in the United States and eventually the British Isles, as well as their appearances (and disappearing acts) in print, visual media, and the kinesthetic medium of performance. In what follows, I not only delineate the Crafts' expertly executed staging of what poet Kevin Young calls "the black art of escape"; I also argue for a reinterpretation of Ellen Craft's graceful gestural vocabularies, both in disguise and out, as quotidian modes of performance art.[14] These everyday acts include buying a train ticket, writing one's signature, and walking. Ellen Craft's aestheticized, serial, and illicit performances as her white male doppelganger (and later, as her equally dangerous white mulatta self) sutured together two seemingly incommensurable traditions: performance art and the everyday disobedient acts committed by black slaves.

For decades, untold numbers of black Americans used their bodies in similarly conscious ways that parallel contemporary notions of performance art. Enslaved blacks broke tools, they prevaricated when talking with their masters, and they skimped on chores. Such sly deeds were numerous; in his autobiography, William Wells Brown admits with glee that he surreptitiously drank his master's mint julep.[15] These routine acts of recalcitrance, or what E. Patrick Johnson calls "embodied acts of resistance," were not just dissident tactics—these furtive moves, I believe, were a kind of performance.[16] I am particularly motivated by Paul Gilroy's outright naming of these subversive methods, such as mimicking masters, as "performance skills." Gilroy goes further, citing Ellen Craft's "thespian skills in crossing the line of both 'race' and gender" as emblematic of such theatrical tools.[17] Both Johnson and Gilroy reframe prototypical understandings of this noncompliance. I hope to push this concept further by calling attention to these stealth actions as not only embodied behaviors, but also forms of black performance art.

Yet, to return to my initial argument, what I term in this chapter Ellen Craft's various *passing performances* were not simply "the actual execution of an action," one definition of performance, but modes of nineteenth-century performance art that effected the most radical of political change: freedom from chattel slavery.[18] As I will discuss shortly, her fluid moves back and forth across class, gender, race, and disability through the simplest of materials—sartorial props and her own malleable body—as well as the insertion of her avatar in aesthetic and quotidian spaces enacted principles that are sine qua non to performance art. Craft's agit-prop stratagems of black performance, in other words, anticipated what RoseLee Goldberg describes as performance art's axiomatic "refusal to separate art activities from everyday life and the subsequent incorporation of everyday actions and objects as performance material."[19] I do not underestimate, however, the danger in Craft's fraudulent embodiments, at least in their earliest incarnations: as a performer on the run, the discovery of Ellen's true identity could have resulted in her and William's captivity and possibly death. Her passing performances are a particularly high-stakes form of antebellum performance art, one in which a fugitive slave enlivened and transformed an object—an imaginary disabled upper-class white slaveholder—into a three-dimensional subject who liberated the Crafts before staging his own vanishing act.

The Parts and Props of Fugitive Performance Art

The hazardous escape enacted by Ellen and William Craft was possible because the duo reconfigured, with tact and artistry, ordinary objects into protean mechanisms that facilitated movement. My use of "artistry" is a counterpoint to its frequent conflation with the merely decorative; rather, "art" here is an active verb, or in the words of Michel de Certeau, "a way of making."[20] I say this to reassert that aesthetic maneuvers are implicit in the entirety of the Crafts' performance oeuvre. Indeed, aesthetics rears its head in what may be the *least* artistic of places: the escape of fugitive slaves. It is exactly here where the Crafts (and later in this discussion, Ellen's devious cousins, Frank and Mary) exact an improvisational, though briefly rehearsed, *art* of escape. The "intense relationship between experimentalism and the everyday" in other words, which philosopher Fred Moten unearths in late-twentieth-century black aesthetic practices, manifests in these carefully sculpted dissident acts as well, more than a century earlier.[21] Practiced by fugitive slaves on the run, however, these artistic devices were closer to tactics, in the way de Certeau framed them, as both "everyday practices" and "clever tricks."[22] The Crafts' status as runaway chattel—"running" by force rather than choice—falls within this logic. As such, from repurposed items-cum-props, and from the quotidian social behaviors delineated below, emerge evidence of their passing performances.[23]

Of all the trespassing and transgressions executed by the Crafts, the pièce de résistance was the sartorial sleight of hand that brought Mr. William Johnson to life; to borrow literary critic Monica L. Miller's idiom, this was Ellen Craft's "crime of fashion."[24] While the elusive avatar repeatedly takes center stage in this book, "his" or "her" bodily doings are always facilitated by a subset of supplemental instruments. In Craft's case, these instruments were the flexible apparatuses of clothing she employed in her escape. They became accessories to her crime, enabling her to pass as her disabled white male avatar. These items, whether utilitarian or mere embellishment, were recoded and put in service of a "freedom drive."[25]

Ellen Craft's "piece by piece" armature of parts and props was extensive, if not idiosyncratic, and further evinced the Crafts' collaborative (and crafty) aesthetic. William purchased different articles of men's clothing in "different parts of the town, at odd times" and gave them to Ellen who, in turn, surreptitiously stored and locked them up in a "chest of drawers" on her plantation, itself constructed by William during his "overtime." Unable to purchase pants, Ellen herself made the "trowsers." Meanwhile, just as "the smoothness" of Ellen's feminine face and her "beardless chin" were obscured by a poultice, the addition of a "pair of green spectacles" purchased by William further shielded her from possible detection. The poultice that hid Mr. William Johnson's damaged hand constitutes another performance of disability, a topic to which I will return. The addition of a "fashionable cloth cloak" further embellished the elegant wardrobe that contributed to Ellen's masterful performance of a master. In a final design flourish, William cut Ellen's "hair square at the back of the head," concluding after viewing her in full disguise that "she made a most respectable gentleman."[26] Armed with these stylish and studied effects, slaveholder Mr. William Johnson and *his* slave William Craft modeled a tailor-made escape.

The Crafts' escape acts via the vehicle of style, however, were not isolated acts of redress; if their performances echoed other black historical figures' skillful sartorial subversion, they also direct our attention to the multiple witnesses who viewed them. In her study of black dandy figures, *Slaves to Fashion*, Monica L. Miller details how hyperbolic forms of racial and class cross-dressing, or "crimes of fashion," were ritualistically staged in African American festivals, such as Pinkster and Negro Election Day, both of which were "regular holidays by the mid-eighteenth century." An amalgamation of British, American, African, and black American aesthetic practices, the participation of slaves and eventually of free blacks in these celebratory events evinced an acute attention to clothing's power to signify. After all, Miller notes, clothing's importance was undeniable, as it swiftly was becoming the means through which the "status of slave and master, whiteness and blackness, masculinity and femininity, Africanness and Americanness was being determined."[27]

William Craft transgressed those very lines while the Crafts were en route to Washington; he donned "a very good second-hand white beaver, an article I had never indulged in before" to disguise himself. William's extravagant hat, though recycled, still enraged "an uncouth planter," who castigated his "master" (i.e., Ellen in disguise) for spoiling that "ere nigger of yourn, by letting him wear such a devilish fine hat." The planter's irate reply, when a friend encouraged him not to speak to a "gentleman" like that, made clear the root of his disgust: "It always makes me itch all over, from head to toe, to get hold of every d—d nigger I see dressed like a white man."[28] While William's elegant attire provoked this lower-class white spectator (who may have lusted after the hat himself), Ellen's equally stylish "persona-play performance" encouraged a more benign curiosity from another anonymous witness.[29]

In a short eyewitness account titled "An Incident in the South," published less than two months after the escape, this "believer in physiognomy" detailed his encounter with Mr. William Johnson, whose "mysterious and unusual" presence led the writer to examine him more closely. Coming in contact with the Crafts onboard the cabin of a steamer in Savannah, the writer's attentiveness to the attire of this odd couple—an "apparently handsome young man, with black hair and eyes, and of a darkness that betokened Spanish extraction" accompanied by his "servant, a strapping negro"—framed how these wearable props worked together. He detailed for his antebellum literary audience how, for instance, this ethnically ambiguous man was bundled in a "capacious overcoat, his face bandaged with a white handkerchief, and its expression hid entirely by a pair of enormous spectacles." Ironically, despite the secrecy and discretion implicit in the escape, the magnetic pull of this conspicuous, layered assemblage *attracted*, rather than repelled, attention. And, as evinced by the author's closing, the unique appearance of this mysterious duo, however fleeting, made an indelible impression: "This morning I cut from the New York Herald the accompanying extract, and there is no doubt in my mind but that William and Ellen Craft are no others than my traveling companions, Mr. Johnson and servant."[30] Yet their appearance did not arouse enough suspicion for the curious eyewitness to report the Crafts. Instead, the writer seems to delight in the trick played upon him, sly enough that, despite his interest in physiognomy, he was unable to detect the truth of the enigmatic presence before him.

Despite, or perhaps *because of,* the Crafts' efforts to partly camouflage Ellen's feminine countenance, Mr. William Johnson's slippery appearance suggested a dandy figure. The Crafts' fugitive performance art, on the one hand, and the carefully cultivated wardrobe of the dandy, on the other, is not incongruous. Rather, the everyday performances of Mr. William Johnson demonstrated, in Monica L. Miller's description, "the fugitive slave's ability to use a gentleman's clothing and attitude to derail the societal expectations of black slaves and the white men who own them."[31] The ambivalence provoked by Ellen Craft's elegant avatar, moreover, was suggested by a puzzling comment made by an additional anonymous figure in this eyewitness account: "We arrived at Charleston, and there lost sight of Mr. Johnson, an acquaintance at my elbow remarking that he was a '*woman* or a *genius*.'"

William and Ellen Craft, moreover, were not the only cultural actors who cut a sharp figure while executing improvised escape acts; Ellen's cousins, Mary and in particular Frank, also enacted passing performances. Thus, what is perhaps most striking about *Running a Thousand Miles to Freedom* is its suggestion that the Crafts' collaborative escape was, literally, all in the family. Ellen Craft's aunt lived in Georgia as the wife of her master, Mr. Slator, with whom she raised several children, three of them "nearly white, well educated, and beautiful girls." When Mr. Slator suddenly died and left no will, Mrs. Slator and her children became vulnerable for eviction from their property when a "villain, residing at a distance, hearing of the circumstance, came forward and swore he was a relative of the deceased." A judge ruled in his favor and the "pusillanimous scoundrel" took ownership of the property, and prepared to sell the mother and all of her children, "except Frank, a fine young man about twenty-two years of age, and Mary, a very nice young girl, a little younger than her brother." When Mrs. Slator attempted to purchase her and children's freedom with money left by "her husband and master," the "scoundrel" claimed the money as his property. Again, a judgment was rendered in his favor, since "According to law, as will be seen hereafter, a slave cannot own anything."[32] The villainous imposter sold the entire family on the auction block—except for Frank and Mary—and a day or two after the sale made plans to return to his home in South Carolina with the siblings, Mrs. Slator's money, and valuables stolen from her household.

In an ingenious improvisational act, Frank and Mary escaped from "the villain Slator." Frank and Mary were handcuffed by one wrist each in a "large light van" pulled by two horses. After treating himself to the "ruined family's best brandy and wine," the imposter became too drunk to drive. The "reins fell from his fingers, and in attempting to catch them he tumbled out of the vehicle, and was unable to get up." Taking the key to their handcuffs from the "drunken assassin's pocket," Frank and Mary undid them and used them to tie the imposter to a tree in the woods. Their owner, William Craft comments wryly, "was better fitted to wear such ornaments." Stealing from him the "large sum of money that was realized at the sale" of their family members, as well as the money stolen from their mother, Frank and Mary used the family imposter's two horses to escape to Savannah. "The fugitives being white, of course no one suspected they were slaves." They promptly sold the horses and escaped to New York and "embarked as free white persons." And if that was not daring enough, Frank returned to aid him and Mary's two youngest siblings—Emma and her twin brother—in *their* escape acts. Frank did this through a dual role-play, utilizing a set of disguises to enhance his "whiteness": "After failing in several attempts to buy them, Frank cultivated large whiskers and moustachios, cut off his hair, put on a wig and glasses, and went down as a white man, and stopped in the neighbourhood where his sister was." After Frank saw them and "arrangements were made for them to meet at a particular place on a Sunday," he returned to escort the "little twins" into freedom's embrace. Frank, however, had "so completely disguised or changed his appearance that his little sister did not know him," speaking to him only after she "showed their mother's likeness; the sight of which melted her to tears."[33]

Like Ellen Craft's seditious acts, Frank's impersonation illustrated how performance was crucial to enacting the spatial imaginaries inherent to freedom and subjectivity, while—as fugitive performance art—they artfully displayed the clever configuration of the white chattel slave's body into an endlessly pliable instrument of escape. Both Frank's and Ellen's subterfuge forcibly claimed the identity and spoils of white subjectivity, and the freedom to travel without surveillance implicit in it, as a means of gaining black citizenship. Performance, in other words, was put in the service of mobility. And this movement not only included the remarkable geographic reach of their quick-witted performances, but in particular the adroit wielding of the elastic matériel of their whitened bodies. Echoing British sociologist Stuart Hall's words in another context, Frank and Ellen Craft deftly used their amorphous bodies as a "'canvas,' light-sensitive 'frame' or 'screen'" whose varied meanings they could manipulate and control.[34] This ability to shift witnesses' perception of their physicality in and out of focus is all the more brilliant considering that they and all fugitive slaves possessed bodies that legally were not their own.[35] Positioning Frank's insurrectionist impersonations alongside Ellen's, I highlight one of the many genealogies—in this case, the literal one of a family tree—of cultural actors who have wielded avatars as a strategy of black performance.

Prosthetic Performances

How does black performance fit with disability? If the Crafts demonstrate that escape can be a form of fugitive performance art, how can their performance—which above all else, relied on movement—rely at the same time on disability? This seeming paradox is essential: Ellen Craft's deft manipulation of disability was yet another dramatic performance enabling the Crafts' escape. These protean ploys included both repurposed objects (such as the green spectacles and two poultices Ellen wore) *and* embodied behaviors (feigned deafness, slowed gait, and frustrated chirography). I term this dynamic matrix of bandages and other ruses *prosthetic performance*. While seemingly antithetical to performance art, these cunning mechanisms enacted its very principles. Performance art's "common characteristics," as Carol Simpson Stern and Bruce Henderson describe, include an "interest in using 'found' as well as 'made' materials," "open-endedness or undecidability of form," and a "provocative, unconventional, often assaultive" stance.[36] Hence, shifting our lenses toward this remarkable nineteenth-century repertoire of prosthetic performances does not require us to forsake performance art's avant-garde roots. However, "to concentrate largely or exclusively upon the avant-garde aspect of modern performance art," Marvin Carlson cautions, limits "understanding both of the social functioning of such art today, and also of how it relates to other performance activity of the past."[37] Ellen Craft's idiosyncratic and experimental bodily expression, via prosthetics, warrants acute attention; an instrument harnessed by her white male avatar, disability here was transformed from mere bodily impairment into an elastic and *mobile* aesthetic device and a set of tactical performances.

This eerie comingling of disability and experimental modes of black performance challenges the discursive boundaries that situate them as seeming opposites. As disability studies scholar Ellen Samuels suggests, this assumption is partly due to a mutual disciplinary erasure, specifically the inattention to disability as a social category in studies of slave narratives and, conversely, the troubling fact that "historians of disability in the US have rarely touched on the issue of slavery." One such result of such critical occlusions is that "disability is never treated as a social identity which can be manipulated or interpreted as can race or gender."[38]

Prosthetics, a term usually associated with a bodily lack, can also be a morphological surplus. Etymologically, the word "prosthesis," used in the beginning of the eighteenth century to "mean an artificial body part," is derived from the Greek *prosthesis* ("addition").[39] These technological devices, such as pacemakers or replicas of bodily appendages, execute acts of surrogation, seeking to literally "embody and replace" the functionality of the heretofore faltering (such as an essential organ) or missing (as with a limb).[40] Yet, Ellen Craft herself was not disabled. Instead, she cleverly employed prosthetic signs as ruses to deflect unwanted attention and simulate the "real" white masculinity of her avatar. Facilitating the Crafts' unlawful escape, these prosthetic performances were literal accessories to a crime. Prosthetics, moreover, are "artificial attachments" manufactured to "suggest a substitute for loss."[41] However, in Ellen Craft's case, they functioned more like supplements. The addendum of these synthetic appendages increased the possible interpretations of Craft's ambiguous body; they also echoed "a certain excess associated with black performance" itself.[42]

I consider the use of "poultices, &c." intrinsic to Ellen Craft's prosthetic performances as quotidian and utilitarian modes of performance art; these bodily maneuvers were meant, paradoxically, to emphasize the everydayness of Mr. William Johnson's disability.[43] These performances are perceived in moments where we witness the Crafts' joint reiteration of Mr. Johnson's illnesses and the *routineness* of their address by "his" valet William. On a steamer bound for Charleston, South Carolina, for instance, after "my master turned in" early, much to the chagrin and puzzlement of passengers who "questioned me respecting him," William enacted a seemingly rote—but of course, fraudulent—algorithm of care. He retrieved the "flannels and opodeldoc" concocted as a prop for his master's putative "rheumatism" and heated them "quickly by the stove in the gentleman's saloon" to bring back to his master's "berth."[44] Later, in a hotel in Charleston, William enacted the laborious task of care again. After William-cum-Ellen "handed . . . [William] the bandages," he took them downstairs "in great haste" asking for hot ones and, when they arrived, placed the "smoking poultices" in "white handkerchiefs" before returning upstairs to his "master's apartment."[45] Both of these passages, detailing the Crafts' animation of "the concept of the invalid—of passing as disabled," have escaped critical attention, I believe, precisely because they describe such ordinary moments.[46] While these two scenes, in other words, are *also* virtuosic passing performances, their quiet everydayness fails to attract the same attention as Ellen Craft's more seductive racial, gender, and class traversals. Their seeming banality, though, is exactly the point. These lesser-noticed corporeal acts may elude critical gazes, but they were fundamental to the efficacy of the fugitive performance art the Crafts enacted, particularly in conjunction with *other* performances.

In short, disability surfaces not as a disadvantage, but as a "doing" that makes actions happen. For instance, when in Charleston, William Craft "took my master by the arm" and they were driven off "to the best hotel, which John C. Calhoun, and all the other great southern fire-eating statesmen" resided in while there. Upon their arrival, the landlord "ran out and opened the door: but judging from the poultices and green glasses, that my master was an invalid, he took him very tenderly

by one arm and ordered his man to take the other." Ellen Craft/William
Johnson's treatment by the landlord was class-based—paid the "attention
and homage he thought a gentleman of his high position merited."[47]
This brief textual interlude, however, does not simply illustrate the effec-
tiveness of Craft's mimesis of white male citizenry; it also demonstrates
how Johnson's ostensible infirmities prompted action. The ability of Mr.
William Johnson's presumed disabilities to effect change is discernible
in the hotel proprietor's literal *moves*, and concomitant order to his em-
ployee to also move and hence act as an accessory to the Crafts' crafty
crimes. Ellen Craft's prosthetic performances, in other words, affected
the bodily movements of others.[48]

[handwritten margin note: performance acted on others]

Yet in the need of disabled Mr. William Johnson to produce a signature, the most famous (and cited) scene of Craft's prosthetic performances, I return to a familiar coupling: avatars as a strategy of black
performance and their intersection with forms of writing. In Charleston,
Mr. William Johnson successively sought to obtain tickets "for himself
and one for his slave to Philadelphia," but post-purchase was met with
a challenge by the "chief man": "I wish you to register your name here,
sir, and also the name of your nigger, and pay a dollar duty on him."[49]
Johnson paid the tax, and "pointing to the hand that was in the poultice,
requested the officer to register his name for him," which the officer
adamantly refused. This potentially hazardous situation, though, was
averted by two witnesses to the scene: a "young military officer" who
had traveled with Johnson for part of the trip, and the "captain of the
steamer, a good-looking, jovial fellow." The former, though slightly inebriated, shook hands with Johnson, and in an act of pretended affinity,
declared: "I know his kin (friends) like a book." The latter, taking note of
this and perhaps not wanting to lose passengers, went even further in his
support—"I will register the gentleman's name, and take the responsibility upon myself"—and promptly asked for and registered the names,
presumably (according to William) "Mr. Johnson and slave." Later, after
this unknowing accomplice's act of kindness, the captain apologized for
the strictness of Charleston's rules, emphasizing that "It was not out of
any disrespect to you, sir," but rather the potential of "any d—d abolitionist" to escape with "a lot of valuable niggers."[50]

Thus, while I and others have emphasized the fantastic technology of
the poultice covering Ellen Craft's hand as a surrogate for her own illiter-

acy, what becomes clear in this passage is even *that* was not sufficient for the Crafts' safe passage; what were needed additionally were able-bodied participants, not only to verify the "complex interdependency of [all the] identities" staged by Mr. William Johnson, but also to execute skills that substituted for "his" putatively missing ones.[51] The late Lindon Barrett remains the literary critic most explicit about the sling's importance in the escape. In his words, "as a substitute for literacy, it is the indispensable correlate to Ellen's racially ambiguous skin . . . it is the ultimate sign of whiteness. It articulates or supplements a literacy that is only for the moment glaringly absent."[52] I have argued elsewhere, concurring with Barrett, that the sling's ironic ability to make Mr. William Johnson's "infirmity *legible*" replaces and represents a "signature no longer required, since 'real' white masculinity was above reproach."[53] Certainly, Ellen Craft's sideways entrance into writing, in the guise of her avatar and through the acts of others, was remarkable considering both the protection of literacy as a form of property exclusive to white citizens and the repeated emphasis on the Crafts' own illiteracy, such as with William Johnson–cum–Ellen's fear of reading a note upside down.[54] Still, Ellen Craft's initial idea of the poultice's function when designing the art of their escape—"I think I can make a poultice and bind up my right hand in a sling, and with propriety ask the officers to register my name for me"—clearly was not sufficient.[55] Instead, the sling acted as what Robin Bernstein calls a "scriptive thing" or a device issuing prompts and invitations to others.[56] In this case, those cues included the verifying of the "realness" of Mr. Johnson's identity as a white gentleman (via the "young officer") *and* the signature-by-proxy enacted for him (by the captain of the steamer). The sling, in other words, was the most salient of synthetic props in this fantastic oeuvre of prosthetic performances, yet its success was not so much in its surrogation, but rather its agile ability to move others (both physically and emotionally) to act on its behalf.

A final instance within this narrative of disability's muscular capability to effect change in others occurred in Baltimore on December 24, 1848. The Crafts were temporarily detained there, because William Johnson attempts to board a train with "his" slave to the free territory of Philadelphia. An "officer, a full-blooded Yankee of the lowest order," upon seeing William Craft and asking his destination, requested he fetch his master out of his carriage, since, he explained, "It is against my rules

[handwritten margin note: protection of literacy as private property]

to let any man take a slave past here, unless he can satisfy them in the office that he has a right to take them along." A conversation between William Johnson and the officer, which "attracted the attention of the large number of bustling passengers," failed to dissuade the latter, after William Johnson proved unable to produce a "gentleman in Baltimore" that could "endorse for him." A stoppage in the Crafts' hitherto successful flight to freedom, though, was averted when the bell for the train's departure sounded and the officer, "in a state of great agitation" acquiesced and told the "clerk to run and tell the conductor to 'let this gentleman and slave past'; adding, 'As he is not well, it is a pity to stop him here. We will let him go.'"[57] Once again, it was the mimesis of disability and the sympathies it induced, rather than simply the whiteness of Ellen Craft's avatar, that greased the wheels on the Crafts' surreptitious journey toward freedom's embrace. The simultaneous movement and immobility that was these prosthetic performances' signature dance may be perceived in the escape narrative's very next sentence, when William tells us, "My master thanked him, and *stepped* out and *hobbled* across the platform as quickly as possible."[58] The Crafts' prosthetic performances took disability, the supposed *least* elastic of identities, as the grounds for their insurrectionist role-play.

Perambulations

It is strange, indeed, to see so many nations assembled and represented on one spot of British ground. In short, it is one great theatre, with thousands of performers, each playing his own part.
—William Wells Brown, *The American Fugitive in Europe; Sketches of Places and People Abroad*

This chapter's recurring chorus—the seeming incongruent fusion of escape from bondage with the avant-garde logics of performance art—arches toward a climax in Ellen Craft's staged appearance at the Great Exhibition of the Works of Industry of all Nations of 1851 in London. In yet another collaborative performance, this time with the assistance of William Craft and a coterie of white British abolitionists, Ellen Craft's white mulatta body became an agit-prop agent that confronted audiences with its confounding racial amorphousness. Like a true performance artist, Craft developed and utilized the "expressive qualities of the body" as an art in itself, her antislavery critique leveled partly at exposing the "inevitable fallacies of a system that relies on the mythical quantification of blood to define racial categories."[59]

The method through which Craft chose to do so—an impromptu happening consisting of three couples walking the Great Exhibition for a whole day—may seem, in its everydayness, to lack the lustrous signature of aesthetics. I counter such assumptions by reconsidering these promenades in time and space, as *ready-mades*. This term, derived from artist Marcel Duchamp's early-twentieth-century experiments with "already-existing objects," embraces the artist's prerogative to select "material or experience for aesthetic consideration" and hence the ability to interpret "real-life activities as art." While Ellen Craft's strolls through the vast spaces of London's Crystal Palace seem quite innocuous at first glance, they are highly aestheticized and experimental self-performances. Though partly spontaneous, Craft's promenades were, nonetheless, still "scripted, rehearsed, and carefully controlled."[60] This coupling of nineteenth-century black corporeal performances and the artistic techniques of performance art made over a century later provide a proper foundation for the performative potential of Craft's peregrinations.

Craft's carefully calibrated—and collaborative—performance was described in a lengthy detailed letter, dated June 26, 1851, that British abolitionist William Farmer, Esq., wrote to American abolitionist William Lloyd Garrison. Farmer notes how "friends [had] resolved that" the Crafts and William Wells Brown "should be exhibited under the world's huge glass case, in order that the world might form its opinion of the alleged mental inferiority of the African race, and their fitness or unfitness for freedom." After a "small party of anti-slavery friends were formed to accompany the fugitives through the Exhibition," they selected Saturday as the date of this interracial coterie's infiltration, since it was the day "upon which the largest number of the aristocracy and wealthy classes attend the Crystal Palace." Their prediction was corroborated when "fifteen thousand" visitors "mostly of the upper classes" converged on the Crystal Palace, "including the Queen, Prince Albert, and the royal children." Each of the Crafts and William Wells Brown was paired with white sympathizers (Ellen Craft with "Mr. McDonnell" and

"Mrs. Thompson," William Craft with "Miss Amelia Thompson" as well as Farmer himself, and Brown with "Miss Thompson"), a strategic arrangement designed, according to Farmer, to both honor "them for their heroic escape from Slavery" and suggest "that we regarded them as our equals."[61] Farmer described what happened next:

> We promenaded the Exhibition between six and seven hours, and visited nearly every portion of the vast edifice. Among the thousands, whom we met in our perambulations, who dreamed of any impropriety in a gentleman of character and standing, like Mr. McDonnell, walking arm-in-arm with a colored woman; or an elegant and accomplished young lady, like Miss Thompson, (daughter of the Hon. George Thompson, M.C.), becoming the promenading companion of a colored man? Did the English peers or peeresses? Not the most aristocratic among them. Did the representatives of any other country have their notions of impropriety shocked by the matter? None but Americans. To see the arm of a beautiful young English lady passed through that of "a nigger," taking ices and other refreshments with him, upon terms of the most perfect equality, certainly was enough to "rile," and evidently did "rile" the slaveholders who beheld it; but there was no help for it. Even the New York Broadway bullies would not have dared to utter a word of insult, much less lift a finger against Wm. Wells Brown, when walking with his fair companion in the World's Exhibition.[62]

This particular iteration of Ellen Craft's repertoire of quotidian performance art, like her four-day journey to freedom, was a collaborative effort. But the differences were equally important. Her perambulation, unlike her escape, was purposely staged for maximum spectatorship. And it did not rely on Mr. William Johnson, Craft's white male avatar.

This seemingly innocuous perambulation may appear, at first glance, ineffectual, if not overly simplistic. After all, interpreting the incredibly quotidian action of strolling as a provocative form of tactical resistance against slavery seems counterintuitive. However, the importance of this fugitive slave performance art was, in fact, its staged everydayness, the seemingly ordinary act of upper-class white British men and women "walking arm-in-arm" with their black American compatriots. Barbara McCaskill describes corporeality itself as a disruptive agent here:

"Though their promenade was unsuccessful in triggering a verbal confrontation between pro- and antislavery factions," she says, "the fugitives once again proved the spectacle of their bodies to be forceful ammunitions against slavery."[63] Thus, in a striking contrast to the Crafts' and Brown's earlier and more aggressively abolitionist efforts, here they silently confronted audiences with a scene of integrated ordinariness.

Yet, Ellen Craft's promenade differed from that of William Craft or William Wells Brown in that its striking visual confrontation was one of *sameness*. The other groupings purposely manipulated the visual mechanics of contrast—black skin/men versus white skin/women and men—to illuminate a plea for equality despite these salient differences. However, Ellen Craft employed a distinct dramaturgical strategy, emphasizing her nearly white skin as an implicit challenge to the white spectators around her: can you distinguish, she seemed to be saying, between a "real" white body and an ersatz one? As an embodied (and impure) copy of whiteness, Ellen Craft troubled the ostensible "pure purity" of whiteness qua whiteness, itself "an impossibility," to quote Jennifer Brody.[64] Thus, while Craft's infamous disabled white male avatar was absent during this six-to-seven-hour live art piece, the method of her perambulations was analogous to the techniques employed in the earlier congealed performances where "he" was present; here, as elsewhere, Craft expertly wielded her pliable physicality, occupying and traversing the realms of subjectivity and objecthood.

Ellen Craft's humble walk is a climactic note in her quotidian performance art as well as an artistically rendered bodily signature. While simplistic in scale and striking a minor key, this perambulation emphasized, in Tavia Nyong'o's words, "the maximal potential of the minimalist gesture."[65] Its aesthetic ingenuity suggests that William Wells Brown should not have fretted over the banal foodstuffs, instead of art, shipped by the United States to Britain for theatrical displays, or *performances*, of nationhood.[66] After all, America's true artistic gifts were not the selected curatorial items on view; instead, they were the everyday movements enacted by its stealth citizens arching toward democracy. Weaving through the elegant halls of London's Crystal Palace, like an errant pen on a page, Craft's promenading "white" and yet black body signed itself in space in those fleeting moments of contact when white spectators momentarily glanced at a woman's body virtually indistinguishable from their own.

Poses, Postures, Performances: Ellen Craft's Escape Art

In 1851, Ellen Craft quietly posed for an engraving in London in her (partial) escape costume, a visual representation that was printed on April 19 of the same year in *The London Illustrated News* with an accompanying story of the Crafts' escape.[67] Yet, like the white male avatar it mechanically reproduced, this seemingly static image generated a remarkable traction,[68] even prior to its use nine years later as the frontispiece that *visually* verified the veracity of the Crafts' escape narrative, *Running a Thousand Miles to Freedom* (rather than the letters of support from white abolitionists that typically accompanied such texts). Craft's portrait was not the first engraving of a black woman used as a frontispiece, a distinction belonging to poet Phillis Wheatley.[69] However, this objet d'art's deeply ambivalent rendering—of a "white" and yet black female fugitive slave in the elegant disguise of her disabled white male avatar—remains unique and remarkable.

In what follows, I aim to reveal the aesthetic labor Craft performed in the artistic arena of visual culture, especially her execution of objecthood. The representational work[70] Ellen Craft enacted was the configuration of her polysemous body and its dandified white male double into visual idioms easily apprehensible to disparate audiences. This corporeal compartmentalization—from a three-dimensional subject to a two-dimensional visual simulacrum and purchasable commodity—circles back to discourses of objecthood.

Similar to her perambulation in the Great Exhibition the same year, Ellen Craft's engraving and eventual frontispiece was not solitary in its pointed antislavery aesthetic; a growing army of black lecturers, artists, and activists were retooling artistic mediums for innovative and resistive ends. A year earlier, in 1850, both William Wells Brown and Henry "Box" Brown displayed panoramas against slavery on opposite sides of the Atlantic. While the former exhibited twenty-four scenes in Newcastle-upon-Tyne, the latter debuted his *Mirror against Slavery* in Boston's Washington Hall; each held up an "unflattering mirror to the nation as a whole."[71] In 1855, landscape painter Robert S. Duncanson and daguerrean photographer James Presley Ball collaborated on an abolitionist pamphlet and panorama, while Sojourner Truth utilized carte-de-visite photographs, a relatively new technology initially designed for

Figure 2.1. "Ellen Craft, the Fugitive Slave." Engraving. *London Illustrated News*, April 19, 1851; later used as frontispiece for *Running a Thousand Miles to Freedom.*

wealthy Italian elites, as a form of self-publicity.[72] These select works by black cultural subjects in the United States as well as fugitive slaves in exile abroad, what Daphne A. Brooks has called a "black abolitionist aesthetic network," deftly manipulated the grounds of the aesthetic as an ideological tool.[73]

These oppositional aesthetic efforts acted as potent visual counterpoints to the sinister (and equally powerful) manipulation of photography as a mechanism to substantiate and sustain racial hierarchies. In this case, photography's supposed transparency was often undermined by its nefarious use to buttress bogus sciences, particularly those concerned with racial difference. In the U.S., a year before the appearance of Ellen Craft's engraving, Joseph T. Zealy made fifteen daguerreotypes of five black men and two black women in Charleston for Harvard University professor Louis Agassiz.[74] These *types*—taken in profile and frontal positions and interpreted as visual proofs of the entire Negro "race"— helped to fortify polygenesis and other discourses that are now recognized as scientific racism. In short, the photograph became, in visual culture theorist Nicholas Mirzoeff's terms, "a prime locus of the performance of the racialized index."[75]

While Ellen Craft's engraving frustrated these explicit attempts to fix racial difference, its most striking feature was that which was *not* represented inside the visual frame. Roland Barthes's typology for interpreting photographs is, again, useful here; if the *studium*, the general "element which rises from the scene," was a portrait of a slender gentleman wearing the sartorial accouterments appropriate to his class position, the *punctum*—the "sting, speck, cut, little hole" that punctures the *studium*—was what was glaringly absent or altered: the original green spectacles (their lenses now clear), the poultice partially concealing the face (removed to better take the portrait, according to William Craft), and the sling that held Mr. William Johnson–cum–Ellen Craft's right hand (now simply hanging around "his" neck, parallel to the tartan sash).[76] The scripting of disability through supplementary aids so central to the escape, what I earlier termed prosthetic performance, is reduced here to one barely noticeable prop. The irony of this "adapted version of the disguise with all signs of disability removed or obscured" was the explicit minimization (and to some degree, erasure) of the theatrical device—performed disability—that facilitated the escape's completion, along with Ellen Craft's mimesis of whiteness and masculinity.[77] Thus, if excess unites black performances, this portrait paradoxically executed the opposite, proffering to viewers a significant set of absences.

It is this very pictorial incompleteness, the portrait's distance from the *real* Mr. William Johnson that it seemingly sought to render, that has led numerous critics to question its purpose, specifically, *who* it is meant to depict. Sterling Bland Jr. rhetorically asks, "Is the engraving intended to represent Ellen, William's wife? Or is the engraving intended to show Ellen in the disguises she used to pass as a white gentleman traveling with his black slave?" Ellen M. Weinauer and Ellen Samuels, in their respective scholarship on the Crafts, attempt to answer Bland's inquiry. Weinauer argues that, due to the absence of the poultice, the engraving's mission "is to represent not 'Mr. Johnson' but Ellen herself." She later contends, though, that the engraving reflects a slippage between "Ellen's true (feminine) self and her fictional (masculine) persona" that thwarts William Craft's efforts in *Running a Thousand Miles to Freedom* to emphasize their discontinuity. Samuels, meanwhile, argues that the portrait's task was to "represent the 'most respectable-looking gentleman' so beloved of critics," emphasizing the gender and racial aspects of Craft's disguise while removing those portraying the "African-American body as unhealthy, dependent or disabled."[78]

These three critics dovetail in their efforts to reconcile the two-dimensional presence of Ellen Craft's now *dis*embodied avatar in what, presumably, would be an otherwise stable image of her. And, as a result, they converge at an unexpected impasse. Despite the acknowledged ontological ambiguity of the image, Bland, Weinauer, and Samuels position the engraving's intentionality (and representation) in a binary that privileges either Ellen Craft *or* Mr. William Johnson. The engraving's slipperiness proves a source of befuddlement, if not contention. Simply put, it is a portrait of one or the other, a white mulatta subject or her disabled white male avatar, but certainly not both.

Yet the poses and postures of subjects in images such as Ellen Craft's engraving are artfully constructed, staged, and performed. Even the seemingly most stable and reliable images of people—portraits—are inherently protean and elusive. "All portrait photography is fundamentally performative," Peggy Phelan writes in her *Unmarked: The Politics of Performance*. Portrait photography, she argues, relies on multiple forms of performance, and costume and fashion are part of its poetics.[79] Black photographers in the early twentieth century employed similar means, manipulating sundry props and elegant attire in their studios as symbols of social status and wealth. In doing so, they deftly shaped the production of new visual images of elegant black citizens, or what Deborah Willis calls a "New Negro visual aesthetic."[80] The seemingly "natural" representation that portraits such as these aspired to, in other words, was the product of an aggressive set of carefully calibrated, and dramaturgical, acts. In the case of black cultural actors, that active shaping of images, again, served a particular ideological function—conveying the dignity, self-possession, and sartorial élan of racial subjects making visual claims to citizenship—that was adroitly staged and *performed.*

The seeming unfinishedness of Ellen Craft's engraving, due to its eerie duality, suggests the performativity of both her *and* her white male avatar. By referring to "performativity," I am explicitly gesturing toward the process by which, as Judith Butler describes, "identity [is] instituted through a *stylized repetition of acts.*"[81] In the case of Ellen Craft, her *doings*—to use Butler's term—haunt the image, even if they are not immediately visible. Stillness, Harvey Young reminds, is an active act, "an enactment of arrest" that is in correspondence with "daily, lived embodied experiences."[82] In that vein, there is a relationship, albeit tenuous, between the ostensibly immobile Craft-in-partial-disguise and Craft, the three-dimensional person; the gestures of the latter aided in the creation of the former. Craft's static posture in the engraving, in other words, is suggestive of how she actively participated in her own visual reproduction; her pose was an artful act, an attempt to "perform (and conform)" to what she imagined audiences saw.[83] This physical enactment of her flexible corporeality is akin to what Roland Barthes likened to, in his own posing for a photograph, as the process of "mak[ing] another body for myself," a mechanizing of the body that becomes even more complex if Craft's duet partner in this portrait, Mr. William Johnson, is considered.[84]

Similar to Craft herself, the engraving renders partially visible the performativity of Mr. William Johnson, or more specifically, Ellen Craft's performative acts that converted miscellaneous props into an enlivened personage. Indeed, the engraving's in-between state lends itself to this very interpretation: like a garment turned inside out (Craft was a seamstress), its incomplete rendering of Mr. William Johnson—with a top hat and spectacles, but not the full poultice—enables viewers to discern the seams of this performance, the *constructedness* of Ellen Craft's white gentleman. His presence in this portrait, though, complicates Barthes's delineation of the prototypical mechanization of the body, specifically from posing subject to consumable visual object. Mr. William Johnson, after all, was an avatar. Thus, if already an object, what did the operation of "making another body" look like for *him*? In contrast to Craft, was this a more idiosyncratic mechanization—the metamorphosis of one object (avatar) into another object (two-dimensional representation)?

In sum, Craft's avatar, however picayune his presence, disrupted notions of the engraving as simply mirroring the cultural actor it attempted to portray. Despite what we can assume to be the engraver's obliviousness to such an interpretation and desire to render to audiences an easily digestible subject, the engraving defies any semblance of ontological certitude.

Likewise, similar to the slippery figure of the avatar itself, the engraving disrupts calcified notions of time, particularly those so often attached to photography. Photography is repeatedly equated with death, as a record that captures and holds a time that is gone, never to return. The very appearance of the photograph signals this, materializing only when a moment is no longer live. Rebecca Schneider resists this temporal logic by considering the still as an *event* that occurs in the live moment of its encounter.[85] The engraving, I would argue, functions by a similar logic. Its use as a frontispiece confirms this; as the very first page of the Crafts' escape narrative, it not only continues to profoundly script how readers interpret the text, but is itself activated whenever readers encounter it in the live. It presents a striking *simultaneity*, of time and "being" itself.

Aesthetics "has always been political, explicitly formulated in close relation to politics, and in some cases more a matter of politics than anything else"; in light of this, let us now attend to the engraving's use as an antislavery emblem available for purchase. Specifically, William Craft notes in *Running a Thousand Miles to Freedom* that through a combination of occasional lecturing, the revenue from sales of the engraving, and the generosity of others, he had nearly raised the necessary funds to purchase his sister out of slavery in Mississippi. Following this, he gives a brief exegesis of laws (particularly Georgia's) that claimed to protect slaves but, in actuality, provided legal loopholes for their mistreatment if not murder, which served only to heighten the urgency of purchasing his sister's freedom, while emphasizing the engraving's utility in such abolitionist efforts prior to the Emancipation Proclamation.[86]

Thus, yoking this visual performance to discourses of crime, rights, and the law, the engraving's visual representation as well as the capital that circulated around it point to the myriad crimes committed by the Crafts. Already, if "real racialized bodies always stand prior to their representations,"[87] the affront of Ellen Craft's very existence as a white mulatta was a crime in itself; it violated the tenets of so-called racial distinctiveness that chattel slavery hinged on and that visual texts like Joseph T. Zealy's aforementioned daguerreotypes sought to perpetuate. Furthermore, if whiteness is a form of property, as legal scholar Cheryl Harris argues, a chattel slave on the run stealing the spoils of whiteness was clearly illegal. If the engraving tacitly expressed the crimes of whiteness committed (and embodied) by Ellen Craft, it also, paradoxically, represented a conundrum: *property appropriating property.* This seeming illogical appropriation resonated in the ability of "runaway property" to purchase a fungible commodity, i.e., William Craft's sister, partly through the capital garnered through the sales and transatlantic circulation of still *another* commodity: the tangible engraving of his wife.[88]

To backtrack, as Michael Ralph explains, the commodity refers to "anything that is bought or sold, borrowed, or traded, suggesting that any entity that can be objectified and reified—and set into an exchange equation—can be commodified (which could conceivably apply to *any* entity)."[89] In light of the above, normally distinct boundaries between subject and object become increasingly blurred, especially if "*any* entity" is applied to a human subject. The Crafts willfully participated in their self-commodification. Through the apparatus of the engraving (and nine years later, their published escape narrative), they engaged in systems of monetary exchange and therefore gained a measure of economic agency, however tenuous, through the sales of these marketed items. The Crafts' ultimate legal transgression, then, might have been their active transformation from items to be "bought or sold, borrowed or traded" to instead what Henry Louis Gates has elsewhere called "speaking subjects," who reaped the economic rewards of their aesthetic labor.[90]

Yet the murky limits between objecthood and an expressly *gendered* objectification in the engraving surface in at least one critic's trepidation that it helped to fix Ellen Craft into a product for her husband and others. Barbara McCaskill argues that, in both the escape narrative and the engraving, William Craft's efforts to appeal to a nineteenth-century market results in a problematic silencing of his wife, an interpretation I concur with.[91] Ellen Craft's representation in the engraving, while provocative, was indeed mitigated by her marriage, her delicate femininity emphasized by her appearances on the lecture stand. Her "white" appearance and William Craft's repeated insistence in *Running a Thousand Miles to Freedom* that his wife wore masculine garb only for the purposes of the escape (and the engraving) aligned her with the behavioral strictures implicit in the cult of true womanhood. This fact alone is notable, considering, as Hazel V. Carby observes, that black women were excluded altogether from that status and instead used to delineate its limits.[92] Still, the ability of multifarious audiences to purchase and take a piece of Ellen Craft with them to stuff in their pockets—whether as sentimental mementoes or for a scopophilic pleasure in looking at and, perhaps, even imaginatively disrobing the woman under the disguise—is redolent of a particularly gendered visual consumption.

The differences between Ellen Craft's sympathetically rendered engraving and Joice Heth's visually crude woodcut and engravings are not as stark as they appear. While Craft possessed measures of agency in her self-presentation that partially paralyzed Heth explicitly lacked, Craft was not entirely free, in Daphne A. Brooks's words, of the "aesthetic complexities rooted in black female performance work under duress in the antebellum era."[93] Ellen Craft's engraving certainly is a site to witness her careful attention to the antebellum politics of women's representation; yet, simultaneously, it also hints at the *doings* of her own polymorphous body, and its slippery white male doppelganger, that exceeded the framings imposed on her (and "him").

Finally, Ellen Craft's engraving was a node in a larger visual economy of other engravings—of both her and her coconspirator, William Craft—that denote the continuation of visual performance art in the Crafts' repertoire. Two engravings of William and Ellen Craft "at the present stage of life (as citizens of the U.S.)" were published, side by side, in William Still's 1872 text *The Underground Railroad*.[94] Facing the viewer's gaze head-on, both dramatis personae made visual claims to citizenship, using clothing as a potent and malleable signifier. While William was elegantly dressed in a suit jacket, crisp white shirt, and tie in his portrait, Ellen was dressed in a dark, high-collared garment and a bonnet wrapped around her head and tied at the neck. Both images, more in line with the tenets of classical portraiture than the engraving of Ellen in disguise, seem meant to emphasize a staged everydayness. Ellen Craft's engraving, though, also traffics in the gendered objectification mentioned earlier, using sartorial cues to affirm her femininity.

WILLIAM CRAFT.   ELLEN CRAFT.

Figure 2.2. "William Craft" and "Ellen Craft." Engravings. William Still, *The Underground Railroad* (Philadelphia: Porter and Coates, 1872). In Still's words, "The portraits of William and Ellen represent them at the present stage of life (as citizens of the U.S.)—of course they have greatly changed in appearance from what they were when they first fled from Georgia. Obviously the Fugitive Slave Law in its crusade against William and Ellen Craft, reaped no advantages, but on the contrary, liberty was greatly the gainer."

Still, the seeming togetherness and yet palpable separation of these paired portraits is intriguing. If this demarcation downplayed the collaborative dynamics inherent in the Crafts' joint escape and the fugitive performance art that facilitated it, it also made tacit the "illicit visual possibilities of William and Ellen's partnering." As P. Gabrielle Foreman argues, the preference for (and popularity of) the engraving of Ellen-in-disguise, in contradistinction to the pair published in Still's text, is two-fold. If the former's containment and singular framing erased the visual "threat that the [latter] image of the phenotypically 'white' Ellen with her phenotypically 'black' husband might pose," the former's singular focus also positioned Craft inside of what Foreman calls "white mulatta genealogies" that place explicit emphasis on the exceptional individual at the expense of the collective."[95] Foreman's arguments again point us toward the scopophilic pleasure in gazing at Ellen Craft's paradoxical "black white form,"[96] perceived by audiences in her repeated self-exhibition on abolitionist lecture stands, and heightened in the mechanical reproduction (and distribution) of the engraving; William's representational presence would, indeed, have disrupted this seductive visual pleasure.

Yet what if all three engravings were positioned together, as a trio? Indeed, what if these three engravings were read as a set of mutable performances that—along with their escape and their perambulations at the Great Exhibition in London—completed the Crafts' journey from runaway objects to subjects and transnational citizens? These images then become the finale act in the couple's dense representational opus. In them, the Crafts adroitly utilized the visual as still another performance space, specifically, as a flexible conduit through which to self-objectify and frame themselves for future visual consumption by their various literary audiences. And while considering all three engravings together certainly does not erase the ideological and gendered discourses inherent in at least two of them, it *does* disrupt efforts to enforce their separation and emphasize an ocular focus on Ellen Craft's whiteness and singularity.

Put another way, to echo the late Eve Kosofsky Sedgwick, when the images' beside-ness (as opposed to the "before," or what came first) is emphasized, a striking reverberation rises.[97] In their two-dimensional flatness, we perceive three subjects—all equal in the visual plane—despite one being a fraudulent persona, if not "being" himself. Thus, while a distinction seems simple—between those whose ontology is stable (the Crafts) and his that is woefully flimsy (Mr. William Johnson, in the midst of transformation nevertheless)—those boundaries collapse when they are read together. Together they emphasize the constructedness of *all* identity, a set of repeated bodily acts enacted here by black and "white" historical subjects (or *tout court*, racial performativity) captured and held steady over a century and half later in the indelible markings of the engraving. The avatar, while ephemeral and vacuous, still *does* something to the visual sphere. Its excessive and misbehaving presence actively shapes, elongates, and messes with the neat tidy frame of the visual sphere, rather than the other way around. In short, the avatar shows, returning to the epigraph that opened this chapter, that black performance—if not blackness itself—includes objects that not only move, but that resist and pose, in the master's clothes no less.

3

Plastic Possibilities

Adrian Piper's Adamant Self-Alienation

In many ways, I regard my marginality as more of a blessing
than a curse, as alienation, too, has it uses.
—Adrian Piper, "Xenophobia and the Indexical Present I:
Essay"

If you were in Manhattan in 1973, walking up Fifth Avenue toward
Union Square, or riding the 6 train up the East Side, or reading the
Village Voice, you may have seen him. Or if you were in Cambridge,
Massachusetts, walking through Harvard Yard on a breezy summer day
on your way to Widener Library, you may have seen him there, too. He
was probably sitting on one of the steps in front of the library, cruising for white women. Surreptitiously, you may have gazed at his various
accouterments—the dark mirrored sunglasses, his curly Afro and bushy
mustache, and, hardest to avoid, his protruding genitalia. Your immediate reaction may have been intrigue, or attraction, or revulsion. Perhaps
you felt all of these things simultaneously. Perhaps you desired to flee in
alarm or thought the whole thing a ruse, a publicity stunt, or yet another
annoying piece of performance art. Perhaps you were bold enough to
strike up a conversation. If so, it would have been of no consequence.
He would not tell you his name, where he went to school, or what he
did for a living. Not even what he thought of the weather. Instead, he
would simply keep repeating the same nonsensical phrase: "No matter
how much I ask my mother to stop buying me crackers, cookies, and
things, she does anyway and says it's for her, even if I always eat it. So
I've decided to fast."[1]

In 1973, conceptual artist Adrian Piper created an avatar she called
the Mythic Being that was her "seeming opposite: a third-world,
working-class, overtly hostile male."[2] She began performing this

Figure 3.1. Adrian Piper, *The Mythic Being: Cruising White Women* (#1 of 3), 1975. Three silver gelatin print photographs; 8 x 10 in. (20.3 x 25.4 cm.). Photo credit: James Gutmann. Collection of Eileen Harris Norton, Los Angeles. © Adrian Piper Research Archive Foundation Berlin.

figure in the streets of New York City and, two years later, in Cambridge, while she was earning her doctorate in philosophy at Harvard.[3] Dressed in blaxploitation-inflected male drag—an Afro wig, mirrored sunglasses, and mustache—the Mythic Being strolled the streets and hung out in public places, acting as "an avatar of stereotypical representations of black men."[4] He rode the subway, leered at white women, and attended art gallery openings, concerts, and films. In one photograph, he is seen from behind, sitting at a desk, writing "BLAH" over and over again on a notepad, next to an envelope addressed to Adrian Piper. In others, he fake mugged a stranger (performed by David Auerbach) in a park and, presumably in Piper's SoHo loft, executed a handstand while doing yoga.[5] In this gender-bending disguise, "My behavior changes. I swagger, stride, lope, lower my eyebrows, raise my shoulders, sit with my legs wide apart on the subway, so as to accommodate my protruding genitalia."[6]

Inscrutable and moody, Piper's flâneur-like double would appear in public several times a month while, simultaneously, she selected a pas-

Figure 3.2. Adrian Piper, *The Mythic Being: Writing* (#4 of 7), 1975. Seven silver gelatin print photographs; 10 x 8 in. (25.4 x 20.3 cm.). Photo credit: James Gutmann. Collection of the Adrian Piper Research Archive Foundation Berlin. © Adrian Piper Research Archive Foundation Berlin.

sage from her journals—what she termed a "mantra"—for publication. These mantras, often adolescent in tone and a few sentences in length, ranged in substance, from the one above about "crackers, cookies, and things" to "Today was the first day of school. The only decent boys in my class are Robbie and Clyde. I think I like Clyde." Each month the selected mantra, and the autobiographical event that inspired it, became "an object of meditation" for Piper.[7] The reproduction of these mantras in the seventeen *Village Voice* advertisements Piper purchased—the first published on September 27, 1973, and the last on February 3, 1975—were a means of reaching both a "non-art-world public" and "an art-world-specific public of artists-participants" simultaneously.[8]

The figure of the Mythic Being, then, served as a psychological, and hence personal, device that aided Piper's efforts to transcend the limits of herself, particularly her personal history. He also operated as a confrontational art object that allowed Piper to engage in physical alterations as a method "of bringing out aspects of my own identity that are not readily available—not only the fact that I am black, because many people do

Figure 3.3. Adrian Piper, *The Mythic Being: Doing Yoga* (#1 of 6), 1975. Six gelatin print photographs; 10 x 8 in. (25.4 x 20.3 cm.). Photo credit: James Gutmann. Private collection, U.S. © Adrian Piper Research Archive Foundation Berlin.

Figure 3.4. Adrian Piper, *The Mythic Being, Cycle I: 04/68*, 1974. #8 of 17 from the *Mythic Being Village Voice Series*, 11 x 16 15/16 in. (28 x 43.1 cm.). *Village Voice* advertisement (April 25, 1974). Photo credit: David Campos. © Purchased with funds provided by Donald L. Bryant Jr., Agnes Gund, Marlene Hess and James D. Zirin, Marie-Josée and Henry R. Kravis, Donald B. Marron, The Edward John Noble Foundation, Jerry I. Speyer and Katherine Farley, and Committee on Drawings Funds in honor of Kathy Fuld. © Adrian Piper Research Archive Foundation Berlin.

Figure 3.5. Adrian Piper, *The Mythic Being, Cycle I: 12/12/64*, 1974. #4 of 17 from the *Mythic Being Village Voice Series*, 14 7/8 x 11 1/2 in. (37.7 x 29.2 cm.). *Village Voice* advertisement (January 3, 1974). Collection of the Museum of Modern Art, New York. Purchased with funds provided by Donald L. Bryant Jr., Agnes Gund, Marlene Hess and James D. Zirin, Marie-Josée and Henry R. Kravis, Donald B. Marron, The Edward John Noble Foundation, Jerry I. Speyer and Katherine Farley, and Committee on Drawings Fund in honor of Kathy Fuld. © Adrian Piper Research Archive Foundation Berlin.

not realize that, but also that I have a very strong masculine component to my character."⁹ Piper's serial enactments of the Mythic Being echoed ethno-linguist Richard Bauman's definition of performance as a "mode of communicative behavior and a type of communicative event."¹⁰

I choose to approach the Mythic Being by, paradoxically, retreating away from it. If Adrian Piper is one of the most accomplished, critically recognized, and controversial artists to emerge in the twentieth century, the Mythic Being is, by far, her most lauded and written-about work. This rapturous critical attention has deflected scrutiny of her earlier, weirder, denser, and harder-to-classify performance work. Yet it is here, I argue, in this "ensemble of objects that we might call black performances," that we begin to perceive the comingling of objecthood, avatars, and black performance art that this book seeks to chart.¹¹

Instead, critical interpretations have hewed so closely to Piper's own later writing on the Mythic Being that seemingly the *only* way to interpret the Mythic Being is (a) as an explicitly "black" male avatar and (b) a set of performances that enabled the light-skinned Piper to experience virulent racism, seemingly for the first time. I concur, in other words, with art historian Cherise Smith: "Much critical dialogue interpellates Piper's work as always and only tackling race and xenophobia, thereby ghettoizing it as 'identity politics.'"¹² I certainly am not negating or denigrating Piper's experiences while in the garb of the Mythic Being. However, the close adherence to Piper's words has resulted in commentary, however well intentioned, that too easily construes it as what it has become—a think piece on race and racism in line with her work since the 1980s—at the expense of what it began as: a bodily and psychological experiment in transcending the boundaries between subjecthood and objecthood to become an art object.

So what if we deferred assent with Piper's later thoughts and instead looked elsewhere? Is it possible that if we juxtapose the Mythic Being against earlier, more bizarre performance works (silently waiting for our attention) and also reposition the Mythic Being as an end point rather than a beginning, that new interpretations may emerge?

While this chapter leaps ahead a century, my pointed move toward Piper in the larger cartography of this book echoes her striking convergence with the corporeal and aesthetic strategies of fugitive slave extraordinaire Ellen Craft; both perform in the service of a certain type of freedom. Craft's transatlantic oeuvre of escape acts, prosthetic performances, antislavery perambulations, and elegant engraving all shared a liberationist impulse. And this propulsive energy, stoked by fellow slaves-in-exile William Craft and William Wells Brown, was directed toward the ultimate of freedoms: escape from chattel slavery and the right to citizenship and self-possession. Adrian Piper's art and performances, I argue, are also intensely interested in the power to determine actions without restraint or interference, including the "freedom from [the] roles induced by other's recognition."[13] In her 1987 essay "Flying," she articulated her specific notions of freedom. She described abstraction as an initial form of freedom, pointing toward both her *art* and her *identity*. For the former, abstraction—specifically, her turn away from representational subject matter in painting to strictly formal concerns—generated Minimalism-derived experiments in space and perception in her late-1960s/early-1970s works. Meanwhile, for the latter, self-abstraction offered the promise of self-transcendence, most especially from her body's racial and gender particularities. To Piper, abstraction was flight; it offered "freedom from the immediate spatio-temporal constraints of the moment," "freedom from the immediate boundaries of concrete subjectivity," "freedom to violate in imagination the constraints of public practice," and finally, "freedom to survey the real as a resource for embodying the possible."[14] Yet, as she notes, her flight was continually grounded by the political upheavals of the 1970s and the affective responses of others to her embodiment as a black woman (most especially in the hallowed halls of academia), both of which trapped her back in her subjectivity. Her art praxis is an ongoing attempt to escape aesthetic and identity-based strictures. Specifically, objecthood, as we will see, is a strategy Piper repeatedly deploys for these ends, a rigorous attempt to render her black female body flexible and polymorphous, and to temporarily escape from it by radical acts of self-estrangement. In short, Adrian Piper's freedom—like Ellen Craft's—is a performance-based assertion of personhood, a push for "new ways of being black and free in public," albeit through willful self-negation.[15]

Craft's utilitarian bodily acts and Piper's tenacious performances of self-alienation, thus, are not as incommensurable as initially meets the eye; Craft's antislavery performances clear the way for Piper's deeply philosophical experiments in black objecthood. This is particularly apparent if we heed philosopher Fred Moten's beckoning that "Piper's performance work moves at the intersection of a feminist anti-slavery aesthetic and the emergence and convergence of conceptual and minimalist art."[16] Certainly, the passing performances and fugitive selves of Craft, and her white male avatar Mr. William Johnson, did markedly different representational work than the multiplicity of embodiments and modes of objecthood we will see in Piper and her various performances with and without her third-world male avatar. Still, the particular relationships of her work to the increasingly canonical field of performance art remain underexplored; the possible links between her work and the everyday performances staged by slippery nineteenth-century black historical actors have gone unspoken. Likewise, if the stubborn refusal of the performances in this chapter to obey any logics or genres other than their own signal a reckoning with artistic freedom (if not ownership), they also share a manipulation of the black female body as protean source material, a strategy explored repeatedly in this book.

Our exploration of Piper will mirror that of the Crafts, with an attention to quotidian bodily acts and visual culture, enabling Piper's particular type of objecthood—more self-conscious, strange, and alienating—to surface. This last adjective is purposeful, as I coax Piper's repeated and complex self-estrangement into conversation with theories of alienation in theater and performance studies. While German playwright Bertolt Brecht's "alienation effect" may be the most obvious focus for this discussion, I direct us instead toward Daphne Brooks's theorization of "afro-alienation acts." While the latter is a less salient term, it importantly tethers self-alienation, as an aesthetic strategy, to black performance practices. Brooks's idiom, specifically, delineates afro-alienation acts as a "specific strategy of cultural performance" through which select black subjects in the late nineteenth century and early twentieth converted the condition of "alterity" into "cultural expressiveness." More simply, these dramatis personae translated "alienation into self-actualizing performance." In this way, afro-alienation, as a concept, attends to how cultural figures like Henry "Box" Brown and Aida Overton Walker wielded "performance tactics" as a means of "critically defamiliarizing their own bodies" (and the spectacle of "blackness" itself) to "yield alternative racial and gender epistemologies."[17]

We will focus in this chapter on Piper's *Aretha Franklin Catalysis* (1972) and *The Spectator Series* (1973), precursors to the Mythic Being. For the former, I delineate Piper's yoking of objecthood to gestural vocabularies of black dance, while for the latter, I direct us to the ecstatic queer pleasure her anonymous "spectator" enables, nudging the aesthetic device of the avatar even more into the illicit zones of sexuality. The third and final part of this triptych will focus on the printed performances of the Mythic Being posters. But before I move to this potent performance trio, we must delineate Piper's remarkable (and rare) traversal across Minimalism, Conceptualism, and performance art in the late 1960s and, later, her tenuous ties to budding notions of black art and feminist art. Piper, as I suggest below, repeatedly breaks loose of taut strictures within (and between) these adamantine aesthetic categories— occasionally to the detriment of her own legacy, as she appears absent from them altogether. Yet, by importing select strategies from each, she constructs a fulcrum for her vigorous art praxis, rendering herself a paradoxical presence.

Paradoxical Presence: Piper's Journey from Minimalism to Conceptualism to Performance

Sandwiched historically between Piper's entrance into the School of Visual Arts (SVA) in New York City in 1966 and the cataclysmic events in the spring of 1970 that jolted her (and, concomitantly, her work), Piper's early artworks were, in her words, "abstract, general, systematic, and formalistic," at first mining the emerging tenets of Minimalism.[18] *Primary Structures: Younger American and British Sculptors*, the pioneering exhibition that debuted at the Jewish Museum in New York in April 1966, is widely regarded as the introduction of minimalist art objects to art-world habitués in the United States. Artworks like these, alongside the growing realm of minimalist dance, radically eschewed traditional art objects and their attendant historical allusions, in lieu of an art elevating the viewer to a new role as an equal player in the aesthetic experience. These performative qualities in the creation and display of art both refuted early assumptions that Minimalism was concerned only with aesthetic questions of style and form, and hinted, rather, at the deeply ideological motives undergirding it. Principally, in the ethos of Minimalism according to Maurice Berger, the "relationship between viewer and art object, when carefully constructed and considered, can empower the social content of art."[19] In contrast to the flat surface of the painting, the minimalist sculptures of artists like Donald Judd and Robert Morris were obdurate and self-referential. They were not rarefied or precious, but rather literal and devoid of narrative, hence the epithet "literalist art." These works were often alarming to formalist art critics like Michael Fried; in a notorious essay, published in June 1967, he chastised their strange theatricality, taking up space on gallery floors and forcing spectators to move around them, as evidence of a vexing "objecthood" that was, to him, the antithesis of art.[20] Piper's artworks from this period—such as *Untitled Constructions* (1967), a pair of similar-looking yet distinct canvases that seemingly announced themselves as sculptural objects—operated similarly to this emergent Minimalism, provoking, in the words of John P. Bowles, "viewers to consider themselves as agents in time and space, realizing and recognizing themselves in the relationships they create with the artwork."[21]

Conceptualism built on these idiosyncratic notions, sharing Minimalism's effacement of the artist and rebuke of hierarchical traditions of art and art making, while privileging concept over material. Conceptualism's radical precept, that the idea becomes the thing of art, enabled artists (including Piper) to imagine artworks too costly or impractical to construct. Its utilization, moreover, of linguistic sources outside the art historical canon—including newspapers, graphs, advertisements, and photographic reproductions—challenged medium-specificity, while encouraging the viewer's self-consciousness.[22] Sol LeWitt's "Paragraphs in Conceptual Art," published in *Artforum* in 1967, provided an early framework for this discourse, and his exhibition *46 Variations of Three Different Kinds of Cubes* at the Dwan Gallery in New York the next year awakened Piper to conceptual art. In 1968, the same year she met LeWitt, one of Piper's untitled conceptual works was published in *0–9*, the cutting-edge mimeographed magazine of poetry and conceptual art edited by Vito Acconci and Bernadette Mayer. Gwen Allen and Cherise Smith describe how print media like *0–9* sought to act as "vital sites of alternative distribution through which artists shed the restrictions of the white cube."[23] Piper's early soundworks of the late 1960s, meanwhile, further evinced her interest in an ostensibly "pure" Minimalism and Conceptualism, while also serving as the type of work that "many art critics can't comprehend being made by a black woman (most people in the art world did not realize I was black or a woman at the time)."[24]

If Piper's parenthetical remarks express her unique dilemma—as a black woman conceptual artist making art perceived (at least initially) as that of a white man—they also allude to the limits of the promise of universalism in these new artistic modes. Piper, discussing her late 1960s conceptual work, remarks that while Conceptualism's ideas were "theoretically fertile," it was a "white macho enclave" emblematic of a "Eurocentric equation of intellect with masculinity."[25] Minimalism, similarly, is still largely defined by the writings of white male artists— LeWitt, Donald Judd, and Carl Andre, for instance—that reinforce the perception of it as an art form dominated by them. Piper's problem, as a black woman, is partly due to the very removal of her presence from the work in order to privilege the viewer, a hallmark of minimalist and conceptual art. In doing so, Piper rendered the work objective and universal while all but ensuring her invisibility as an artist, which only worsened her marginalization, like that of other women artists. That erasure, moreover, is heightened by the likelihood that curators, collectors, and other artists excluded her work from certain exhibitions (and publications written about them) because a black woman made it. These dual negations—Piper's own purposeful self-alienation and the racism and sexism of the art world—render Piper, in Bowles's words, a "doubled absence in the history of Minimal and Conceptual art."[26] This omission is particularly troubling, art historian Kobena Mercer admonishes, considering Piper's role as "the only African American artist involved in the New York milieu of first-generation Conceptualism and the only member of this generation who actually became a philosopher."[27] In short, Piper's dilemma was her commitment to the ideal of objective universality espoused by Minimalism and Conceptualism and, at the same time, her embodiment of a certain particularity: she was unavoidably a black woman.

The most intriguing of these early works is Piper's *Hypothesis* series (created between the fall of 1968 and April 1970), which inserted information—in this case, her everyday tasks—into the art object, attempting to extract the universal from the mundane. Piper called nineteen of these works *Situations*, further exemplifying how she might have envisioned them, converting aspects of her quotidian life (shopping for groceries, for instance, in *Hypothesis: Situation #16*) from the specific into the paradigmatic, a theme of her later work. The dry documentation of some tasks considered "women's work" lent them an unexpectedly feminist edge. This is perhaps most apparent, Bowles argues, in *Situation #14*. It is a study, accompanied by photographs, of two "co-existing space conditions," the "office" and a female secretary, "Sandra Livingston," a friend of Piper's, who was the receptionist at the personnel agency where Piper worked as the bookkeeper. Charting Livingston's secretarial tasks and the unchanging office space at different times, it "universalizes the working woman's situation"; likewise, it also critiques a sexual division of labor, whereby women conceptual artists often had to take such jobs in order to support their art careers, which enabled their male counterparts to derisively label them "dilettantes." In 1969, the same year she worked for Cameo Personnel Agency, Piper was also a receptionist and administrative assistant for Seth Siegelaub Gallery, underscoring the predicaments faced by women who aspired to become artists.[28]

Foreshadowing Piper's later use of performance art, the very first piece in the *Hypothesis* series, *Meat into Meat* (1968), was a performance. *Meat into Meat* documented the transubstantiation of a quarter pound of meat, as it was cooked and ultimately consumed by her boyfriend at the time, David Rosner. It became a "confrontation performance," as she described it, because Rosner's dismissal of Piper's "feminism, vegetarianism, and 'avant-garde' art sensibility (that is, about all the things that were important to me)" provoked her "confrontation, ridicule, and objectification of him through the piece."[29] Rosner was a professed Marxist, but also a "rabid carnivore," and hence the piece upended his authoritative and patriarchal dismissal of Piper by putting his contradictory stance on display *as* art. A loft performance, Piper's *Meat into Meat* presciently echoes artists' manipulation of alternative spaces in the 1970s, such as private/work lofts and storefronts in SoHo, as sites of a burgeoning underground performance art scene, a milieu in which Piper was an early participant.[30]

The spring of 1970 demarcates two major shifts: both when Piper's political inclinations, until then vague, became suddenly more overt and when Piper's body, until then absent, was forcefully inserted into her art. In her essay "Talking to Myself: The Autobiography of an Art Object," Piper remarks that four particular events "changed everything for me: (1) the invasion of Cambodia; (2) The Women's Movement; (3) Kent State and Jackson State; (4) The closing of CCNY, where I was in my first term as a philosophy major, during the student rebellion." Amid these upheavals, she pondered her unique subjectivity "as an artist, a woman, and a black" and the "natural disadvantages of those attributes," an effect of her realization that she was "in situations which were themselves deeply affected."[31] According to her personal chronology, she joined the interracial Art Workers' Coalition that year—an organization that specifically targeted the Museum of Modern Art and that, as I detail in chapter 4, Howardena Pindell also joined. In April 1970, as well, she withdrew her *Hypothesis* from the *Conceptual Art and Conceptual Aspects* show at the New York Cultural Center, in protest against President Richard Nixon's invasion of Cambodia as well as the Kent State and Jackson State massacres.[32]

Piper's actions mirrored the political foment in the New York art world, as a large group of politically active artists chastised museums for conceiving of themselves, and hence aesthetics writ large, as "pure" entities distinct from the realm of politics. As Kellie Jones notes, "withdrawal had become one very visible means for black artists to register their disagreement with institutional actions and real world events."[33] In this way, Piper's removal of her work was in sync with the politically overt acts of black artists as well as the New York Artists' Strike against Racism, Sexism, Repression, and War (known simply as the Art Strike) that began on May 18, 1970. Four days later, five hundred artists protested outside the Metropolitan Museum of Art and the Museum of Modern Art (MoMA) when both refused to close as requested by artists who chose to withdraw their work from view for the day as a symbolic act of solidarity with the victims of the numerous national and global atrocities occurring at the time.[34] In a letter to the director of MoMA, dated May 26 and simply signed "Art Strike, N.Y. N.Y.," artists applauded the museum's suspension of admission charges "on these occasions of dissent" while critiquing MoMA's failure "to understand the meaning of symbolic denial (closing the museum for ONE day), which speaks to the actual denial of life by forces of violence." The letter continues, "Artists must have the right to decide how art is to be used. What are you afraid of? Artists don't destroy art. War and racism destroys art.

War and racism destroys people."[35] While these artists-activists argued that museums—MoMA and others—should not act, in the words of the Guerrilla Art Action Group, as "a diversion from the realities of war and social crisis," they also forcefully stated that the artist should have the last word on how art is utilized by arts institutions, a view that most museums, understandably, took umbrage at.[36] Though she attended AWC meetings, Piper appears not to have been involved in either the May 22 protest or the drafting of the May 26 letter. And despite her withdrawal from the New York Cultural Center exhibition, she still participated in the groundbreaking *Information* show at MoMA later that year, one of the first museum exhibitions of conceptual art in the United States, showing her *Context #7*.[37]

In addition, Piper shifted her praxis away from the "self-enclosed aesthetic concerns" that previously motivated her, as she abandoned "traditional art media" and instead embraced the "plastic possibilities" of her own body.[38] She writes that the "political and art-political realities" of the time made her realize that her "earlier, conceptual work was too rarefied and socially isolated to be personally meaningful any longer."[39] By becoming the artist-as-artwork, Piper hoped to induce a catalytic change in the viewer; meanwhile, she aspired to more directly engage the public by taking art out of the elitist surroundings of the museum and the gallery and, instead, into more ordinary scenarios, from subways to buses, from Macy's to Union Square. In doing so, she hoped to test the perception of her viewers, risking not only their interpretation of her as more of a public disturbance than artist, but also their possible conflation of Piper-the-artist with the body she used as a support for the artwork.

The provocative *Catalysis* series pushed the limits of all these artistic philosophies at once, as Piper manipulated strange amalgamations of fascinatingly mundane materials to render herself a truly paradoxical presence. She made what she called "artificial and nonfunctional plastic alterations" to her body—including bubblegum bubbles she loudly popped and let smear on her face, helium-filled Mickey Mouse balloons that she attached to her body, and clothes submerged in a mixture of vinegar, eggs, milk, and cod liver oil—staged in the "same time and space continuum as the viewer."[40] Armed with these alterations, Piper executed seemingly ordinary tasks, but always with a bizarre twist. For instance, in *Catalysis III* (1970), she painted her clothing with wet oil

Figure 3.6. Adrian Piper, *Catalysis III* (#1 of 3), 1970. Three silver gelatin print photographs on paper; 16 x 16 in. (40.6 x 40.6 cm.). Photo credit: Rosemary Mayer. Collection of the Generali Foundation, Vienna. © Adrian Piper Research Archive Foundation Berlin and Generali Foundation.

paint, put on the still-dripping clothes, attached a sign on her chest that read "WET PAINT," and went shopping at Macy's for gloves and sunglasses. The same year, in *Catalysis IV* (1970), she rode the bus while dressed in a conservative outfit, except with a white bath towel stuffed into, and spilling out of, her mouth; she repeated this action while riding the subway and the elevators at the Empire State Building.[41] The *Aretha Franklin Catalysis*, which I discuss later in the chapter, continued this perceptual disorientation, albeit via the vehicle of black dance.

Figure 3.7. Adrian Piper, *Catalysis IV* (#2 of 5), 1970. Five silver gelatin print photographs on paper, 16 x 16 in. (40.6 x 40.6 cm.). Photo credit: Rosemary Mayer. Collection of the Generali Foundation, Vienna. © Adrian Piper Research Archive Foundation Berlin and Generali Foundation.

Piper's seminal *Untitled for Max's Kansas City* (1970) pushed the artist-as-artwork paradigm to the outer reaches as she experimented with sensory deprivation in the service of her increasingly edgy art. Staged on May 2, 1970, as part of *The Saturday Afternoon Show*, a hour-long exhibition organized by Hannah Weiner, Piper's performance had a particularly unusual goal: to fully transform herself into an art object. She sought to accomplish this by walking around the bar in everyday clothes, long gloves, a blindfold, and ear and nose plugs; in this act of removing herself from virtually all tactile, visual, or aural stimulation, she would embody objecthood. Piper purposely staged this exercise at

Max's Kansas City, a SoHo establishment popular with the art world cognoscenti; she described Max's as "an Art Environment, replete with Art Consciousness and Self-Consciousness about Art Consciousness."[42] Howardena Pindell seconded this view; she remarked in an interview that while she knew of those—like influential art dealer Leo Castelli and artists Robert Rauschenberg and Robert Morris—who frequented Max's, she "always consider[ed] it death row. You go in and there are all these artists sitting there waiting for someone famous to come in and discuss with them, its like Hollywood."[43] Piper strategically alienated herself from Max's affected atmosphere, so as not to have her "own consciousness co-opted and modified by that of others," while also attempting to transcend her own subjectivity. She presented herself as a "silent, secret, passive object, seemingly ready to be absorbed into their consciousness as an object."

Yet such absorption proved impossible, in large part, because Piper learned that her extreme attempt at self-alienation did not render her a docile inert sculpture, an object devoid of subjectivity; quite the contrary, her striking ontological experiment was a forceful form of agency and, in Judith Wilson's words, a "radical assertion of 'subjecthood.'"[44] Hence, in Piper's counterintuitive description, "My objecthood became my subjecthood." Moreover, the absorption Piper had intended proved impossible because her "*voluntary* objectlike passivity" implied aggressive choice. Her emphasis on the adjective "voluntary" suggests the perplexity (and suspicion) with which patrons likely experienced a blindfolded Piper; many might well have wondered: why is this woman seeking to willfully jettison her subjectivity? Furthermore, Piper writes, "unbeknownst to me the bar had turned into a stage,"[45] hinting that, to her dismay, her atypical actions were recognized, and categorized, by denizens of Max's as *performance art*; all this suggests that, despite her efforts, her aggressive acts may have been co-opted by and absorbed into Max's self-conscious art consciousness after all, suggesting that her ability to provoke the self-reflection of her audience may have been blunted by the self-awareness of that audience.

Piper's seeming aversion to the label "performance art" here is emblematic of her later, more overt efforts to distance herself and her work from such terminology, even while she has made repeated use of the form in her work (and in her essays) over several decades. After all, as

RoseLee Goldberg has observed, performance art was often a natural extension of conceptual art, particularly in its critique of the commodification of art by an increasingly competitive brokering of power between galleries and museums. Performance art's inability to be bought or sold resisted such market imperatives, an anticapitalist logic Piper has elsewhere concurred with.[46] Its ephemeral form also enacted, to use Lucy Lippard's verbiage, the "dematerialization of the art object," a leitmotif of conceptual art.[47]

Despite this apparent aversion, in her 1984 essay "Performance: The Problematic Solution," Piper praises performance art as an answer to interrelated quagmires that arise from the gap between audiences and art objects. Specifically, she delineates the problems that arise from audiences and artists not communicating in the same idiom. The discrete art object is somehow supposed to bridge the gap between the two, but is itself of a different ontological status than both. Performance art, she argues, solves many of these dilemmas, especially because artist and art object are collapsed into one human entity. Its immediacy allows artists to calibrate their effect on audiences immediately, while its flexibility enables artists to constantly refine it to suit the demands of each particular set of audiences. Its status remains problematic, however, due to the fact that most artists are trained to "pummel, slash, and besmirch objects in the isolation of our studios" rather than engage audiences, and hence lack the expertise that the form demands.[48]

Piper's thoughts here suggest that a proper interpretation of the chronology I have charted above—her sui generis traversal from Minimalism to Conceptualism to performance art, and also back and forth between these fields—requires an understanding of her fluid moves to the aesthetic form that is most suitable for her artistic and ideological purposes, extracting foundational ideas from each to build her potent praxis. She implies as much, in a 1992 lecture, noting that despite her frequent misclassification as a performance artist, she self-identifies as a conceptual artist, for two reasons. The first is her use of the medium that "best realizes the ideas I am exploring"; the second is "the priority of strategic over aesthetic considerations," hence her employment of "whatever media resources are best suited to achieve those goals."[49] Piper's remarks here are useful, *not* as an ironclad distinction between Conceptualism and performance art, but rather as a hermeneutic—they shed light on *how* she singularly maneuvered emergent, yet seemingly distinct, aesthetic categories. Piper, as noted above, at first adhered to several axiomatic principles associated with Minimalism and Conceptualism, including the self-effacement of the artist and the deemphasis on art objects, in exchange for an art giving precedence to ideas and the prioritization of the viewer. Her eventual amalgamation of conceptual art and performance art, after the tumultuous political events of spring 1970, stretched these newfangled ideas to their extreme endpoints as she sought to aggressively produce catalytic change in her viewers. She experimented with harnessing the possibilities offered by her plastic-like corporeality, utilizing her body as a buttress for her art. In this substitution of her altered physicality for the discrete art object, and self-staging in the everyday locales of New York City in lieu of museums and galleries, Piper accomplished several things at once. If her art became much more confrontational and performative, it also purposely tested her audiences' ability to recognize her *as* art. After all, her prescient *Catalysis* pieces were conducted prior to the eventual codification by critics of performance actions enacted by artists as "performance art" as well as its recognition by the art world, which would not occur until February 1976 at the Whitney Museum of American Art—Piper, of course, was a participant.[50] Performance art's insistent focus on the artist's body, moreover, eased the strain Minimalism and Conceptualism's aspiration toward universalism placed on Piper's vexing particularity "as an artist, a woman, and a black." And, finally, it further concretized the themes of absence and presence (as well as self-alienation) that became signatures of her subsequent work. In all these ways, Adrian Piper emerges as an artist "simultaneously upfront, underground, and ahead of her time."[51]

Feminist Art, Black Art, and the Predicament of Black Women Artists

In the early 1970s, as Piper tentatively developed an art praxis in the interstices between Minimalism, Conceptualism and performance art, she also moved in and out of two additional aesthetic categories—feminist art and black art—that were even more fraught. If these nascent formations were, undoubtedly, by-products of larger sociopolitical upheaval, specifically the feminist and civil rights movements, they were also symptomatic of the aforementioned micro-tensions between artists and art institutions that, as I discuss below, presaged aggressive demands for greater inclusion of female and black artists. Despite their lack of overt feminist themes, Piper's early works, as well as her later ones, were featured in several exhibitions and publications that framed them as feminist art. Her work, for example, was included in two of the earliest exhibitions of feminist art in the United States—*26 Contemporary Women Artists* (1971) and *C. 7500* (1973)—each of which sought to define what exactly feminist art was; in the latter, John P. Bowles remarks, one of Piper's early artworks was included and understood as feminist despite its complete lack of reference to gender or sexuality. In a 1972 interview with Lucy Lippard, Piper was asked if the aggressions in her *Catalysis* pieces had anything do with her being a woman or being black. Piper partly sidestepped the question, ignoring the issue of race while insisting the work was apolitical. She did remark, however, that the "work is a product of me as an individual, and the fact that I am a woman surely has a lot to do with it. You know, here I am, or was, 'violating my body'; I was making it public. I was turning myself into an object." Three years later, in an article for *Ms.*, Lippard discussed Piper's *Mythic Being* alongside the work of other female artists—including Eleanor Antin, Lynda Benglis, and Judy Chicago—focused on the self as subject matter; all utilized costume, disguises, and fantasy to enact striking new selves—or, in Lippard's parlance, "transformation art."[52]

Piper's relationship to black art and art-world activism of the time, however, is more vexing. Her entrance into SVA in 1966 mirrored an influx of black artists who gained admission to prestigious MFA programs in fine art on the East and West Coasts as a result of desegregation efforts begun in the 1950s. By 1970, for example, graduates of Yale University's elite MFA program included black artists Howardena Pindell ('67), Barbara Chase-Riboud ('60), and William T. Williams ('68). Meanwhile, incipient notions of black art were anchored on the West Coast by two key exhibitions in 1966—*The Negro in American Art* and *66 Signs of Neon*, both at UCLA—and on the East Coast by the opening of the Studio Museum of Harlem on 125th Street in New York on September 26, 1968.[53] The Studio Museum's social mission explicitly sought to connect black artists to the local Harlem community, echoing efforts by other black artists to render more permeable the boundary between the studio and the street. In 1969, the Metropolitan Museum of Art's egregious failure to include black artists in its *Harlem on My Mind* exhibition led to protests at its opening and occasioned the Studio Museum's exhibition *Invisible Americans: Black Artists of the 1930s*. The latter's pointed title seemed designed as an explicit corrective not only to the Met's flagrant oversight, but also the erasure of black artists from narratives of American art writ large. Piper, as noted earlier, attended meetings of the interracial Art Workers' Coalition (AWC). She was not directly involved, however, in their art actions. Nor was she an active member of the Black Emergency Cultural Coalition (BECC), yet another by-product of the Met debacle, or Women Art Revolutionaries (WAR), organizations that demanded greater institutional representation of black artists and women artists, respectively. In short, Piper did not participate in black artist-organized collectives and exhibitions in the late 1960s and early 1970s, and race was not explicitly invoked apropos of her work until 1972 (by a critic) and 1973 (by herself).[54] Thus, with the exception of Pindell, her fellow AWC member, Piper appears to have been isolated from her black art world contemporaries until at least the early 1970s.

In 1970, other black women artists—often doubly excluded from the male-dominated Black Arts Movement and white-dominated feminist (and feminist art) organizations—began forming their own groups and curating their own exhibitions. For example, the 1970 *Sapphire Show* at Gallery 32 in Los Angeles, a short-lived gallery run and funded by artist Suzanne Jackson, was the city's first survey of black woman artists. Meanwhile, in New York, artists Kay Brown, Faith Ringgold, and others organized the group show *Where We At: Black Women Artists 1971*, which quickly led to the formation of the collective "Where We At" Black Women Artists (WWA). In 1973, the Woman's Building, a nonprofit feminist arts organization, was founded in a vacant structure near the Los Angeles neighborhood of MacArthur Park by former California Institute of the Arts (CalArts) teachers Judy Chicago, Arlene Raven, and Sheila Levrant de Bretteville; that same year Betye Saar organized the exhibition *Black Mirror*, focused around black women artists, in the Womanspace Gallery, a leased venue within that same building.[55]

At the very least, the rigid tenets of the Black Arts Movement may be partly to blame for Piper's absence from such conversations, since its demands for art that was didactic and figurative were at odds with her early oeuvre. After all, Piper's purposeful self-alienation and perceptual disorientation flouted such conventions. Her artistic preoccupations refused to easily coalesce inside what was starting to be called "black art," or at the least the definition of it outlined by Larry Neal in 1968, in which he imagined the Black Arts Movement as the aesthetic corollary of the Black Power movement and, hence, black art as a pursuit that must be yoked tightly to racial uplift. Far from a fait accompli, though, black artists heavily debated whether there was such a thing called "black art" and, if so, what its essential properties were. Moreover, several black artists, including Richard Hunt, Barbara Chase-Riboud, and, as we will see, Howardena Pindell, rejected such dogmatic tendencies and were henceforth accused of making art that was not sufficiently black.[56] These renegade artists, whether intentionally or not, eschewed the facile equivalency of black artists with "black art"; the repercussions of this, as Darby English reminds, continue to be vastly important for how we interpret the works black artists make.[57] For an artist like Piper, as well as her contemporary Pindell, this point is particularly important; in her own life, Piper became increasingly active starting in 1970—after her initial involvement with AWC, she soon moved into the realm of feminist consciousness-raising, for example[58]—even when her political inclinations, and her identity as a black women artist, were not salient in the works themselves.

While Piper is a doubled absence in Minimalism and Conceptualism— once by her willful self-erasure from her work, and again by the exclusion of her work from histories of these aesthetic movements—her relationship to feminist art and black art is neither clear-cut nor conspicuous (even while her work has been identified, retrospectively, as both). As Kobena Mercer has argued, Piper was rarely in sync with 1960s and later identity politics, practicing an approach to art and politics that has always been askew.[59] While Piper occasionally discussed her work in ways that related it back to her experiences as a woman, she did not identify it as feminist art. And while she has retroactively discussed *The Mythic Being* (1973–75) in terms explicitly tethered to race and racism, she has neither aligned earlier works in her oeuvre in such distinct language nor claimed them as black art. Simply put, the nexuses between Piper's early artworks and embryonic notions of feminist art are at best oblique. Their ties to the enterprise of black art, meanwhile, are virtually nonexistent. As a result, they require us to place more pressure on the capacious but capricious term "black art," a category, I argue, that does not fully capture Piper's early artworks, or perhaps, any of her artworks. This is despite ongoing efforts to squeeze them into the category and claim them as such. Rather, her early minimalist and conceptual works, as well as her early performances, might be understood as outliers that help define the outer limits of "black art" (and perhaps also "feminist art") by their seeming absence from its sphere. Akin to Piper the artist, these works are a paradoxical presence, intermittently detectable but not always visible within these emergent aesthetic categories.

Piper has recently claimed that these early works must reflect the historical moment they are situated in, suggesting that they *do* reflect the terror she faced as a black woman, unconscious or not, as well as the politics of civil rights and Black Power activism.[60] Her candor underscores the risks black women in this historical period faced, especially those who dared to identify as artists. However, the argument that these early works, many assumed to be made by a white male, *must* reflect these perils seems an abrupt about-face for an artist insistent that interpretations of her work not be overdetermined by her personal biography (especially her race). Granted, her reluctance to identify her art objects as black art at the time was perhaps due to the fact, as Bowles suggests, that curators, galleries, and artists had a difficult time interpreting her art as anything *but* black art once they discovered that Piper was a black woman.[61] Indeed, her ability to make art crossing a remarkable number of otherwise distinct fields at once—Minimalism, Conceptualism, performance art, and in less discernable ways, feminist art and black art— hints at the biggest challenge she may have faced as an artist who also happened to be a black woman: her very attempts at aesthetic mobility, at crossing the well-guarded boundaries between genres and at making work not easily categorized or understood. The tricky predicaments, apropos artistic freedom, she encountered are ultimately effaced (like the artist) from the early objets d'art she deftly constructed.

We will see Piper's signature self-alienation from her work become even more complicated, as I shift from these early works to the mid-1970s and her increasingly daring attempts to wield her body-as-art-object as a slippery instrument. In these performances, I lead us to a bank, the New York Public Library, and an empty parking lot—among other places—as Aretha Franklin's righteous "Respect" provides the soundtrack for our trek.

Dancing in the Streets: The *Aretha Franklin Catalysis*

In September 1972, Piper first wrote about the *Aretha Franklin Catalysis*, a piece that she had performed in various guises and spaces that year. The piece was simple: she would confront unbeknownst spectators with a dancing, but silent, body. To prepare, Piper "listened to Aretha's version of 'Respect' until I had it completely memorized" and could play it in her head "at will," when desired. Then she went outside. In her words, "The piece consisted of my listening to the song in my mind and simultaneously dancing to it. I did a mixture of the Bugaloo, the Jerk, the Lindy, the Charleston, and the Twist, with a high degree of improvisation. I performed the piece while waiting on line at the bank, at a bus stop, and in the Public Library." Piper would perform a version alone in an empty parking lot the same year, and a "second version" in her "loft, in complete solitude."[62]

The subtraction of the external audience in later versions may have been a strategic response to the discordance between street audiences and Piper's artistic intentions, most especially the expectations of male spectators. On the most basic level, audiences may not have been aware that her actions were "art." After all, the pieces in the *Catalysis* series were purposely performed in non-museum contexts to avoid their easy delineation as such as well as any semblance of premeditated theatricality (i.e., that they were "happenings" or performance art). As a result, while Piper's dances may have invited misinterpretation as a weird public disturbance (and of her as a kooky social misfit), she also willingly abdicated a degree of control, trusting audiences, in her words, "not to destroy or attack me." In this way, her radical self-abnegations in the *Catalysis* acts hint at multiple palpable risks—the nonrecognition of passersby of these self-stagings as art, the possibly outright animosity of urban denizens, and even the threat of arrest—all of which left her "always petrified while doing those pieces."[63]

These performances also invited a different risk: her sexual objectification by men. She had already been shocked to discover that this objectification occurred even when she appeared the most revolting. In an interview with Effie Serlis, Piper discusses the puzzling reactions of businessmen to an early *Catalysis* performance when she wore a set of clothes soaked in a "very disgusting mixture," coated her arms in cod liver oil, and decided to ride the subway: "I was very passive (just standing there), and they would look at me like they really wanted to fuck me. This friend said that by walking around that way, it seemed that I didn't have any respect for my body, so why should anyone else?" She goes on to suggest that since her public appearance was not an issue in the *Aretha Franklin Catalysis*—since she was dressed normally (sans vile substances)—she assumed her actions would be more acceptable and, presumably, not engender powerfully misogynist behavior. Instead, she garnered very particular gendered responses from men who wrongly assumed her dances were for their pleasure.

> I'd attract the attention of a different kind, because I was dancing [,] from men; they'd clap or try to pinch me, and that made me very angry. I knew that I brought it on myself, but it seemed to me [that] if a guy had done that, no man or woman would come by and try to pinch him or think that somehow the performance was being done specifically for that person's benefit. These men would feel justified in responding, and when I'd say something really harsh, they'd get all hurt. "Why are you doing it then?"[64]

This description suggests an alarming chasm between her self-exploratory dances and the uninhibited responses of her male viewers. The anonymous man's self-reflexive question implies that public acts staged by women have no utility, let alone as art, unless they are designed explicitly for the gratification of men. Otherwise, why perform them? Piper's remarks betray her possible naiveté at that time, particularly if she was in fact performing primarily for herself, but in the presence of others. Yet they are also indicative of the dangers of performing objecthood. This is especially true with the often hard-to-classify performance work of black women. Rendering oneself an object can swiftly lead to sexual objectification. It can also provide license for audiences to cross the invisible threshold between them and the artist, poking and prodding the black female performer on self-display. The late Joice Heth, and her early-nineteenth-century bodily phantasmagoria, provides a lasting (and ultimately tragic) example of this pernicious dynamic. Similarly, with Piper, male spectators seemed all too willing to transgress the limits of respect (to invoke Aretha), an inclination heightened not only by the freedom of a non-museum environment, but also by the gendered norms of power that, too often, place authority in the hands of men.

Piper's improvisational executions of black American dances in mundane public spaces undoubtedly bear traces of Minimalism and Conceptualism. This is particularly true in her use of the kinetic vocabularies of dance as an artful practice or a "way of making," to quote Michel de Certeau.[65] These funky everyday acts, moreover, are also oft-elided precursors to her more notorious "dance-lesson-as-performance-art-piece" *Funk Lessons*.[66] Staged between 1982 and 1984, these later performances were collaborative; spectators-made-dancers participated as Piper confronted overwhelmingly white audiences with a black musical and dance form they usually regarded with antipathy. By "making accessible to them a common medium of communication—funk music and dance—that has been largely inaccessible to white culture," Piper aspired for the performances to "restructure people's social identities."[67] Both sets of dances, despite the temporal distance and divergent aims separating them, echoed the embrace by Minimalism, and later Conceptualism, of the "new dance" of choreographer-dancers like Yvonne Rainer and Trisha Brown and their methodology—pointedly saying, to quote Rainer, "NO to spectacle, no to virtuosity, etc." in favor of banal, everyday movements.[68] Still, if the *Aretha Franklin Catalysis* (and its various permutations) utilized specifically *black* dance forms—a radical departure from the artistic preoccupations of the predominately white avant-garde documented in Sally Banes's canonical *Greenwich Village 1963*—they also gestured elsewhere in their explicit explorations of objecthood.[69]

In the aptly titled essay "Talking to Myself: The Ongoing Autobiography of an Art Object," Piper discusses how she became increasingly able to substitute her "own self-consciousness of me as an object" for that role, what she calls the "reflective consciousness," once supplied by an external audience. In being able to absorb this role into herself, she was able to achieve a dual set of perceptive lenses—both subjectivity (as artist) and objecthood (as art object)—or more simply: "I perform,

reflective consciousness

and simultaneously perceive myself as performing object."[70] Here, Piper perhaps comes the closest to telling us what the intricate textures of objecthood *feel* like:

> I have assimilated an "other" into my sense of self, which is that reflective perceiver consciousness. I perform, and simultaneously perceive myself as performing object. . . . But if this is so, and if I am able to be reflective about my actions in the manner of a perceiver, then of what value is an external audience? . . . One Sunday evening I was doing the Aretha Franklin piece in the deserted trucking district, and I found myself to be entirely self-conscious of my actions, even while being fully involved in performing them. My perceiver consciousness expanded to fill the immediate spatiotemporal environment, even though there was no external audience. The more I substituted solitary environments, the more I was able to permeate those environments with my perceiver's self-consciousness of me as acting object.[71]

This dense but intriguing description of the *Aretha Franklin Catalysis*—itself a minimalist art object—delimits how objecthood *works*.

Piper succeeded in the dematerialization of the art object by becoming an art object while eliminating the external audience altogether. If the "primary structures" of Minimalism confronted spectators via seemingly alive sculptural forms, Piper wielded the medium of performance to enact objecthood through *herself*. This self-referential process was embodied in the phrase "acting object," which she used to describe her process of endowing an (art) object with life through her literal embodiment of it. This occupation of subjectivity and objecthood simultaneously, links Piper, however delicate and gossamer-like the thread, with Joice Heth and Ellen Craft's experimental and quotidian performance art, manufactured over a century earlier in the shadow of slavery.

Yet the more Piper decided, in her words, to "fuck it" and just boogie,[72] the more she diverged from her unlikely antecedents. That divergence came in the seductive properties of her particular objecthood and its saturation of the "spatiotemporal environment" that ultimately eliminated a viewing public altogether. If performances are always for someone, as Marvin Carlson has argued, the silent and fluid moves of the *Aretha Franklin Catalysis* that Sunday evening in 1972 existed solely for

Piper herself. Still, "herself" is misleading in its simplicity. For, as Fred Moten notes, easy delineations between artist and art objects become tricky for a historical figure like Piper, where "object, person, commodity, artist, and artwork converge."[73] All this to say, while what was lost in this empty industrial zone was a collectivity of external witnesses, what was ultimately gained was a thrilling extension of objecthood as Piper's "voluntary self-objectification" condensed the entire art experience inside herself.[74]

The lack of witnesses for Piper's loose improvisations, as well as the erudite prose of so much of her writing, occasions a simple inquiry: can we (or should we) take Piper at her word? She has, after all, used the word "solipsistic" in reference to her art, suggestive of its heavy focus on the internal processes of the self; that solipsism sometimes came with detriment to Piper herself, who was not always cognizant of how others viewed her artistic praxis.[75] This schism, apparent with the male *Catalysis* audience on a New York City subway described above, reoccurs with *The Mythic Being*. Piper's essays, written after the fact, aim to render her perplexing actions as art, using the aloof tone of an academic to make salient their premeditated quality. In doing so, her writings become a site at which to witness her "rhetorical personae," specifically the persona of "Adrian Piper, Conceptual Artist and Philosopher." This idiom, Cherise Smith argues, is useful for artists in inventing and developing writerly personas distinct from the ones they enacted in their performances, as an intentional method of presenting themselves as whole individuals. Her tone also reveals how these texts are not only tethered to her performances, but are themselves performances as well.[76] Furthermore, in their self-consciousness, drawing attention to the act of reading, they are minimalist art objects—they mirror the proliferation of text in art galleries in the late 1960s as the page became a site for art as legitimate as the blank canvas.[77]

The echo of Aretha Franklin's throaty vocal intonations, silent though it may be here, also signals how Piper's approach is coterminous with a black avant-garde aesthetic. Granted, Piper's early work "continually erupts out of its own categorization," in Moten's words, and she would undoubtedly bristle at this perception.[78] Not to mention, as I noted earlier, the black avant-garde of the 1970s was not particularly inclusive of artists not making prototypical "black art," or of women making art of any kind. Still, Piper's use of Aretha Franklin's "Respect" is a notewor-thy, if not curious, choice. A cover of an Otis Redding single, Franklin's far more famous (and sassier) version, released in April 1967, would go on to become her signature song, earning her two Grammy awards the following year. It is this rhythmic, brassy, and unmistakably black Amer-ican tune that Piper memorized and sutured to her deeply philosophi-cal explorations of objecthood. The *Aretha Franklin Catalysis*, in other words, stretched the borders of conceptual art; it combined the avant-garde and blackness together in a new morphology. The avant-garde, and its attendant class pretensions, was thus linked—whether it liked it or not—to rhythm and blues and the soulful gestures of black dance.[79] If each—blackness and the avant-garde—"depends for its coherence upon the exclusion of the other," Piper's *Aretha Franklin Catalysis* can be in-terpreted as asserting, albeit unintentionally, that "the avant garde is a black thing" and, conversely, that "blackness is an avant-garde thing."[80]

Aretha Franklin's "Respect," as a clarion call for the feminist move-ment, leads to another shared border, however amorphous, between Piper's dancing in the streets and feminist performance art. Prior to Piper's *Aretha Franklin Catalysis* in 1972, other artists—particularly women—began using their physical bodies as artistic material. Carolee Schneemann's *Eye Body: 36 Transformative Actions* (1963) presented viewers with a sculptural-like presence cast not in clay, but rather her own female body. Yayoi Kusama's *Naked Event* (1968) also manipu-lated the terrain of her naked body (and others), covered in polka dots.[81] Piper's gestural acts in the empty trucking district, as well as banks, bus stops, and elsewhere in 1970s New York City, employed qualities similar to the politically charged aesthetic works created by these and other artists as described by Josephine Withers, especially their "improvisational character," "deliberate transgressions of the art/life boundaries," and "openness to the banal and everyday." The medium of performance art was distinguished from more traditional forms of art by its distinct "unruliness" and axiomatic "resistance to tidy boundaries"; yet feminist performance art went even further in "its creator's desire to communicate an alternative vision of themselves and the world they lived in—sometimes dystopic, more often utopian and transformative."[82] In Piper's case, and as further evidence of her askew relationship to art and politics, that world was one in which a black woman artist dancing in the streets could happily exist, for in those silent moves were the poetic residues of objecthood's pleasures, its alluring promise of new forms of being.

In both the *Aretha Franklin Catalysis* and Piper's brief employment as a discotheque dancer in the New York City nightclubs Entre Nous and Ginza, beginning in 1965, "the infinite freedoms offered by dance" gave her the opportunity to transcend self-consciousness as her body guided itself to its own tempos.[83] In the former, Piper danced silently in the street, while in the latter, she danced alone suspended in a glass cage above clubgoers, letting her body be a proverbial slave to the rhythm. But whether or not she had spectators seemed of little consequence: "it just doesn't matter whether there is an actual audience there or not. I have assimilated its double vision into my own consciousness."[84] Existing simultaneously as subject, artist, art object, and now audience, in the *Aretha Franklin Catalysis*, Piper used dance as a method to explore objecthood's limits and render her physicality a moldable, plastic presence.

In/visible Stagings: The *Spectator Series*

As Piper continued her "complete and intense alienation from my audience" in these rigorous bodily acts, her experiments in generating an inner audience moved her into the realm of impersonation and disguise.[85] She alludes to such a shift in an illuminating moment in the essay "Preparatory Notes on the Mythic Being," dated July 28, 1973. In her words,

> I was trying to develop my arena by becoming an object in it. I now want to become the arena itself; I want to be, for a while, a consciousness within which I view myself and other objects. I'm thinking of the ghostly spectator, eternally viewing, taking in everything, recording and reflecting on everything, but not being an object of refraction him-herself because invisible.[86]

This train of thought suggests Piper's desire, which becomes more pronounced as she develops the *Aretha Franklin Catalysis*, for a type of objecthood through which she could not only "be" an object, but also internally perceive herself while operating as this performing object. In

be an object while conscious

short, she aspired to be an object among "other objects." Yet, now, she wanted to go even further, as the passage above implies: Piper desired to become a "ghostly spectator," an ersatz omniscient narrator able to perceive everything, while completely invisible to (and unable to be perceived by) others. The only way to accomplish such an improbable feat was through disguise, specifically a "witness disguise." Hence, in the very next sentence, she declares, "I'll have to completely change my appearance in a permanent but recognizable way." It is here where an assemblage of disconnected items—a wig, tinted sunglasses, dark lipstick, and platform cork shoes, among others—began to come together into what became the *Spectator Series*.

The birth of the *Spectator Series*, dated August 3, 1973, provides a glimpse of a still inchoate avatar. Its surface was composed of a "disguise: short auburn wig, reflecting sunglasses, white turtleneck/shirt, black pants." The exterior of this persona, its stylish surface immediately perceivable by audiences, was intended to preserve "the inner cohesion of myself as enclosed object." This camouflage, in other words, was to aid in the clean cleavage between performing object and inner self, or in Piper-speak, "external consciousness of an object; internal consciousness of self." "Phase 1" was to occur in "public events: gallery openings, concerts, dance concerts, panels, museums, etc.," and the piece, was to oscillate "from kitsch to avant garde," while this in/visible witness was intended to act as "pure spectator: freedom from roles induced by other's recognition." Two weeks later, the witness disguise was amended somewhat to "black pants and turtleneck, brown boots" (wig and sunglasses the same), while Piper added a new dimension: she planned to have "fifty reproductions" made of a "b & w front face photo" to be "scotch-taped wherever I've been sitting" (presumably taped by her) in advance of each performance. At the proposed end of the performances—in April 1974—she would have one of the photos run as an advertisement "in the *Village Voice* in the Exhibitions Section for the month."

The final components of the *Spectator Series* were the most recognizable to later viewers of the Mythic Being: "I should be in DRAG, dressed as a *boy*. Another possibility. Take sentences from each year of my journal, from 1960 on," she wrote in her preparatory notes. Below this, a drawing (dated August 25, 1973) shows a figure in sunglasses and a mustache with an "empty thought balloon" above him, accompanied by instructions to fill it in with a quote for the month and possibly submit it to the *Village Voice*. These short journal selections were named "MANTRAS" in an entry six days later, further defined two days after that as aids in Piper's "identity dispersion" or "transcendence of the personal."[87] With the chanting of these mantras, whose spiritual origins we can tentatively trace to the principles of yoga, Piper's performance took a particularly personal turn. The mantras, in other words, were a specific, intense strategy of objecthood, utilized to purge the past of meaning; unsurprisingly, due to their efficacy, they were later delineated as "pathways into the identity of the Mythic Being: I can, through careful concentration on them, transcend my own."[88] When yoked together with the sartorial trappings of disguise, this layered assemblage composed the script of the *Spectator Series*, designed to propel the dissemination of an in/visible persona through early 1970s New York City.

By late September 1973, the fertile DIY aesthetics of Piper's witness disguise began to bloom in unexpected thoughts and peculiar erogenous zones. Her essays detail her extreme poverty at the time—with $10 in her bank account, for example, Piper decided to ask Sol LeWitt for $100 to make the piece—suggesting the necessity of affordable clothing articles and accessories for the increasingly complex series. It is here where, as with Ellen Craft in chapter 2, we witness an artful deployment of what Karen Tongson has called "making do" in the conversion of banal "pre-fabricated" and everyday "materials into art and performance."[89] Moreover, while Piper seesawed with whether or not to give her avatar a personal history—a "mythology of the witness: his background, tastes, family, friends, pursuits"—she began taking him out in public. On September 30, for instance, she wore her "witness disguise to the Lincoln Center Film Festival to see Straub's *History Lesson*" and, when asked a question by someone when leaving the film, she "answered with the mantra."[90] In some fascinating passages, Piper ruminated on her feminine physicality, took her persona on the subway, and marveled at his erotic energy:

1. Felt extremely self-conscious about my mustache—must put it on better next time. Also about the fineness of my eyebrows, which tend to raise, and the possibility of my protruding breasts (just

when I don't want them, they show up . . .). So I've adopted a very hunched posture to rectify that.

2. When I was waiting for the subway, I found myself deliberately aping more "masculine" body movements and behavior to be convincing. I deliberately contemplated a sexploitation film ad for a few minutes.

3. Felt really horny. If I'd had a cock, I would've surely had an erection. But I couldn't keep my mind on it for very long periods of time because of the mantra.[91]

Piper's performances as her avatar, a detached yet hypersexual spectator, were queer in their sexual expressions and pointedly action oriented. For the latter, the *Spectator Series*, similar to the *Aretha Franklin Catalysis* preceding it, embraced the elusiveness of performance, especially its "reversal of the traditional precedence of the object over the act," following the tenets of Minimalism and Conceptualism. Paul Schimmel describes that elusiveness as follows: "Actions performed with the goal of producing objects gave rise to the execution of performative actions whose primary goal was the process of creation rather than the production of objects."[92] In that regard, the bodily actions in the subway and elsewhere discussed here are a continuation of Piper's efforts to keep her art both ephemeral and out of the milieu of the museum. Meanwhile, I conceive of Piper's performances as queer not in the sense of laying explicit claim to her own sexual preference, but rather in how they veer away from, and violate, conventional orderings of sex, reproduction, and intimacy and the normativities they produce, underscoring again her askew relationship to traditional linkages of art and politics.[93] We can perceive this in the thrilling illicit eroticism of point 3 above, as Piper's embodiment of her anonymous male avatar produces a fecund sexuality that, ironically, filters down to her. Though "he" is imaginative and immaterial, "his" queer energy has palpable effects: through performing objecthood, Piper expresses a startlingly explicit sexuality in public space that infiltrates her own psyche.

If the openness of Piper's sexual expression here—and later, more formally, in the Mythic Being—contrasted sharply to the restrictions black women felt within the feminist and black radical movements, this profusion of phallus-centered sexuality was undeniably a black masculinity.

After all, the most popular exploitation films at the time were blaxploitation films,[94] and the germinating sexual charge radiating throughout the *Spectator Series* seems, in large part, derived from representations that were largely gendered and raced as black male. The macho gesticulations and hypersexuality of this "witness disguise" endowed Piper with a multipronged freedom of movement. If she was able to traverse the streets differently—unrecognized (presumably, by her neighbors and art world friends) and thus able to pursue objecthood as an anonymous moving object in space—she was also able to escape artistic and political strictures placed on black women artists.

Yet, in Piper's rigorous objecthood, if the avatar was deployed as a synthetic device that enabled and reinforced her "internal transformations," its efficacy was also in its ability to resolutely remain an object, albeit an amorphous one.[95] Piper's avatar, in other words, was designed to be "a nonmaterial art object, unspecified with regard to time or place."[96] Furthermore, while Piper wrote how he (the avatar-spectator) "is more than an outer shell, surprisingly. It takes more energy to sustain his attitudes, mannerisms, movements, etc., than I thought," his purpose was to further her self-estrangement, or afro-alienation. In her words, "I find myself very involved in his mental framework. Chanting the mantra suspends me in a tightrope between two personalities. Perhaps I'm driving myself to schizophrenia."[97] Here we can perceive how Piper's intense dedication to her particular brand of objecthood, perhaps more so than any other figure in this book, illustrates the extreme mental stakes of performing objecthood. Purposely disorienting to audiences and, more importantly, herself, Piper's performance strategies furthered her "voluntary self-objectification" that we witnessed earlier in the *Aretha Franklin Catalysis*, letting objecthood's heavy hand guide and infiltrate her inner self and bend the pliable surfaces of her body to its will.

Alienating Acts, Visual Remarks: The *Mythic Being* Posters

In writings dated December 14, 1973, Adrian Piper not only first used the phrase "mythic being," defining such a figure in general terms, but also the more formal appellation "Mythic Being" to refer to a specific persona she had begun deploying in street performances and visual reproductions three months prior. In these preparatory notes, she described a mythic being in supernatural terms, specifically, as both a "fictitious or abstract personality" used in folktales as well as a "timeless" figure whose personal history superseded that of the history of the world.[98] Both of these portrayals of a mythic being, whose fictive and temporal qualities are suggestive of avatars, were repeated in Piper's characterizations of *her* Mythic Being, as we will see below. Birthed in September 1973, the Mythic Being was an inscrutable male persona—one she initially called "an alternative of myself" and later "a masculine version of myself; myself in drag"—complete with curly Afro wig, mirrored sunglasses, and a bushy mustache, as evinced by later photographs.[99] Piper appeared in public several times a month in the guise of the Mythic Being, while she was living in New York City, in street performances that were, according to her, undocumented except by her own retrospective writings; she began photo-documentation of the performances only after she moved to Cambridge, Massachusetts in 1974 to begin her graduate studies at Harvard and resumed the Mythic Being performances there a year later.

While Piper later remarks that the Mythic Being was an outgrowth of her *Food for the Spirit* and *Catalysis* series that she performed between 1970 and 1972, and indeed her self-objectification in both suggests as much, the date of its start makes it obvious that its closest antecedent was the *Spectator Series*. Overlapping with the *Spectator Series*, *The Mythic Being* was a further refinement of it, exchanging the auburn wig for an Afro wig, as her ghostly spectator morphed into "an abstract entity of mythic proportions."[100] Piper exuberantly detailed the effects of her external transformation in the Mythic Being performances in her later writings, the way her physical body seemingly gave way to his loose-limbed swagger and her fascination with his potent sexuality, emblematized by her fantasy of his bulging genitalia. Piper's early writings on the Mythic Being, ironically, infrequently mention the physical disguise Piper donned in public or the street performances themselves, instead, privileging the Mythic Being's visual presence and his utility as a *"medium"* or *"device"*[101] to free Piper of her past, both of which I detail below. Despite this, Piper's repeated embodiment of the fictional Mythic Being on the streets of New York City (and eventually in Harvard Yard) is particularly significant, hinting at one of her initial goals: using art to partially veer away from the particulars of her personhood, and the stultifying present, in order to imagine "alternative modalities of freedom" and being in the world.[102]

Piper attempted to further facilitate the process of reincarnation by pairing her outer accouterments with an internal metamorphosis, using what she termed "mantras"—passages selected from her personal journal between September 1961 and December 1972—to divest her experiences of personal meaning and, instead, reroute them through the Mythic Being. By chanting a mantra repeatedly for a month, Piper sought to render her past foreign to herself while, simultaneously, using it as pathway into the Mythic Being. In her words, the mantra "becomes an object for me to contemplate" that, once erased of personal significance, "loses its status as an element in my own personality or subjecthood." Meanwhile, a visual image of the Mythic Being appeared in the *Village Voice* on a monthly basis. The assigned mantra surfaced as content inside the "thought balloon" attached to the Mythic Being, concretized to readers of the *Village Voice* as the feelings of the shadowy presence lurking on the page.[103] In short, her personal experiences prior to the Mythic Being's birth—purged through careful concentration, reassigned to the empty shell of the Mythic Being, and published in the public forum of the newspaper—would, ideally, scatter into myth. Piper, thus, conceived of the widespread distribution of her past, an idea implied by her original title for the work, *Dispersion: The Mythic Being.* And as the mantras circulated, becoming the common property of those who read them, their weakened connection to her, conversely, bolstered the Mythic Being as an independent presence. In all these senses, Piper's aspiration for the Mythic Being was a radical, if paradoxical, act of self-negation: achieving self-transcendence through a purposeful enervation of her subjectivity.

The Mythic Being, as a visual phenomenon, first appeared in purchased monthly advertisements in the "Exhibitions" section of the September 27, 1973, issue of the *Village Voice.* On a full page of the newspaper, Piper's advertisements were a small square (perhaps a inch or two in width and height) nestled among equally miniature ads for exhibitions—such as an Alvin Loving show on Broome Street in SoHo or one of Tantric Buddha art on East 65th Street—and events at performance spaces, like Ellen Stewart's La MaMa E.T.C. (Experimental Theatre Club) on the Lower East Side. The *Village Voice* might seem an unusual forum for the display of Piper's experimental self-estrangement. After all, as opposed to an art magazine like *Artforum,* the *Village Voice* might not appear to be part of what she earlier delineated as "the art establishment" through which an "artist's activity is *validated* as art by a limited, informed public," as important as more traditional sites like "galleries" or figures such as "dealers" and "collectors."[104] Yet again, Piper's ad-works were advertised along with other exhibition notices, implying they reached an art-specific audience as well as nonspecialized readers simultaneously. Moreover, as a cheap and widely distributed publication with a circulation of 145,000—at the time, eight times that of *Artforum*—the *Village Voice* also fit Piper's desire for a site potentially "as accessible as comic books or television," in contradistinction to the "recondite and elitist character of contemporary art."[105] Not to mention, the paper's liberalism made it an appropriate forum for Piper's quirky, racially ambiguous avatar. The Mythic Being, which she referred to as both an "abstract personality" and a "folk character," the raw material of myth, was designed to seep into reader's consciousness, to become "part of the common folklore and folk consciousness of all who read the *Village Voice.*"[106] Piper's ad-work was similar to other artists' use, in Cherise Smith's words, of "art-specific publications" as sites to dialogue with "each other (and potential patrons)."[107] The artist's body itself was often its own site of publicity, whether naked and brandishing a dildo like Lynda Benglis in her notorious 1974 advertisement in *Artforum* or, in Piper's case, clothed and insistently standoffish. As I noted earlier, if Piper's reincarnation as her male avatar in her street performances were an experiment in what *not* being tied to personhood—specifically, Piper's personhood—might look like, her public dissemination of "his" thoughts in the *Village Voice* was an effort to render him a universal, if unusual, presence.

Piper's experimental photographic work with the Mythic Being in the mid-1970s was emblematic of conceptual artists' avant-garde and idiosyncratic use of photographic technologies from the 1960s forward. Following the inventive use of print media as its own form of art, conceptual artists continued using the traditional canvas of the painter, but replaced the prototypical brushwork with "photographic emulsion." Robert Rauschenberg's *Combines* (started circa 1954) are a key example of this; their collage-like painterly surfaces incorporated cartoons, photographs, and paper clips as artistic material underneath textured layers of paint, becoming more "performance-oriented" in their early 1960s iterations. Likewise, in lieu of the "standard gelatin silver print," conceptual artists of the 1960s manipulated alternative photographic forms such as "books, canvases, slides, and magazine pieces."[108] For instance, Andy Warhol's early silkscreens (begun in 1962) of icons and ordinary objects like Coca-Cola bottles transformed banal images into colorful Pop art. These and other works refashioned photography in the service of an improvisational conceptual art aesthetic.

Meanwhile, feminist artists wielded the camera to illuminate the cultural portrayal of female bodies. In Abigail Solomon-Godeau's words, many feminist artists imaged "themselves in the medium of photography" as a means of exploring and often contesting "various conceptions of the self and its representation."[109] As Anne Rorimer describes, the "camera's ability to arrest movement and single out a moment within a temporal continuum of an action or activity," evident below in the Mythic Being advertisements and later in posters, was also evinced in other intricate performance art pieces, such as Eleanor Antin's 1972 *Carving: A Traditional Sculpture*.[110] The latter, a photo-diary of Antin's naked body as she progressed through a thirty-six day diet, sutured feminist concerns of representations of the female body with the "mythos of the sculptor who creates perfect form by eliminating errant material from a hunk of stone," in Peggy Phelan's description.[111] If conceptual art doyen Sol LeWitt, likewise, "began to experiment with the serial form as early as 1963," performance artist Cindy Sherman—influenced by Piper's "subversiveness" while an art student in Buffalo, New York—took it to fascinating feminist extremes.[112] Similar to Andy Warhol's and Antonio Lopez's use of photographic technologies (the Polaroid and Kodak Instamatic, respectively) to capture seemingly candid and yet highly stylized serial portraits of celebrities and undiscovered mavericks, Sherman staged a dizzying portrayal of various cinematic female "types" in the photographs from her best-known work, the *Untitled Film Stills* (1977–80). However, Sherman's interest in role-play (or "transformation art," to use Lucy Lipppard's phrase) appeared even earlier, as evident in much of her experimental photographic work from 1975–77, dovetailing with Piper's visual work using the image of the Mythic Being, in the same period. The camera's supposed neutrality, therefore, was tested as feminist artists manipulated the photographic lens for polyvalent articulations of female subjectivity.

In 1975, after three years of street performances, Piper suddenly ceased staging the Mythic Being in public and reoriented the avatar and his relationship to potential spectators by focusing exclusively on visual representations in the form of posters. While the *Village Voice* advertisements, according to Piper, were discontinued in May 1976 due to lack of funds, financial motives do not seem the sole reason, if they are one at all, for the ceasing of the advertisements and the advent of the posters. In fact, the shift is hinted at earlier in her retrospective writings, dated January 1975, in which she deemed the Mythic Being's fleeting material existence as unnecessary for the piece's success, a guise that now served as little more than a "pleasurable behavioral reinforcement" of her more profound internal shifts. Instead, as an art piece, the Mythic Being had metamorphosed from a vaguely material persona to a "visual and pathological entity," whose visual characterization was primary. Piper's delineation of the Mythic Being as essentially surface, "for there is nothing further within him, and nothing further behind the iconographic surface he projects," is echoed in a statement that now reads as yet another clue to this shift, as she cryptically noted her "transition into a work in progress, *Surfaces*, which utilizes the Mythic Being in a different but related capacity."[113]

Piper's new approach also seemed to proceed from the idea that the uniqueness of performance art had become insufficient for establishing a shared medium of communication between artist and audience. As Piper described her move to a different and more appropriate form,

> The themes of confrontation, objectification, and estrangement keep resurfacing in my work whether I think about them consciously or not. The format of the work has changed from a dynamic mode (street performance) to a multiple static mode (posters, postcards), but the basic concerns of the work seem merely to assume different guises in response to the particular medium at hand. I doubt whether I'll street-perform the Mythic Being again in the near future. For the time being, I've opted against the spatiotemporal limitations of the medium—its unique-object requirements still reminiscent of the gallery as esoteric shrine, its de facto accessibility only to those adequately "prepared" for it—and in favor of a more public, common, accessible medium. I've been doing posters in unlimited editions, centered around the image of the Mythic Being as a static emblem of alien confrontation.[114]

Piper, who moved toward performance art precisely because of its divergence from formalist art objects, now came full circle, returning

to discrete art objects, while endowing them with a confrontational and
performative edge. On one level, she seemed to jettison her street performances because they had lost their initial promise, specifically their
inability to be categorized. Recall that in her *Catalysis* series, Piper noted
her efforts to not define herself "to viewers as artwork by performing any
unusual or theatrical *actions*," and hence distinguish herself and her art
from the more recognizable categories "of 'guerrilla theater,' 'event,' 'happening,' 'streetwork,' etc."[115] Her attempt to "resist, trespass upon, as well
as transgress the categorical imperative," as Sarah Jane Cervenak puts
it, was successful with that series, the experimental wanderings of *The
Mythic Being*, and the *Spectator Series* that immediately preceded it.[116]
Yet Piper's provocative use of herself in her flâneur-like peregrinations—
often understood as a merger between artist and art object, though not
a seamless one—was overshadowed by a reinforcement of the gulf between herself and her spectators. This was particularly true when that
schism was exacerbated, in Cervenak's description, by the "disparity
between Piper's own self-image" as a performing and self-estranged object and the designation of identity categories (race, gender, etc.) that
resulted in a labeling of "her objecthood by others."[117] However, the
Mythic Being seems designed, at least in part, to elicit the very reactions it received. Did she not think that passersby would judge her based
on the identity markers she was performing? Recall that Piper's precise,
intellectually dry words above are designed to have retroactive force,
rendering her unusual street performances not only as premeditated,
but also as *art*. As such, what appears as transparent documentation and
Piper's testimony—implying that we should take her at her word—is
not. Instead, the words above intellectualize and render coherent what,
undoubtedly, were profoundly messy (and personal) experiences, even
more so because Piper could not control her audiences' reactions—to
her, the conceptual artist, or to the Mythic Being, her strangely irate
third-world male avatar. Similarly, as Piper noted in a 1987 essay, her
gender, race, and even her "'weirdo' art" provoked antipathy from men
(whether her college boyfriend, fellow male students, or her professors),
and these interpersonal conflicts and "failures at communication" were
reflected in the "later *Mythic Being* performance and poster pieces, 1975–
76."[118] In doing so, she implied that the shift to visual representations
was also, in part, initiated by her experiences in academia, specifically

the ostracism and misrecognition (as well as downright racism and sexism) she faced while a college student and later when working toward one of the first Ph.D.s in philosophy granted to a black woman in the United States. Performance art in the "alternate contexts" of the streets—which just a few years earlier seemed the "more public, common, accessible medium"—was, therefore, jettisoned for the static, confrontational (and I would argue, controllable) medium of the poster.[119]

Piper's strategic move from street performances to visual portraiture was thus not a strictly aesthetic decision, but rather a far more personal response to racism while in the guise of the Mythic Being. As mentioned above, in 1992 she described her displeasure in experiencing the vitriol directed toward "visibly black Americans" while performing the piece. In her words, since "I was showing certain visual cues of a black person, I was responded to in that way and it was truly horrible: I felt objectified over and over again in subtle ways that I, to this day, believe people have no control over." Put differently, the liberating potential of performing objecthood, as an "altered object of perception" that confronted audiences with the Mythic Being's "permanently hostile gaze," shifted to a debilitating objectification—the Janus face of objecthood—as Piper-the-art-object was confronted with the equally hostile gazes of passersby.[120]

Piper's language of racialized "visual cues" is telling, since her remarks above allude to the distance between her own self-image and spectators' perceptions of her adopted sartorial signs. As Cherise Smith notes, while Piper understood her use of those iconographic symbols—cigar, sunglasses, and the curly Afro—there was also a "profound misrecognition" that those "iconographic fictions of race, gender, and class" referred "back to black men and the actual historical, social, economic, and political circumstances of their lives. When performing Mythic Being, Piper seemed to work under the assumption that black masculinity was merely a set of signs she could mobilize on the surface of her body."[121] As Kobena Mercer observes, Piper, as a "light-skinned woman of African American and Jamaican parentage," was accustomed to being perceived as "neither 'black' nor 'white' within the polarized visual topography of 'race' in American society."[122] Piper-in-disguise, however, was unavoidably black and male. Or was she? The Mythic Being's bodily insignia indeed sampled from stylized archetypes of black men in blaxploitation films like Shaft (1971) and Superfly (1972). Likewise, the avatar's bushy Afro trafficked in the hairstyle's late-1960s status as the *ur*-symbol of black militancy, à la the Black Panthers, fueling interpretations of the Mythic Being as "embody[ing] the threat of Black Power."[123] At the time, however, the Mythic Being was described by Piper as "third-world, working-class, overtly hostile male"; he did not become "a young black male" until 1992.[124] I note this to highlight a by-now obvious point—Piper-as-commentator on her own work—and to suggest that the now-rote understanding of the Mythic Being as a black man is partly inaccurate, even though Piper herself uses this language later. The two-decade gap between her creation of the Mythic Being and her description of him as a young black male, moreover, differs from her viewer's understandings; the objectification Piper faced, in other words, implies that the disparate audiences who witnessed her performances had no such gap—they perceived Piper as a young black man almost immediately. Yet such a specific designation belies the racial indeterminacy of her avatar's earliest iterations. He more closely resembles, to paraphrase Mercer, a groupie of the Latin rock band Santana.[125] Likewise, his mien recalls icons of international radicalism—Che Guevara and Fidel Castro, for instance—suggesting Piper's designation of "third-world" indicates a purposeful diasporic alliance with "developing" countries in Latin America, Asia, and Africa.[126] In photographs, his artifice is salient. In fact, in their parody of stereotypes of black men, the excessive Afro, bushy mustache, and mirrored sunglasses appear campy, rather than authentic. In this way, as the Mythic Being, Piper theatricalizes the visual tropes of black masculinity, revealing—in her hyperbolic performance of them—its profoundly mythic character. After all, the Mythic Being does not represent any particular person, but is rather a fantasy, an avatar of third-world (later, black) masculinity in the national imaginary.

Objecthood, if we recall the *Spectator Series*, generated a freedom of movement for Piper; it enabled an alienation from her body, and thus a tactical move from the specific, localized experience of personhood to a nonspecific embodiment. Objectification, however, produced opposite effects. When Piper was perceived as the actual, specific, and mythic-like presence of a black male in America—or, more accurately, perceived others perceiving herself that way—the Mythic Being's (and Piper's) steps slowed, stuttered, and stopped.

Movement, and racism's effect on it, is important here. The Mythic Being's subjection to racism exposes race's quotidian function in Ameri-

Subjection to racism

social organization [handwritten marginal note]

can life or, to quote sociologists Michael Omi and Howard Winant, its role as a *"fundamental* axis of social organization" so basic that "race becomes 'common sense'—a way of comprehending, explaining, and acting in the world."[127] It is this prejudice, caused by the perception of Piper's wandering body-in-performance as a black or third-world man, that literally grinded the Mythic Being's moves to a halt. If racism is an "ongoing and unfinished history, which orientates bodies in specific directions, affecting how they 'take up' space," in Sara Ahmed's words, Piper's *dis*orienting experiences impeded her physical moves.[128] Yet they also occasioned a new form of movement, albeit aesthetic, from one mode of address to another, suggesting how, as Kobena Mercer puts it, "Piper's double moves of withdrawal and confrontation—retreating into interiority, then aggressively moving outward—underpin all of the works involving the Mythic Being."[129]

Evincing an evolution in her thinking, Piper delineated two specific aesthetic techniques in the Mythic Being posters: what she terms "the frontal gaze" and the "indexical form of address." The former positioned the Mythic Being in a pose facing the front of the image head-on; it was designed to aim Piper's avatar directly at viewers. The latter, then, utilized this pose, with the viewer and the Mythic Being facing each other head-on, to stage a conversation between the parties. Piper also termed this "the I/You first-second person singular, personal form of address."[130] According to Cherise Smith, "The strategy of staging a dialogue—whether presented as a conversation between like-situated interlocutors, a proclamation to adversaries, or an argument with rivals—was not lost on artists" and was particularly effective in calling attention to "intersectional identities," a tactic we will see again with Howardena Pindell in *Free, White, and 21.*[131] In the case of Piper, the dialogical imperative was represented by her "mantras," reproduced as textual dialogue in "thought/speech balloon[s]" drawn over photographs of Piper in her Mythic Being disguise.[132] The mantras, as we have seen, were a rhetorical method of Piper's afro-alienation from herself, attempts to purposely evacuate her subjectivity. And they were successful to the point that when Piper encountered the mantras later, while she recalled the "personal situations" they arose from, they were "as cryptic to me as they must seem to anyone else."[133] Reproduced as visual remarks in the Mythic Being posters, where they were wielded in a more self-aware and confrontational manner than in the *Village Voice* advertisements, their new use became a convenient conduit for Piper's belief that the solution to the nefarious workings of racism and xenophobia was a dialogue rooted in "the specifics of the particular, concrete solution that is occurring between two people who are interacting in the indexical present."[134]

In the posters, Piper further transformed her avatar into a "static emblem of confrontation" and a "permanently hostile object" through a third technique: reconceptualizing the relationship between audiences and her male drag. Earlier, in the murky period between the *Spectator Series* and *The Mythic Being*, her playful donning of a male disguise in New York produced a surplus of queer erotic energy. In these aggressive printed performances, by contrast, Piper adroitly utilized a version of what José Esteban Muñoz has called "terrorist drag" to render her body, in Brechtian parlance, "*strange* and even *surprising* to the audience."[135] In contrast to traditional drag "invoking glamour or 'realness,'" "terrorist drag" is a "guerrilla style" that is engaged in "creating an uneasiness, an uneasiness in desire, which works to confound and subvert the social fabric." Piper's mercurial third-world male persona can be interpreted here as practicing similar methods of "ground-level cultural terrorism" in her efforts to, again, hijack a traditional (read: passive) aesthetic experience.[136] Thus, if the Mythic Being's Afro, cigarette, and mirrored sunglasses were pragmatically utilized to distance "you"—the viewer—from "him," they were also designed to aid and abet Piper in harnessing the negative affects experienced while performing and, in a tactical redistribution, impose that apprehension on passive spectators.

The deployment of these three aesthetic techniques was designed to promulgate a new "ethics of seeing," to borrow Susan Sontag's term, around racial perception. To Sontag, photographs are didactic. Photographs teach viewers a "new visual code"; they "alter and enlarge our notions of what is worth looking at and what we have a right to observe."[137] Elsewhere, Piper expresses her keen interest in visual perception. "Racism (like sexism) is primarily a visual pathology," she writes, which "feeds on differences in perceived appearance"; similarly, she expresses her belief (by way of Kant) that xenophobia stems from the "innate tendency to categorize."[138] The Mythic Being posters, in particular, were methods by which Piper attempted to deconstruct the visual field that racial formation, racism, and xenophobia depended on and maneuvered in. Aggressively worded thought-bubble phrases—such as "I EMBODY EVERYTHING YOU MOST HATE AND FEAR" or the sexually suggestive "IT DOESN'T MATTER WHO YOU ARE/ IF WHAT YOU WANT TO DO TO ME/IS WHAT I WANT YOU TO DO FOR ME"—sought to do this work at the micro-level of racial formation where "race is a matter of individuality, of the forma-tion of identity."[139]

In this manner, according to Piper, the thought-bubbles were pointed in their dialogues—largely *imagined* conversations, I argue—with white as opposed to black viewers. For instance, the posters can be interpreted as having a "cathartic function" for black spectators in their expression of "shared emotions," while for white audiences they potentially had a more "didactic function," specifically in their challenge to "preconcep-tions about oneself and one's relation to blacks."[140] Piper's remarks as-sume not only a white audience, and a hostile (or at least politely racist) one at that, but a set of empathetic black spectators as well, assump-tions that are strangely simplistic and unfounded. Moreover, as I suggest above, these potential pedagogical effects and affective charges are not only entirely imagined by Piper, but presumably take place only in the museums or galleries where the posters were shown. While this does not entirely blunt Piper's artistic aspirations, it does complicate their ef-ficacy. Still, Piper's "ground-level cultural terrorism" was the adaptation of her wandering experimental male persona into a two-dimensional, macho, black figure asking for, if not demanding, a new means of seeing and being seen. In this merging of art and the moral politics of racial perception, Fred Moten's words on Piper's praxis resonate: "You don't have to privilege the ethical over the aesthetic in art if the aesthetic re-mains the condition of possibility of the ethical in art."[141]

Likewise, the amalgamation of the real and the sketched in the Mythic Being posters seems also partly aimed at avoiding the risks associated with photography, especially its suggestion of mastery. The photograph, by default, arrests motion, as the camera freezes gestures and mechani-cally transforms them into a still. In the case of the Mythic Being, Piper may have chosen not to make her avatar strictly photographic for sev-eral reasons. For instance, she may have decided that photography's documentary-like realism might too easily isolate and "frame" her ges-tures (similar to her avoidance of the *appearance* of theatricality in her

Figure 3.8a–c. Adrian Piper, *The Mythic Being: It Doesn't Matter*, 1975. Three gelatin silver print photographs altered with oil crayon; 8 by 10 in. (20.3 x. 25.4 cm.). Collection of the Spencer Art Museum, Lawrence, Kans. © Adrian Piper Research Archive Foundation Berlin.

Catalysis series).[142] Similarly, photography's ability to freeze action could potentially undermine a more sophisticated understanding of her street performances. Put another way, photographs would present the ostensible "truth" of Piper's idiosyncratic acts to viewers and, hence, possibly distract from the raison d'être of the Mythic Being (and most of her work since then): to induce audience self-reflection. Still another possibility is that photography, at the time, was too closely aligned with the focus on realist representation that the Black Arts Movement claimed as the impetus for black art. All of these are viable rationales for eluding the capture of the camera, and hence might partly explain the complete lack of photo-documentation of the *Aretha Franklin Catalysis*. In the case of the Mythic Being posters, their oil crayon embellishment and thought-bubble phrases, I argue, are a distinct method by which Piper not only circumvents the mastery of photography, but also continues to render the Mythic Being—and possibly herself—slippery.

Meanwhile, if the posters' components are in line with the repeated emphasis on objecthood in this book, their visual interventions were not as distinct from modes of performance as Piper leads us to believe. I conceive of the posters as extensions of her earlier wish, in the *Spectator Series*, to become the "arena" in which she views herself and "other objects." In this case, however, that embodied arena—of her mythical avatar—was flattened into the two-dimensional. Still, in this realm, one object (the Mythic Being) was situated inside *another* object (the poster). Piper remarks, in an essay on performance, that "like human beings, objects have identities."[143] The Mythic Being was a fictional and racially ambiguous avatar designed to possess no history. Yet he not only possessed an identity but also often described adolescent experiences that were Piper's, rather than his own, and thus situated in a particular historical moment. Which is perhaps why these posters present the viewer with a perplexing quandary: what is the proper retort to an expressive object that is nothing but mere "verbal and visual surface"?[144] After all, these posters were art objects independent of Piper, encasing an avatar whose thoughts often revealed, in Bowles's words, "less about the artist than about the viewer's attitudes toward race, gender, and sexuality."[145] Piper, let us recall, praises the unique ability of performance art to speak the same idiom of communication as its viewers. Her printed performances, however, were not straightforward in their communications,

Figure 3.9. Adrian Piper, *The Mythic Being: I Embody Everything You Most Hate and Fear*, 1975. Gelatin silver print photograph altered with oil crayon; 9 15/16 x 7 15/16 in. (25.3 x 21.1 cm.). Collection of Thomas Erben, New York. © Adrian Piper Research Archive Foundation Berlin.

but rather strangely opaque; they distanced, rather than embraced, their interlocutors. In that regard, while these posters again assist Piper in her self-alienation, they also illustrate her deployment of language that, despite its intimacy, also worked as a tool to further estrange viewers from the intimidating Mythic Being.

We see this opaqueness at work, for example, in *The Mythic Being: I Embody Everything You Most Hate and Fear* (1975). In the poster, the Mythic Being is glancing at the viewer, his right eye visible under tinted sunglasses, while smoking. The smoke from his cigar becomes a fleeting frame for his declarative statement: "I EMBODY EVERYTHING YOU MOST HATE AND FEAR." Here, as in all the posters, hand-worked photographs of Piper-in-disguise are drawn over with black oil crayon and enlarged. Along the borders of several of the posters, if one looks closely enough, are visible black scribbles escaping over the photograph's edges. The mix of the photographic and the drawn lends the posters a hazy, mysterious, and mythical quality. These smoky visual objects can be interpreted alongside feminist performance art, as a tactical move away from "realism to express new forms of dramatic subjectivity and emotional encounter," in the words of Peggy Phelan.[146] Their opaqueness is also an aesthetic tool specific to the art of black performance, hinting at how black historical actors have wielded, as Daphne A. Brooks puts it, "anti-realist forms of cultural expression" to "disrupt the ways in which they were perceived by audiences."[147]

These posters also undoubtedly deployed forms of performance. The photographs underneath the oil crayon clearly suggest that Piper posed for them, restaging the Mythic Being in the two-dimensional realm. "All portrait photography is fundamentally performative," Peggy Phelan reminds, and this is true of these posters as well.[148] I am focusing, in other words, on Piper's aesthetic labor in configuring her body to be captured by and replicated via the photographic lens. Granted, there is no description from Piper of this bodily process or details of these photographs' staging. Who took these photographs of Piper in the guise of the Mythic Being? Were they staged, like the *Food for the Spirit* series, inside her SoHo loft? Despite these omissions, however, I emphasize this process of posing-as-performance because it again confounds, or at least blurs, the too-easy demarcations between three-dimensional street performances and two-dimensional visual representations Piper delineated earlier. The posters of the Mythic Being were not "static" per se, the adjective she used to describe them, but rather incredibly flexible and performative sites of address.

As a final contrast, let us position Piper's serial representations of the Mythic Being alongside the engraving of fugitive slave Ellen Craft in disguise from over a century earlier to consider the likenesses and yet striking dissimilarities in their poses, postures, and performances. Both women, often taken for white, were dressed in the sartorial props of their male avatars, one a white male slaveholder and the other an unruly third-world man. Both, to employ Piper's term, were positioned in a "frontal pose" inside their respective frames, facing the viewer directly, while wearing glasses that partially obscured their respective gazes. The ambivalence of Craft's image sans head poultice—i.e., the engraving's tension between Ellen Craft and Mr. William Johnson—is similar to the ambiguity of Piper's. After all, to see the Mythic Being is also, inevitably, to recognize Piper's shadow body underneath the mirrored glasses and oversized Afro wig. Moreover, both initially appeared in newspapers, Craft's in *The London Illustrated News* in 1851 and Piper's in the *Village Voice* in 1973.

However, the willful self-commodification enacted by Ellen Craft and the "voluntary self-objectification" exacted by Adrian Piper arch in wildly different directions. Craft became a visual object of perception as a means to achieve freedom from her status as a fungible commodity, and to fulfill her desire to be a "speaking subject" and American citizen.[149] Piper, on the other hand, executed almost the exact reverse process. She became a static visual object as a means to achieve a much different type of freedom: the will to preserve one's subjectivity while, simultaneously, embodying and performing a dense objecthood. The Mythic Being's audible speech, moreover, rivaled Mr. William Johnson's virtual (and necessary) silence. Mr. William Johnson's polite quietude under the mask of disability ensured Ellen Craft's safety from detection as a runaway piece of property. The Mythic Being's vocal dissonance, on the other hand, helped Piper experience or achieve several different things: the transformation of "actual feelings of macho masculinity" into art; a freedom that, she noted, "even the women's movement hadn't facilitated"; and, in the posters, a challenge to the potential racism of spectators.[150] Commerce-wise, Phelan argues, "Performance, as object-less art, works against (if never fully eliminating) the commodification of the art object."[151] Piper surely utilized performance art partly for this very reason, its ephemerality enabling her to resist, as quoted earlier, the "esoteric shrine" of the gallery and the "recondite and elitist character of contemporary art."

In 2009, the Museum of Modern Art, the signature institution of contemporary art, acquired a full set of the seventeen Mythic Being advertisements; they were displayed to the public the following year, suggesting that Piper's efforts to avoid the institutional grasp were ultimately unsustainable, if not unrealistic. Still, the printed performances of the Mythic Being, like the other performances described above, demonstrate just how far cerebral experiments around various aesthetic and ontological impasses—art and artists, subjectivity and objecthood, self and audience, and embodiment versus a type of afro-alienation—can go, especially when all of these appear to be condensed inside one person.

Coda

While the Mythic Being will remain an inscrutable presence, we are able nevertheless to briefly see and hear his urban jaunts, as well as Adrian Piper's accompanying efforts at self-transformation. In a sharp break from the other historical actors (and their avatars) discussed thus far, the movements of the Mythic Being were preserved in moving-image media. Piper, as the Mythic Being, appeared in Australian artist Peter Kennedy's 1973 film *Other than Art's Sake*.[152] In an excerpt from the film, she is seen tying her ponytail back and attaching or slipping on the accouterments of the disguise—a meticulously applied mustache, a large curly black wig, and mirrored sunglasses—as she discusses her motivations for the work.

> The idea is very much to see what would happen if there was a being who had exactly my history, only a completely different visual appearance to the rest of the society. And that's why I dress as a man. And I find that when I put on the garb, somehow it transforms the nature of the experiences I'm thinking about.

Piper, the disguise complete, opens a notebook—one of her journals, presumably—and begins reciting the mantra quoted in the first paragraph of this chapter. She paces around what appears to be her SoHo loft and smokes a cigarette. After a quick cut, she walks down the street continuing to recite the mantra, while various onlookers—elderly white bystanders, young black children—walk beside or behind her. The camera momentarily pans to their uniformly befuddled faces. The most humorous, an elderly white woman in a coat with a fur collar, glances at Piper walking ahead of her and asks the camera, "Movie?" Her perplexity is spot on: is the person holding the camera directing an actor in a scripted Hollywood scenario? How should she interpret this unfamiliar figure in a black curly wig wandering down the street, repeating phrases with the cadences of womanly speech? Receiving no answer, she turns around and walks in the opposite direction. The scene ends with Piper, in the guise of the Mythic Being, continuing to recite the cryptic passage about his mother buying him "crackers, cookies, and things" while walking down a narrow city street, surrounded by amused and intrigued spectators.

Figure 3.10. Adrian Piper, *The Mythic Being* (video still #10), 1973. Video, 8 min. Collection Adrian Piper Research Archive Foundation. © Adrian Piper Research Archive Foundation Berlin.

In an unforeseen twist, the aforementioned film excerpt has taken on a new resonance that—due to recent actions by Piper—occasions a meditation on black performance art, specifically Piper's position in that genealogy. In late October 2013, Piper withdrew her work from the major exhibition *Radical Presence: Black Performance in Contemporary Art*, organized by curator Valerie Cassel Oliver, at New York University's Grey Art Gallery just off Washington Square Park. The aforementioned excerpt from *Other than Art's Sake*, until then shown on a loop via a television monitor in the gallery, was turned off and a white typed page placed over the now-black screen. The note—dated October 24, 2013—included remarks from Piper, drawn from her correspondence with Oliver, that allude to the reasons for the removal of her work:

> I appreciate your intentions. Perhaps a more effective way to "celebrate [me], [my] work and [my] contributions to not only the art world at large, but also a generation of black artists working in performance," might be to curate multi-ethnic exhibitions that give American audiences the rare op-

portunity to measure directly the groundbreaking achievements of African American artists against those of their peers in "the art world at large."

Oliver then responds to Piper with an excerpt from her essay in the exhibition catalogue about resisting "reductive conclusions about blackness," and her choice to show artists who "have challenged both the establishment and at times their own communities"—a very accurate description of Piper herself.[153] Oliver follows with a more direct and terse rebuttal. "It is clear, however, that some experiences are hard to transcend," she writes, "and that stigmas about blackness remain not only in the public's consciousness, but also in the consciousness of artists themselves. It is my sincere hope that exhibitions such as *Radical Presence* can one day prove a conceptual game-changer."

This ideological skirmish, unsurprisingly, raises more questions than it answers; it also unearths some knotty contradictions. Principally, considering Piper's remarks, is an exhibit limited to black performance art necessarily a ghettoizing affair? Put differently, does an exhibition of black performance artists, cleaved apart from their non-black peers, risk reinforcing their marginalization within the art world writ large? In addition, in line with what I have discussed above, does including pieces from Piper's oeuvre in such an exhibition risk overdetermining her work, either reducing it ostensibly to a contested subcategory *within* black art or placing more attention on the artist's identity (as a black performance artist) than on the art artifact she has created? Furthermore, what is to be made of Piper's inclusion of this video art piece—along with five works from the *I Am the Locus* (1975) series, deemed too fragile to travel to New York—in the original run of the exhibition at the Contemporary Arts Museum Houston in late 2012 or in the accompanying exhibition catalogue, printed the following year? In other words, Piper's very public withdrawal of her work—once the exhibition had arrived in New York City; a few weeks before Part I was to close, and Part II was to open at the Studio Museum of Harlem; a month after a review in the *New York Times* called it "an entertaining and philosophically stimulating exhibition" that could also be interpreted as an "allegory about being black in today's America"—seemed a deliberate, and expertly timed, exercise in self-promotion.[154]

Despite (or perhaps because of) these many questions, there is one thing we know for sure: Adrian Piper's staging of her withdrawal from

Radical Presence is, in itself, a brilliant black performance art piece. Her fight with Oliver provocatively restages the dyad between presence and absence that is a hallmark of her aesthetic praxis. In this way, this much-publicized tussle is not a distracting aberration from Piper's work, but rather a bold act of self-estrangement that is the latest incarnation of an essential theme of her work. If this maverick move, moreover, extends to Piper's paradoxical presence in the exhibition catalogue—now, simultaneously, strangely present and a vanishing point—it also stretches to the humble sheet of paper taped over the muted television monitor. Similar to Piper's voluminous writings, in themselves minimalist art objects, the typed sheet is an edgy performative document, "a physical trace of a past action," to quote Debra Lennard. "A canny conceptual addition to the exhibition, this unassuming sheet of paper has become the highly charged locus of a fierce critical debate" over the very terms that constitute black performance art.[155] Piper's forcible removal of her work from the show did not succeed in alienating her from genealogies of black performance art. Quite the contrary, simply by this ambiguous act of self-erasure, Adrian Piper may have made herself into the materfamilias of contemporary black performance art.

Yet the Mythic Being was no ordinary (artistic labor of) love. Rather, Piper's "transformation art," to again use feminist art critic Lucy Lippard's term, was multipronged and remarkably pliable in its modes of inquiry. In the *Aretha Franklin Catalysis*, the *Spectator Series*, and finally *The Mythic Being*, we perceive the many uses of the object. It and/or "he" are at once a psychological device, methods of staging the artist as (dancing) artwork, producers of queer erotic energy, survival strategies, confrontational instruments, and above all, apparatuses of self-alienation. Black performance art, via Piper, is stretched to radical ends as her purposeful self-effacement is often coupled with the erasure of all witnesses, beside herself. Resembling a merging of artist, art object, and audience, her work is unabashedly solipsistic (a word she herself uses), obstinate, and obsessive; consequently, she is often the first and last authority on her art. Through her brainy deployment of objecthood and avatar production, Piper superseded the limits of her body and converted herself into art and representation. She became a catalytic agent, a ghostly spectator, a mysterious avatar, and, finally, a staged absence. Indeed, alienation has its uses.

4

Is This Performance about You?

The Art, Activism, and Black Feminist Critique of
Howardena Pindell

It was so strong, this idea about having myself in a blond
wig . . .
—Howardena Pindell[1]

Deep in the hot, sweltering summer of 1980, a black woman artist in
New York was fed up. Howardena Pindell, a trained painter and a curator at the prestigious Museum of Modern Art until 1979, was active in
the politicized and increasingly fractious climate of the New York art
world. While, earlier in her career, Pindell was primarily involved in
the feminist movement—specifically, the radical efforts of women artists to establish and run their own exhibition spaces—she had recently
shifted gears to rebuke the racism permeating the New York contemporary art scene, a focus she would return to later. After "yet another
run-in with racism in the artworld and the white feminists," she made a
twelve-minute videotaped performance in her top-floor SoHo loft entitled *Free, White, and 21.*[2] Pindell played all the characters. In the video,
she portrays at least two versions of herself, detailing autobiographical and familial encounters with racism and sexism, all intercut with
an anonymous character in cat-eye sunglasses and a short blond wig—
"White Woman"—who debunks Pindell's experiences as mere paranoia
and berates her for her ingratitude. Also present in this televisual tableau are eerily silent and abstract avatars of Pindell: one wraps herself
mummy-like in strips of cloth, while another peels a sticky translucent
mask off her face. The experiences Pindell describes in the video include
her being granted and then denied placement in an advanced history
class in high school, receiving five hundred job rejection letters after her

graduation from the Yale University School of Art, and sexual harassment at a friend's wedding reception in Maine.

Free, White, and 21, easily Pindell's most famous (and controversial) work, prompted pointed reactions from different constituencies. The video was first shown in September 1980 in *Dialectics of Isolation: An Exhibition of Third World Women Artists in the United States*, a group show organized by three artists (including Pindell's colleague, the late Ana Mendieta); the exhibition was staged in SoHo at the A.I.R. (Artists in Residence) Gallery, the first all-female artists' co-op gallery in the United States.[3] The mise-en-scène was especially ironic: both the A.I.R. Gallery, with its "openness to experimental, ephemeral, and often practically unsaleable artwork"[4] by women artists, and the feminist movement more generally were the first proponents of Pindell's work.[5] While Pindell's video was in sync with 1970s women artists' view of performance art and happenings as "new forms for the exploration of the intersection between the political and the personal," in the words of Peggy Phelan, the content of *Free, White, and 21* was inflammatory.[6] The tape provoked outrage from various white women, including fellow A.I.R. artists, and even a white male colleague of Pindell's who did not believe the experiences narrated in the piece—Pindell being denied jobs or treated as inferior simply because she was black and a woman—actually happened. Artists of color, conversely, felt the video "was not forceful enough," according to Pindell's later recollections, and judged that "my experiences were in environments of privilege." When it was included in an exhibition at a museum in New Jersey, black security guards refused to turn it on "because they felt it was offensive to people of color." When it was shown in Japan the following year, wrote Pindell, audience members laughed at "how Jewish I looked in white-face," suggesting its seriousness did not translate to audiences abroad. By the late 1980s, both because of its content and because of the reactions it aroused, Pindell's oft-derided piece had become "an underground cult tape" shown primarily in universities.[7]

More recently, though, the reception of Pindell's pièce de résistance has undergone a notable shift. In 2007, *Free, White, and 21*, along with one of Pindell's earlier paintings, was included in the traveling exhibition *WACK! Art and the Feminist Revolution*, touted as "the first comprehensive, historical exhibition to examine the international foundations and legacy of feminist art."[8] The Kitchen, the legendary art and performance space in New York City, currently owns the tape. It has been added to the behemoth permanent collections of two art institutions, both with ties to Pindell: the Studio Museum of Harlem, where her *War Series* was part of the landmark 1988 exhibition *Art as a Verb*,[9] and MoMA, where she had worked for twelve years, by 1977 rising to the rank of associate curator in the Department of Prints and Illustrated Books.

In the queer paths of this book, Howardena Pindell and her white female avatar serve as a particularly provocative node, both gesturing backward to historical actors (and their avatars) that have preceded them as well as forward to those yet to come. As we shall see, Pindell's "identity-switching masquerades" are not dissimilar to Joice Heth's over a century earlier in their deployment of versions of herself, rather than male personas, in the art of black female performance.[10] And Pindell's short blond wig morphs into a long Day-Glo pink one, among other neon permutations, in the figure of Nicki Minaj, one of the subjects of this book's conclusion. The most striking comparison, though, is Pindell's contemporary Adrian Piper, whose discarded, mysterious, mirrored sunglasses are picked up and redeployed as Pindell's vintage 1950s cat-eye lenses. What occurs at the intersection where the third-world male avatar on the streets of early 1970s New York crosses paths with the white female avatar on film?[11] While both artists were certainly aware of each other—both were included in the aforementioned exhibition *Art as a Verb* and referenced each other's respective essays in the 1980s—their careers, political activism, and disguises were markedly different.[12] On a surface level, they are polar opposites. Piper, often mistaken for "white," performed as the hostile, third-world (later, black) Mythic Being, while Pindell, visibly black American, staged a caricature of a white feminist. Moreover, as will soon see, while Piper's dense and brainy conceptual art experiments carried over into her performances, Pindell's work prior to *Free, White, and 21*, the only performance in her oeuvre, was resolutely abstract. However, what will become clear as Pindell's artistic and activist acts spool out across this chapter was her ferocious commitment to exposing racial inequities specifically in the art world, a role that I argue—in contradistinction to Piper—is partly to blame for Pindell's relative obscurity and, arguably, alarming erasure.

In order to do proper justice to this erasure, I position *Free, White, and 21* as the middle panel in this chapter's aesthetic triptych. The first panel traces Pindell's participation in, exclusion from, and movement between various artistic and political communities in New York in the late 1960s and 1970s, while the third panel discusses her activist work in the virtually unknown PESTS. The three parts of this chapter blend into and across each other; the resulting cross-pollination of texts, mediums, genres, and identities mirrors the ontological and aesthetic labor undertaken by the other mavericks in this study. We begin with Pindell's arrival in New York City in 1967, fresh from Yale with an MFA degree, traversing an increasingly segregated and politicized art world. As we move south, flâneur-like, from the Studio Museum of Harlem on 125th Street to the A.I.R. Gallery in SoHo, what surfaces are the stakes of a black American woman participating in the potent merging of art and politics, while struggling to make and exhibit work derisively deemed non-black art.

"I Wasn't One of the Boys": The Place of a Black Woman Artist in New York

Howardena Pindell's employment at the Museum of Modern Art in 1967 proved quite beneficial, if not for key contacts, then for providing a much different type of art education than the formal one she had received at Yale. The same year she was hired, a guard by the name of Sol LeWitt—one of several MoMA employees who eventually became bona fide artists—published his infamous "Paragraphs on Conceptual Art" in *Artforum*.[13] While Lewitt's tutelage was particularly important for Adrian Piper, it is unclear if he and Pindell ever crossed paths at the museum. In Pindell's case, the mentoring figure was curator Lucy Lippard. In addition to her duties at MoMA, Lippard was an activist and early champion of feminist art; she would win a Guggenheim fellowship in 1968 and in 1973 publish the widely influential *Six Years: The Dematerialization of the Art Object*. Pindell later noted that Lippard was the only coworker who really treated her as an equal and that they were also in the same consciousness-raising group, wryly remarking that these activities—art and feminism—generally overlapped during this time period.[14] It was through collaborations and conversations with Lippard, Pindell said much later, that she met "European American feminists as well as Adrian Piper."[15] While Lippard's and Pindell's paths eventually pivoted in different directions, Lippard's combination of art and activism was a model for Pindell's later pursuits and presaged the incendiary art actions and protests staged by Pindell and other New York artists, many of them centered on MoMA.

Across the dozen years that Pindell worked at MoMA, a growing number of artists—black artists in particular—blended art and politics to challenge the elitism of museums, demanding equitable representation and distribution of wealth and resources. In 1968, following the assassination of Dr. Martin Luther King in April, the shift from the passive resistance of the civil rights movement to the provocative aggression of Black Power was encapsulated in Black Panther leader Eldridge Cleaver's run for president that fall on the Peace and Freedom movement.[16] Coincidentally, that fall, a loose group of thirty artists and critics called the Black Emergency Cultural Coalition (BECC) picketed the Whitney Museum's exhibition *The 1930s: Painting in Sculpture and America* for its failure to include any black artists, and issued three demands, centering on the inclusion of black artists in the Whitney's offerings.[17] According to its flyers, BECC was an "action-oriented watchdog organization" whose mission was the due recognition of the cultural contributions made by black Americans; its counterexhibition at the newly formed Studio Museum in Harlem—pointedly titled *Invisible Americans: Black Artists of the 1930s*—provided exactly that, suggesting a taut relationship between African American artists and historiographies of American art.[18] This "comingling of protest, race, and aesthetics" produced remarkable results—a groundbreaking *twelve* exhibitions of black artists at the Whitney from 1969 to 1975, six of them solo shows by abstract artists—though not without incident.[19] Similarly, on March 31, 1969, three hundred demonstrators protested the Museum of Modern Art's inadequate showing of black art; the group of artists and critics heading the demonstration issued a "13 Points" manifesto, which included demands for free admission, a section of the museum dedicated to black artists, and a retrospective for black American artist Romare Bearden.[20] In October 1969, the "Manifesto for the Guerrilla Art Action Group" demanded that MoMA sell a million dollars of art and give the proceeds to the poor, decentralize and communalize its power structure, and close until the end of the war in Vietnam.[21] While at MoMA, Pindell met several black artists—such as Vivian Brown, Camille Billops, Richard Hunt, and Mel Edwards—and "to MoMA's dismay," as she put it, joined the Art Workers' Coalition, where she met Faith Ringgold.[22] While, as Kellie Jones notes, several of these artists (especially black abstractionists, like Pindell) were deeply "committed to their right to aesthetic experimentation," they were also fierce advocates for representation in the major museums in New York, holding these publically funded entities as responsible for their apolitical stances as for their active marginalization of black American artists.[23]

An even smaller subset of these artists—both black *and* women— joined forces with other groups advocating for greater representation of women artists and, in some cases, formed their own spaces. A group of four artists representing Women Artists in Revolution (W.A.R.), for instance, in June 1970 sent a letter to John Hightower, then MoMA's director. Their four demands included that every museum in New York City have a woman's exhibition by 1972 and that, by 1975, *all* art institutions— museums, galleries, foundations, etc.—have fifty percent representation of women artists.[24] Meanwhile, Ringgold and filmmaker Camille Billops (along with two other artists) sent a letter to Governor Nelson Rockefeller proposing the installation of a Women's Wailing Wall in Rockefeller Center with twelve to-be-chosen artists of varying ethnicities and a three-day conference for the spring of 1971 on the role of women in art. In their provocative words, "The answer to the question of 'What do women want?' is a very simple one. Women want fifty percent of everything men artists have and black women want fifty percent of that."[25] Meanwhile, in 1971—a year before Pindell cofounded the A.I.R. feminist co-op—Ringgold, Kay Brown, and other black women artists arranged the group show *Where We At: Black Women Artists 1971*, which led to the formation of their own organization, "Where We At" Black Women Artists (WWA). WWA was particularly important for black women artists who were "doubly challenged," Valerie Smith notes, by the assumption that neither "blacks or women could legitimately claim to be artists."[26] Both A.I.R. and WWA's community-based models for exhibiting the art of women artists were paradigmatic of the ethos of "participatory democracy" that pervaded this politicized branch of New York's art scene.[27]

While these coalitional alliances echoed the white avant-garde's revaluation of the relationship between art and community, their interests importantly differed from the latter's predominant concerns. Cultural historian Sally Banes discusses how Greenwich Village was a central site for the proliferation of art activities and groups, including Fluxus, art cooperatives, café theater, and underground film. Meanwhile, artist Andy Warhol's rented space, dubbed the Factory, served as "site and symbol of the alternative culture's disdain for the bourgeois ethic" and an alluring devotion to the pleasure principle, as he silkscreened images of celebrities and made experimental films.[28] Yet while Warhol and other white avant-garde artists were "sympathetic to black social movements and to black artists," according to Banes, their aims were largely insular. In her words, "their own forms of symbolic leveling were first and foremost expressions of their own situation—that is, their aim was the democratization of the avant-garde in terms of class, and sometimes gender, but not race and ethnicity."[29]

In the early 1970s, as Pindell's artistic praxis shifted toward experimental materials, the possible venues for exhibiting her art shrunk, instigating her arrival at A.I.R. Initially, Pindell worked at MoMA during the day as an exhibition (and eventually curatorial) assistant, and at night painted in a studio on 28th Street and Seventh Avenue.[30] While she had strictly been a figurative painter at Yale, her circumstances now occasioned a radical shift; the combination of her meager salary and being unable to paint with natural light led her to a more idiosyncratic practice. In a 1990 interview, she explained, "I found if I cut the canvas to a certain size, I would have all these scraps. I figured I couldn't throw them out. I took the scraps and sewed them together." The results of this organic improvisation were "soft sculptures, " including a "soft portable grid."[31] She later noted, in a 1997 panel discussion, that she would also take home the beveled mats discarded by the "museum frame shop" and use them as the background base for other pieces.[32] This strategy of converting everyday materials into art was also evinced in other black abstractionists' inventive substitution of the paintbrush for scissors, sewing needles, or (in painter Ed Clark's case) a push-broom.[33]

However, Pindell's movement away from figurative work to an adroit usage of detritus for art making—a black avant-garde sensibility Kobena Mercer has elsewhere called "the poetics of the found object"—led her away from "black art" to the auspices of A.I.R.[34] It is worth quoting her at length:

I didn't really get involved in the women's movement until the early seventies. That was really a direct response to taking my work to the Studio Museum. I was told by the director at the time (late sixties) that I was not doing black art because I was not using didactic images. I was not dealing with information that would be helpful to the black community. I also felt that there was bad feeling because I was a woman. I wasn't one of the boys. So I was told to go downtown and "show with the white boys." I felt real depressed about that because I knew how I was closed out downtown. I had no recourse. So I ended up showing with multicultural groups of artists that were forming and renting spaces in Soho when it was affordable. This was when Soho was empty except for factories and folks who bought lofts for $3,000 and were living very, very secretly. . . . The people who were just forming the idea for A.I.R. Gallery came to me. They approached me through a registry, ironically, at Artists Space. This was 1969 or 1970. They saw my work and invited me to be one of the founding members. That's how I started showing on a regular basis. I think I was the only black member.[35]

Pindell evokes the intersecting exclusions that she faced, while also highlighting her evasion of the strictures of a proper (read: male, didactic) "black art." These multiple negations initiated Pindell's movement from the Studio Museum, in the so-called "black mecca" of Harlem, to the very different world of a pregentrified SoHo, more than a hundred blocks south.

In a milieu inflected by both black nationalism and the Black Arts Movement, figurative work was deemed the preferred medium of a "black aesthetic." Active roughly between 1965 and 1976, the Black Arts Movement was closely tethered to (and named by) poet and playwright Amiri Baraka (formerly LeRoi Jones); it espoused a focus on vernacular and populist forms that were easily apprehended by black audiences across music, theater, literature, and the visual arts—the latter exemplified by the aesthetic principles set forth by Chicago art collective AfriCobra.[36] Unlike the assumed elitism of abstraction, realist representations of black subjects were perceived as the "more useful way to combat centuries of derogative imagery."[37] Pindell's rejection from the Studio Museum was the first of many reminders of her apparent distance from "black art." In 1971, she took part in a joint show; here too the exhibition materials indicated that sense of distance, although in a somewhat more critical way. Hans Bhalla criticized the term "black art" as being "grossly misused and ill-defined to describe the vast proliferation of art works by some black artists." He seemed to backtrack, however, when it came to

the "well-controlled colors" and surrealist landscapes of Pindell's paintings: "Her works in no way relate to the themes of Black experiences or
Black awareness."[38] These words seem to suggest a gnawing disappointment in Pindell's paintings and their obstinate refusal to self-identify as
"black" or specifically as "black art."

That disappointment would only grow. Pindell's art in the mid-
1970s, specifically the *Untitled* series, continued this drift against the
tide of realist representations, instead moving toward experiments in
texture, form, and color. *Untitled #4* (1973) was a dense system of meticulously numbered hole-punched holes, while *Untitled* (1977) presented an almost undulating multicolored landscape, the entropy of its
hole-punched holes contrasting with the rigorous order of the grid-like
canvas. Unlike the literal and political emphasis of certain black art objects from these same years, such as Betye Saar's *The Liberation of Aunt
Jemima* (1972), Pindell's art beat to the pulse of an abstractionist drum.
As art historian Darby English has recently argued, if the givenness of
"black art" as a framework still needs to be rebuked, so too do the expectations attached to art objects placed under this umbrella term. Black
artists' work, in his words, is seldom the subject of "rigorous, object-
based debate," but rather is expected to "show-and-tell on behalf of an
abstract and unchanging 'culture of origin.'" If Pindell's objects seemed
(and for many, still seem) at odds with the category of black art, the
blame for such a schism was misdirected. Instead, "the given and necessary character of black art—as a framework for understanding what
black artists do—emerges as a problem in itself."[39]

At the same time Pindell's art was deemed not "black" enough, the
white women artists looking to establish A.I.R. became interested in her
work. In her most extensive discussion of her time in A.I.R., an interview
published in 1981, Pindell remarked that Lucy Lippard had earlier seen
her work and tried to get her involved with the Ad Hoc Women's Committee, which Pindell declined. Later, "the four or five central members
of A.I.R. were looking for members for the group of twenty" and made
an appointment to see Pindell's work after looking through "the wom-
en's slide registry and through catalogs of shows, Lucy's catalog, and the
annual." When a month later, she received a call asking her to join the
gallery as a member, Pindell accepted and, immediately it seems, participated in a smorgasbord of tasks. In her words, "At that point they

were just forming discussions about what name we would call the gallery and how we would structure it. We had meetings to find a name for the gallery. We built the space, which was very hard. I think there was a lot of attention focused, because this was the first attempt women had made on their own to show their work outside the system."[40] While, as Martin Beck remarks, the "industrial spaces of SoHo lofts" were "spatial blueprints for a break with the gallery establishment," A.I.R. was not, he suggests, completely cleaved off from this system. Instead, "A.I.R.'s model of an alternative space was based on mimicking the conditions of the art market and thus attempting to create an alternative *inside* the system."[41] Nevertheless, if the time-intensive labor required of the artists in A.I.R. to operate it was one of the main reasons Pindell eventually left the co-op, it served as an important space where her art was finally accepted as is.

The foundational principles of A.I.R., and Pindell's key involvement in it, are observable in a little-seen foldout poster A.I.R. produced. On one side, "A.I.R." was printed in large black print above an oversize black-and-white photograph of the gallery from outside with its door slightly ajar, its address—97 Wooster Street—printed below. The other side included an announcement for an exhibition of ten women artists, pictures of other artists' work in A.I.R. above the dates their exhibitions would take place, and photographs of the space *in medias res*. For the latter, among twelve images of electrical cords, beams, and unpainted walls is a portrait of Pindell—the only clearly identifiable image of an artist's face—with glasses and an Afro. Meanwhile, in a mission statement of sorts delineating the gallery's workings, its labor and commitments were made clear. A.I.R. sought to offer women artists "a space to show work which is as innovative, transitory or unsaleable as the artist's conceptions demand, a rare opportunity for women artists" through an equitable system, including a rotating exhibition schedule to begin September 16, 1972.[42] To maintain this system, artists were expected to "be financially able to contribute to the maintenance of the gallery and willing to work on one of A.I.R.'s committees" as well as be available to "meet whenever it is necessary, i.e. whenever group decisions have to be made."[43]

The throwaway nature of this ephemera belies its importance; I emphasize this handout's photographic and textual contents to counteract Pindell's repeated erasure from A.I.R's cultural history, but also to emphasize class—rather than simply race—as the main contributor to

OPEN A.I.R.

A.I.R. artists invite 20 women artists

DEC. 30 - JAN. 10

Dotty Attie	Saundra Gellis	Diane Levin
Judith Bernstein	Mary Grigoriadis	Emily Mason
Shirley J. Bernstein	Harmony Hammond	Rosemary Mayer
Blythe Bohnen	Anne Healy	Patsy Norvell
Maude Boltz	Linda Howard	Howardena Pindell
Mirium Brumer	Iria	Anne Sharp
Rachel bas-Cohain	Laurace James	Dinah Maxwell Smith
Agnes Denes	Ellen Kaufman	Jenny Snider
Donna Dennis	Nancy Kitchel	Nancy Spero
Daria Dorosh	Louise Kramer	Amy Stromsten
Sarah Draney	Pat Lasch	Joan Thorne
Loretta Dunkelman	Juliet Leff	Susan Lewis Williams
Louise Fishman	Michelle Lester	Barbara Zucker

A.I.R. Gallery 97 Wooster St. New York, N.Y. 10012

Gallery hours: 10 - 6, Tues. - Sat.

Figure 4.1. "Open A.I.R." gallery announcement, n.d. Courtesy of the A.I.R. Gallery Archives, Fales Library, NYU.

her eventual departure. The two most widely circulated photographic images of A.I.R. members—both from 1979—do not include Pindell, who left A.I.R. four years earlier. (Among the members photographed in both of these group portraits, the most recognizable one is the late artist Ana Mendieta.) An obscure photograph from 1973, showing Pindell and her colleagues at artist Daria Dorosh's loft, is a rare exception to this omission.[44] If Pindell's shadow body haunts the visual insignia of her colleagues, so too does her careful class critique of A.I.R. In the 1981 interview, she described class as the distinguishing marker between her and some of the other members and linked it to a broader argument about the feminist movement. In her words, "It does distress me that a situation like A.I.R. demands that you have to have a certain financial freedom to be able to participate. That to me is a paradox in the women's movement. It means that only middle-class women, or only married women whose husbands are making enough money to support them, can be in the gallery."[45] This cautious criticism, even when pressed further by the interviewer, was lodged solely against the class privileges

Figure 4.2. A.I.R. members, 1973. Photo credit: David Attie. Courtesy of the A.I.R. Gallery Archives, Fales Library, NYU.

both of Pindell's colleagues and the feminist movement writ large. It was only later, in Pindell's white feminist impersonations in *Free, White, and 21*, that she retuned her critique to an anti-racist frequency.

Prior to her departure from A.I.R. in 1975—which would eventually relocate to 63 Crosby Street—Pindell's ingenious *Video Drawings* series

Figure 4.3. A.I.R. Gallery at 63 Crosby Street, n.d. A.I.R. moved to this location in 1981, staying until 1994. Today, it is located in Brooklyn's Dumbo neighborhood. Courtesy of the A.I.R. Gallery Archives, Fales Library, NYU.

anticipated her later attraction to video technologies and performance in *Free, White, and 21*. In 1972, concurrently with her budding involvement with A.I.R., she continued her experiment with new materials— this time, acetate, ink, and a television screen—again out of necessity. Her eyes becoming "damaged from the detailed work" of the numbered "oaktag pieces" in her *Untitled* series, Pindell's eye doctor advised her to "concentrate on something moving in the distance." In her words, "I felt that it was a good excuse to get a color TV." In a painstaking process, she drew "vectors and numbers" onto the clear acetate and then placed them over the television screen.[46] Then, as Kellie Jones notes, Pindell photographed the acetate "at slow speeds so the video image became blurred while the solid ink drawing remained constant."[47] The *Video Drawings*, in their singular glory, were shown mostly in Europe, including Berlin and Copenhagen.

At the conclusion of the 1970s, prior to Pindell's (and our) arrival at *Free, White and 21*, a highly controversial exhibit at the nonprofit Artists Space in SoHo prompted her to action. A series of charcoal pieces entitled *Nigger Drawings* by an artist named "Donald" (later identified as Donald Newman), was exhibited at the cutting-edge gallery from February 16 to March 10, 1979. On March 5, a twelve-person coalition of artists and other art world figures—including Pindell, artists Faith Ringgold and Carl Andre, curator Lucy Lippard, and writer Ingrid Sischy—signed a letter sent to Artists Space expressing their outrage at this "puerile bid for notoriety" and the support by "one of our leading alternate spaces" for such a "racist gesture." A protest in front of Artists Space was held on April 14 and reported by the *New York Times*, while letters were sent to the New York State Council of the Arts condemning its allocation of public funds that, in part, financed the exhibit. In an ironic turn of events, however, Pindell and her compatriots were accused of trying to censor Newman and deny his right to free expression.

In an essay published almost two decades later, Pindell remarked at length on the exhibit's frustrating turn of events. While she was certainly perturbed by Newman's pointed use of a racial epithet, she seemed equally if not more concerned with how the concerns of artists of color were dismissed. In her words, if "some of the Left, the Right, and liberals expressed their belief that (white) artists have a First Amendment right to express their racism," they also did not seem "bothered that artists of color were excluded from defining themselves in the same arena, although white artists could 'define' them as subject matter in their work."[48] The Artists Space controversy signaled the beginnings of the "culture wars" that defined the late 1980s and early 1990s and, as we will see, presaged Pindell's later collection of statistics documenting what she called "art world racism."

While this was a particularly jarring affront, particularly for an artist like Pindell who struggled throughout the 1970s for places to exhibit her works, an even more personal (and painful) injury occurred in October of the same year. By then, Pindell had quit her associate curator position at MoMA and was a month into a job as an associate professor at the Stony Brook campus of the State University of New York (a position that, at the time of this writing, she still holds).[49] While riding with her department head and two critics in a Volkswagen Bug, she was involved in a "freak accident as a passenger in the back seat [. . .] on the way to my job." Pindell sustained a brain injury and temporary memory loss. As a result of the accident, both of her parents moved into her SoHo loft and lived with her for several months.[50] All of these events were ingredients in the emotional cauldron out of which Pindell created *Free, White, and 21* in the summer of 1980, as both the aesthetics and content of her work took a sharp turn.

White Feminist Impersonation: The Performance of Memory, the Uses of Anger

My work was primarily about process until a car accident, in
1979, then my theme became autobiographical.
—Howardena Pindell

If *Free, White, and 21* depended on a repurposing of sundry items into performance material, Pindell's gesticulations were also supported by unseen others. In a method that sounds eerily similar to Ellen Craft's more than a century earlier, Pindell described her gathering of the accoutrements of cross-racial disguise:

> I bought a blond wig at Woolworth's. My mother had given me clothes
> because she would hear me complain about having no money for clothes.

She would send me clothes from Sears Roebuck, which I hated. I kept
bags of these things. I used some of the clothes for the tape. If you've seen
the tape you see I change my clothes for each segment. Well, those are all
the clothes that my mother sent me. [. . .] I bought stage makeup. I put
white makeup on, lipstick, and the dark glasses from my teenage years.
So I had the black glasses and the blond wig. A photographer friend gave
me backdrop paper . . . seamless paper in different colors.[51]

Pindell's accumulation of both sartorial and video-oriented props mirrored her earlier organic approaches to art-making. And simultaneously,
we perceive a kind of temporary disassembly of Pindell's white female
avatar into the various parts—blond wig, cat-eye sunglasses, white
makeup, and clothes from Sears, for example—that script "her." Here
again, this reduction of the anonymous white lady character into her
various gears mirrors the description of Mr. William Johnson in the
opening pages of the Crafts' *Running a Thousand Miles to Freedom*, but
their aesthetic and social provocations diverge. Most importantly, Ellen
Craft's antislavery ready-mades were an illegal embodiment performed
by a fungible commodity; Pindell's, by contrast, were an inflammatory
antiracist critique staged by an Ivy League–educated artist-curator-
activist-professor. And if William Craft was the shadow prop enabling
Ellen-cum-William's transgressions, in Pindell's case, her invisible
supports were camerawomen provided by a "woman at Downtown
Community Television" who also assisted in "editing the piece I called
Free, White, and 21."[52] Thus, while it was staged as a solitary performance in Pindell's loft, the dematerialization of the art object in this
piece did not preclude, in Shannon Jackson's words, "the material relations that support the de-materialized act. Ephemeral forms still need
their stage managers and their run crews."[53]

In the case of Pindell, that material support also included her parents, and it is perhaps therefore fitting that the antiracist current of *Free,
White, and 21* commences with the physical trauma of her mother, rather
than herself. The opening credits—the words "FREE, WHITE, AND
21 by Howardena Pindell" typed on white paper—run before the image
of the white lady character appears. We see Pindell in whiteface, short
blond wig, a yellow sweater, and opaque black sunglasses against a blue
background—the aforementioned White Woman. She sits silently. The

Figure 4.4. Howardena Pindell, *Free, White, and 21* (video still), 1980. Video, 12 min. Courtesy of the artist and The Kitchen, New York.

scene suddenly shifts to Pindell, sans disguise, facing the camera as she begins a monologue, implying that the white lady character is quietly listening. Without pause, Pindell-as-narrator tells the following story:

> When my mother grew up in Ohio, her mother would bring in various babysitters. There were about ten children in the family and one of the babysitters happened to be white. My mother happened to be the darkest of ten children, so when this woman saw my mother's skin she thought that she was dirty and washed her in lye. As a result of this my mother has burn marks on her arm.

If the babysitter's belief that black skin was equivalent to filth was not sufficient, the act of seeking to eradicate it through a harsh solvent certainly conveyed the depth of her beliefs. Racism, Pindell's mother learned early on, is far more than skin deep. Pindell's mother was born in 1902 or 1903, suggesting the extent of her exposure to the sticky residues of the national trauma of slavery.[54] As Ann Cvetkovich observes, "Genocide, slavery, and the many other traumas of 'American' history [...] are part of its founding and yet have too often been ignored and forgotten, especially as trauma."[55] Thus, in one incident, we have the comingling of a national trauma and the (literal) scar tissue of its ideological effects.

In the context of the video, Pindell's recollection of this torturous incident is made even more shocking by the deceptively calm way she conveys it. Her theatrical casualness suggests, in Cvetkovich's words, "a sense of trauma as connected to the textures of everyday experience."[56] Through this scene of subjection (*pace* Saidiya Hartman) that transmitted its quotidian abjection to Pindell, racism surfaces as a genealogical process, passed down through generations like a family heirloom. Put simply, Pindell and her mother both harbor scars, even if Pindell was not there to witness her mother's desecration. Telescoping backward to Joice Heth's sonic of dissent, Elizabeth Alexander's words resonate here as well: "Hearing, too, is central to witnessing. Heard images haunt the mind as much as visual ones."[57] If *Free, White, and 21*, moreover, transmits this trauma to a third party—the viewers of the video—then audiences too become aural witnesses to the actions against Pindell's mother, and visual spectators of Pindell's pain, if not silent rage.

Next, Pindell-as-narrator shares two more encounters with racism, this time her own. In the first, she recounts the childhood experience of asking her kindergarten teacher to go to the restroom during afternoon naptime. Out of a class of forty, she was one of two black students. Her teacher, "who was not very fond of black children," refused to let Pindell go, then yelled, "I can't stand these people," as she used sheets to tie Pindell to a bed. The teacher kept Pindell tied up for a few hours before releasing her. As she speaks, in a seeming pantomime of what occurred, the adult Pindell begins wrapping a long white gauze-like strip of material around her head. Kellie Jones has noted that the texture of this material is "eerily close to the white canvas strips from which Pindell had been creating her paintings up to that moment," suggesting a cross-pollination between painting, performance art, and video art.[58] The use of gauze was not only aesthetic but personal, directly related to Pindell's physical injuries sustained during her car accident. She notes, "I had a concussion, and that's part of the reason why I wrapped my head in the video; it was an unconscious reference to the car accident."[59] Eventually, the material covers her entire face and the narrator sits silently, face obscured. After another cut, Pindell-as-narrator appears again, in different clothing and a differently colored background, and tells a story about Pindell asking her high school history teacher to place her in an advanced class. The teacher, at first, conceded that her grades were high enough and agreed, but then remarked that a "white student with lower grades would go further," and thus denied the request.

In these scenes, Pindell's body enables us to witness not Pindell per se, but rather her avatars. Thus, even though she narrates in the first person, her autobiographical encounters are spoken through performed *versions* of herself. These avatars, in other words, are digital simulacra of Pindell. This avatar production is partly signaled by the video's theatricality. The vibrant colored backgrounds and the outfits Pindell wears, both of which slightly shift between characters, suggest a multiplicity of personas coexisting in this video dreamscape. In her discussion of the various definitions of "support" utilized in aesthetic practices, Shannon Jackson describes the characteristic use of a supporting performer in theater, or "the actor who 'supported' the characters s/he played. 'Support' referred to the act of act of 'sustaining a character in a dramatic performance.'"[60] I conceive of Pindell as performing a similar function in *Free, White, and 21*, portraying a panoply of dramatis personae that not only include the anonymous white lady character who appears later, but also these more plaintive characters who happen to be likenesses of herself. We can enlarge the category further, moreover, to include weirder manifestations, like the appearance of the silent avatar whose head is wrapped almost completely in gauze, except for sections of Pindell's puffy Afro that escape the taut strips. In this regard, Pindell's body-in-performance operates as a type of support "holding up the entire performance event" that is *Free, White, and 21*.[61] These avatars perform, as in *execute*, the aesthetic labor of Pindell's magnum opus.

This tricky business of avatar production becomes even more complex when the white lady character, seen in the beginning of the video and intermittently in the scenes above, stages a seemingly exasperated response to what she has heard. After Pindell's first avatar details the lye incident, we see the white lady biting her thumb, as if she is ruminating on the veracity of the memory just described. She seems on the verge of a response, when the second narrator appears. By the time the third, high school narrative is related, the white lady character finally has the opportunity to speak. She replies, with undisguised frustration: "You know you must really be paranoid. Those things never happened to me. I don't know anyone who's had those things happen to them. But then, of course, they are free, white, and 21, so they wouldn't have had that kind of experience." As the video continues, and more avatars of Pindell enumerate experiences of discrimination—the five hundred rejection letters she received when applying for jobs after graduation; being stared at at a wedding reception—White Woman continues to berate her in a nasal, condescending voice. She tells Pindell, "In fact, you don't exist until we validate you. If you don't want to do what we tell you to do, then we'll find other tokens." She even belittles Pindell's art: "I hear your experiences, and I think, 'It's got to be in her art.' It's got to be in your art. And, it's got to be in your art in a way that we consider valid."

Toward the end of the video, Pindell details one more incident at the same aforementioned wedding. There is a live band and no one asks Pindell—the only non-white person present—to dance, until the very end. The minister, a man in his mid-sixties, makes the invitation and whispers in her ear, "I come to New York often, why don't we get together, we can have some fun." White Woman continues her mantra-like refrain: "You ungrateful little . . . after all we have done for you. You know we don't believe in your symbols, they are not valid unless we validate them. I have never had experiences like that. But, of course, I am free, white, and 21." Pindell's biting embodiment of White Woman in this taut twelve-minute video and its debut in the compact confines of a group exhibition at the A.I.R. Gallery contributed to the atmosphere of "dense and sustained confrontation" that was (and is) this video's leitmotif.[62]

Pindell's strategic white feminist impersonation is suggestive of theories of cross-racial embodiment in both psychoanalysis and art history. I am thinking, respectively, of Diana Fuss's notion of the "miming masquerade" and Cherise Smith's "radical mimicry." In her *Identification Papers*, Fuss paradoxically conjoins two words, the former—"miming"—associated with hyperbole and parody, and the latter—"masquerade"—with the unconscious assumption of a role. Discussing unveiled Algerian women who passed as European during the French occupation of Algeria (1830–1962) to avoid inspection by French soldiers, miming masquerade is a "deliberate taking up of a cultural role for political ends," or

a "tactical mimesis." Its success "depends not upon excess, but equivalency." It imitates an identification that, in actuality, is not there. Instead,
Fuss writes, it "install[s] a wedge between identification and imitation,
in its suggestion that not every imitative act harbors a secret or unconscious identification."[63] By contrast, the trope of radical mimicry articulated by Smith in *Enacting Others* is a performance strategy not based
in the sameness of actor and role, but rather the excess between the two.
Put differently, radical mimicry performs an "other," but without the
impetus of exact replication. Instead, as Smith discusses in the complex
performance work of Anna Deavere Smith, "the actor's difference from
her subjects is always on display."[64] Pindell's portrayal of White Woman
in *Free, White, and 21* is a perfect example of the idiom described by Fuss
in its deliberateness and its aggressive nonidentification with the character. And the political edge to Pindell's performance is located in the distance between identification and imitation that Fuss describes, the gap
between Pindell's identifications and her imitation of the "feminist," a
gap that exists because racial and class differences render the latter term
insufficient for describing all women equally. However, Pindell's excess,
her distance from the character she is playing, is always present; in this
way, her performance is closer to Cherise Smith's radical mimicry. Put
simply, even with the various sartorial and cosmetic props, Pindell is
always recognizable under the whiteface make-up. The grain of Pindell's
voice, in particular, in its high-pitched supercilious politeness, performs
this surplus; this excess is a hallmark of black performance in general
and shared by each of our black women performers.

It is through her cohabitation of a white feminist and other, more
recognizable, versions of herself that Pindell staged a dialogue manqué:
a conversation between white feminists and feminists of color, one that
is unfulfilling and disappointing because the former refuses to empa-
thize with (or believe) the experiences of the latter. In short, the words
of White Woman, in their polite dismissal of Pindell's (and her mother's) experiences, were indicative of Pindell's critique of white feminists'
shortsightedness. The "strategy of staging a dialogue," between interlocutors or otherwise, was "not lost on artists"; as a tactic for staging
"the politics of identity" it was particularly utile, Cherise Smith argues,
for shifting "the terms of intersectional identities, making them productive rather than destructive."[65] In the case of *Free, White, and 21*, the

film technique of shot/reverse shot was used to stage this conversation between two parties within the video, while the one-sidedness of the real-world manifestations of this conversation was evident in the content of White Woman's responses. White Woman's rejection of racism as simple paranoia, for instance, located the "truth" in her own position precisely because the incidents Pindell described were not experienced firsthand by herself or people this character knew. The etymology of the phrase "free, white, and 21" is unclear, though a 1963 film shares the title.[66] Yet we can infer that Pindell is referring to its colloquial meaning: possessing the ability to do whatever one wants, being beholden to no one. In the context of the video, "free, white, and 21" suggests the only people the white lady character knows are similar to herself, unable to feel the slights experienced by Pindell and her mother because they are "free, white, and 21." Pindell's subversive embodiment of a caricatured white feminist was her means of critiquing, via performance, the feminist movement's myopic vision of what constituted experience. However, while the refrain "free, white, and 21" appeared to be a blanket categorization, it indexed a specific identity: white feminists (and Pindell's peers) who were not only spared the experience of racism, but also persistently lacked the ability (or simply refused) to *see* it. For white feminists, to put it differently, to be "free, white, and 21" was to lack perception or knowledge outside of their own identities as "white" and "women." Concomitantly, it was also to fail to recognize how those blind spots were actively utilized to suppress and negate the experiences of those who were not free, white, and twenty-one. Hence, the opaque black sunglasses worn by the white lady character in the video were not only a prop, but also a metaphor for the impaired vision of white feminists.

The decidedly didactic tone of *Free, White, and 21*—ironic since Pindell's art was earlier rejected from the Studio Museum for *not* being didactic enough—and its critique of white feminists anticipates black feminist scholarship and its attention to the ways that American culture in general and white feminism in particular excludes black women and their "herstories." I borrow this phrasing from Marxist feminist Hazel Carby, whose influential essay "White Woman Listen! Black Feminism and the Boundaries of Sisterhood" was published in 1982, a mere two years after the debut of Pindell's fiery video. In it, Carby sharply argued that black women's "herstory," though "interwoven with that of white women," was not "the same story" and black women were more than capable of writing it themselves. To quote her: "However, when they write their herstory and call it the story of women but ignore our lives and deny their relation to us, that is the moment in which they are acting within the relations of racism and writing *history*."[67] Carby's thoughts on the tactics of erasure regarding the experiences of women of color dovetailed with Pindell's, both in the video and even more strikingly in a later essay, where Pindell said *Free, White, and 21* was about "domination and the erasure of experience, cancelling and rewriting history in a way that made one group feel safe and not threatened." She went further, calling it a "Hatshepsut maneuver"—referring to the efforts of pharaohs in ancient Egypt following Hatshepsut's reign to excise her from historical records and thus "cancel out her place in history"—in which "white women were removing the cartouches of women of color."[68]

Carby's "White Woman Listen!" was joined by foundational texts by Angela Davis, Audre Lorde, Cherríe Moraga and Gloria Anzaldúa, and bell hooks.[69] Pindell's performance was in dialogue with many of the tenets of these texts, like Lorde's sustained call to recognize the very *differences* between women as foundational to any political coalition.[70] Even more relevant is Lorde's discussion of the "uses of anger":

> Women of Color in america have grown up within a symphony of anger, at being silenced, at being unchosen, at knowing that when we survive, it is in spite of a world that takes for granted our lack of humanness, and which hates our very existence outside of its service. And I say *symphony* rather than *cacophony* because we have had to learn to orchestrate those furies so that they do not tear us apart. We have had to learn to move through them and use them for strength and force and insight within our daily lives. Those of us who did not learn this difficult lesson did not survive. And part of my anger is always libation for my fallen sisters.[71]

Free, White, and 21 also trafficked in this strategic managing of anger's mercurial effects. Pindell's deceptively calm and plaintive utterances, in other words, smooth over the discordant echoes of a profound rage, suggesting a symphony rather than a cacophony. This fury, I argue, is not directed simply at white feminists. Instead, it is the product of an accumulation of abuses, from Donald Newman's *Nigger Drawings* in 1979 at Artists Space to the Studio Museum's rejection of Pindell's work in the late 1960s for not being "black art." In her "public articulations of trauma," Pindell's calm demeanor may have masked the effects of these multiple physical and emotional injuries, but did not erase them.[72] *Free, White and 21*, instead, places the production of "herstory" in the hands of the black woman artist. The echoes of Lorde are evident in the video not only as a model for navigating anger, but also as a simple testament to surviving. In Pindell's words: "Act on your feelings for your own survival and priorities."[73]

Free, White, and 21 and its "televisual dissemination," to quote José Esteban Muñoz, renders possible black feminist counterpublics, collectivities aligned against the racism and sexism of the "dominant public sphere."[74] "A counterpublic," Michael Warner argues, "maintains at some level, conscious or not an awareness of its subordinate status"; in this case, *Free, White, and 21* explicitly expressed what the Combahee River Collective described as "the manifold and simultaneous oppressions that all women of color face."[75]

Black performances, as survival strategies with a surfeit of aesthetic energy, lead to the tenuous nexus between Howardena Pindell's whiteface female avatar on film in 1980 and Adrian Piper's black male avatar on the streets a few years earlier. Both sets of ephemeral performances are what Ann Cvetcovich calls "archives of feelings" that serve as "repositories of feelings and emotions, which are encoded not only in the content of the texts themselves but in the practices that surround their production and reception."[76] Both, moreover, bleed across genre distinctions—between painting, performance art, and video art (Pindell), and performance art and conceptual art (Piper)—while also serving as sites where "aesthetic and social provocations coincide," in Shannon Jackson's words.[77] Unlike in Pindell's, however, the feelings encountered in Piper's work (at least initially) are oblique. The Mythic Being's emotions are not his own, but rather the quirky adolescent emotions of Piper's journal entries, which she alienated herself from through her repeated mantras. While Pindell similarly channeled her critique of white feminists through her role-playing of White Woman, her other filmic avatars (specifically the versions of herself I noted earlier) directly addressed audiences with her grievances—in Anne Anlin Cheng's terms, the "intangible wounds" that played a "constitutive role" in her identity

formation.[78] Alongside Pindell's frustration with the class privilege embedded in A.I.R., *Free, White, and 21* can be interpreted as an extension
of her careful criticism, albeit one that did not sacrifice aesthetics for a
vociferous political push. As an artist during the turbulent 1970s, Pindell's work—starting with *Free, White, and 21*, and even more so with
her involvement with PESTS—grew from the seeds of art activism. In
light of her temporary amnesia, *Free, White, and 21* is also an explicit
exercise in memory-work: not only the recollection of her embodied
and ancestral pasts, but also, more rudimentarily, an expression of the
literal will to remember.

In the concluding moments of *Free, White, and 21*, we are presented
with a conundrum: three figurative and yet abstract beings, who draw
our attention away from the explicit realm of politics and toward the
surface textures of masks. In the final three scenes we witness three avatars of Pindell who appear in succession, each peeling off a surface or
putting one on. The first one is a version of Pindell, wearing the yellow
turtleneck sweater of White Woman but minus the whiteface makeup.
She slowly and methodically peels a translucent mask off her face, in-
timating not only that she was playing the character all along but also,
paradoxically, that the differences between Pindell and the white feminist caricature are not as stark as they first appeared. The second avatar, sitting against a bright orange background, in a blue shirt and her
head fully covered in the white gauze-like material, slowly unwraps the
cloth until it is completely off and then sits silently, looking into the
camera. The third avatar, in the last scene of the film, is White Woman.
She places a taut white stocking completely over her head and says, in
a high voice, what has become by now a comical refrain: "You ungrateful little . . . after all we have done for you. You know we don't believe
in your symbols, they are not valid unless we validate them. And you
must be really paranoid. I have never had experiences like that. But of
course, I am free, white, and 21." The first two avatars can be interpreted
as Pindell's efforts to unmask and reveal herself to the audience, while
the third might indicate White Woman's recalcitrance toward both seeing and being seen, a defense against the mounting evidence put forward by Pindell's avatars of her willful blindness and lack of sympathy
toward Pindell's grievances. Pindell remarked in an interview that the
idea of the stocking came from "bank robberies [and] people who want

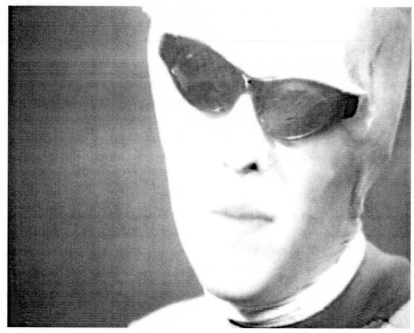

Figure 4.5. Howardena Pindell, *Free, White, and 21* (video still), 1980. Video, 12 min. Courtesy of the artist and The Kitchen, New York.

to disguise and hide themselves."[79] White Woman, already hiding be- hind dark sunglasses and now masked further by the pantyhose-like material, is rendered virtually impenetrable to the viewer, impervious to scrutiny, and obstinate in her refusal to reverse her position or utter anything other than a standard set of responses.

Stuart Hall famously remarked that black diasporic peoples have "worked on ourselves as the canvases of representation." These final moments of the video are where Pindell's deft manipulation of her physicality—her actual skin—as a textured, almost painterly, canvas is most clear. According to Hall, writing about black popular cultures, black cultural actors skillfully manipulated their bodies "as if it was, and often it was, the only cultural capital we had."[80] We can look else- where, to an essay by Pindell on African adornment, to delineate the nexuses between her multiple "flirtations with the surface," borrowing Anne Anlin Cheng's phrase, in *Free, White, and 21* as well as her other work.[81] In the essay, written in 1984 to accompany an exhibit entitled

The Aesthetics of Adornment in African Art, Pindell says that she had not conceived before of adornment as a serious art practice. Formerly associating it with the "vagaries of fashion-world sensibilities," she reconsidered only when she positioned adornment alongside the context of her "own work—that of the textured accumulated surface." As she continues in the essay, her own artistic practice and the "adornment-enhanced body" she perceives in African art begin to merge. For instance, she identifies "the accumulation and aggregation of elements" as a "distinctive characteristic of African aesthetic." Near the end, she remarks that the adorned African body is identical to a "living canvas, on which each individual constructs his or her own image."[82] I want to suggest we similarly perceive Pindell's body in *Free, White, and 21* as an iteration of this "living canvas."

In these scenes, I perceive Pindell as performing a sculptural objecthood, an embodiment as an aesthetic art object as well as an object pivoting between the figurative and abstract. Her autobiographical experiences related in *Free, White, and 21*, in other words, were about the totalizing effects of racism, the reduction of herself and her mother to the visible color of their skins; the final scenes, by contrast, represent a partial reversal of the "visual certitude and readability" sutured to racialized bodies, the false simplifications that racism pivots on.[83] In that schema, blackness and skin, or interior essence and outer surface, are collapsed into each other. Instead, in these concluding scenes, skin becomes a pliable "support" for the undoing and redoing of other flexible surfaces. These surfaces include the sticky plastic-like "white" skin, rendered opaque as it is removed from Pindell's skin; the white gauze-like strips wrapped around the head of one of Pindell's avatars that are unwound; and, in the final scene, the stretchy pantyhose of the stocking cap suffocating the whitefaced skin underneath. Pindell, as an embodied prop, supports a proliferation of stretchable, plastic materials. In short, we witness the revenge of the "textured accumulated surface," albeit in the ductile skin(s) covering the "living canvas" of the body, rather than the canvas support of the painting.

Speaking of painting (and plastic), the same year as *Free, White, and 21*, Pindell exhibited *#104 Memory Test: Free, White and Plastic* in a self-titled show at the Lerner-Heller Gallery in New York. Measuring eighteen by seventeen inches, it is a densely layered black-and-white assemblage of acrylic, watercolor, gouache, ink, thread, nails, mat board, spray adhesive, and plastic on cardboard.[84] The painting, according to Pindell, "mock[s]white supremacy and has a white gorilla in it. African American people were always stereotyped and made fun of. In this case, I am calling the whites also monkeys."[85] The painting perhaps signals further the "aesthetic conviviality" between Pindell's painting and video art (and between her figurative work and abstraction); moreover, its title suggests that it and *Free, White, and 21* were coordinates in a larger project combining memory-work with social confrontation.[86]

Art Activism, Visual Ephemera: "Art World Racism" and the Legacy of PESTS

In 1989, nine years after *Free, White, and 21*, Howardena Pindell struck the art world again with her article "Art World Racism: A Documentation." Straightforward in its aims, the essay and its accompanying statistics sought to reveal a lack of support for non-white artists across New York City's major museums. Pindell used the *Art in America* 1986–87 annual, "where artists names were provided by each gallery for listing," as a primary source, and also requested exhibition lists from 1980 to 1989 from New York City's seven major art museums.[87] As a confrontational action, though a textually based one, "Art World Racism" was similar in tactic to (and a spawn of) the activism of groups I described earlier, including the Art Workers' Coalition, W.A.R., and the Black Emergency Cultural Coalition (BECC). As artist Julie Ault notes, "the proliferation of alternative structures through the mid-1980s can also be portrayed as the legacy of cultural and political activism of the late 1960s and early 1970s."[88] Pindell was a participant in a couple of these groups while a curator at MoMA, and "Art World Racism" exposed the persistence of the very same biases these groups aimed to eradicate two decades earlier.

In 1987, Pindell first presented the material from "Art World Racism" in a lecture delivered at Hunter College.[89] Subsequently distributed in Xerox form, it was widely circulated among artists and other art world cognoscenti, and eventually published in the *New Art Examiner* in 1989. A year later, Adrian Piper referenced the article in her essay "The Triple Negation of Colored Women Artists." Coincidentally, the artists had intersected two years earlier, in the 1988 exhibition *Art as a Verb*, when Piper's *The Big Four-O* and Pindell's *The War Series* were two of four pieces censored by the "corporate fathers" of the sponsoring company, the Met Life Foundation. Undoubtedly, the censorship of Pindell's drawing series for its treatment of racism and U.S. foreign policy shaped the activist impulse of "Art World Racism" and her thoughts about her still-tenuous footing as a black woman artist in New York (*The War Series*, as well as the other censored work, was eventually exhibited at the Studio Museum of Harlem).[90] In 1997, the essay was reproduced in her own collection, *The Heart of the Question: The Writings and Paintings of Howardena Pindell*, where she expanded it to include statistics from ten years later (using the 1996–97 *Art in America* annual), and featured quotations from notable artists, curators, and critics on how little things had changed in the art world.

In the essay, which converses both with Pindell's earlier critiques and what was still to come, she outlined the "closed circle which links museums, galleries, auction houses, collectors, critics, and art magazines." Art institutions founded to address the needs of "Black, Hispanic, Asian, and Native American artists"—since "racial bias had closed them out of the primary network"—were "rarely, if ever, permitted to enter the closed circuit." The consequences of this "closed, nepotistic, interlocking network" were severe: an "industry-wide 'restraint of trade,' limiting their ability to show and sell their work." The persistence of "art world racism" was made particularly stark in Pindell's extensive statistics. While all seven museums she examined had at least one exhibition by an artist of color between 1980 and 1989, the data percentages were quite low, if not alarmingly so. The Whitney Museum, for instance, had not mounted "a one-person exhibition of a black, Hispanic, or Native American painter or sculptor since 1980," while at MoMA only two exhibitions—out of 242—were one-person shows by artists of color. Pindell's article also offered important questions for museums to grapple with. For instance, what was the cultural diversity of the curatorial staff, how did the exhibition statistics reflect the community and borough the respective museum was located in, and was there was only "token representation" on both boards of trustees and acquisitions committees? The charge of tokenism was seconded by artists in the expanded version of the article, most notably via a satiric quotation taken from the Guerrilla Girls'

"Token Times" poster: "Person of color needed to intimidate foundations, corporations, and collectors into giving large amounts of money. Successful candidate must relish being only minority staff member. High visibility in public, silence at staff meetings required. Photogenic a plus." And finally, Pindell questioned the running of public institutions as if they were "restricted private clubs, [not] held accountable for the public funds and the tax benefits" they received while, conversely, museums and galleries run by people of color lobbied "for dwindling funds" while being "constantly scrutinized." When she updated and expanded the article to include both museums *and* galleries from 1986 to 1997, the latter fared even worse in their representation of artists of color. If "Art World Racism" aggressively argued that "business drives what is documented as art history," it made clear that the failure to represent artists of color resulted in their omission from both.[91]

Meanwhile, Pindell's attention to the manifestations of "art world racism" put her at odds with the very person who introduced her to art activism: her former MoMA colleague Lucy Lippard. In 1986, Pindell voiced her disapproval of *The Law and Order Show*, a silent auction and exhibition at three prominent galleries in SoHo to benefit the Center for Constitutional Rights.[92] While the list of donated works included a veritable who's who of famous artists—Vito Acconci, Cindy Sherman, Robert Rauschenberg, Jasper Johns, and Barbara Kruger, for example—all the artists on its publicity material appeared to be white. Pindell's critique of both the Center and the three-person organizing committee that included Lippard is evident through letters addressed to Pindell by the Center's executive director (who received Pindell's letter through writer Alice Walker), as well as Georgia state senator Julian Bond, a sponsor of the show. Pindell noted in her letter to Bond that she was informed there would be two black artists in the show and later was asked to participate but declined because she did not "want to be included under these conditions as an after-thought." Meanwhile, the organizing committee signed a form letter, presumably sent to the various sponsors of the events, taking responsibility for the selection of the fifty artists while also arguing that Pindell, their "friend and co-worker against racism in the art world," had her facts a bit "skewed." The tension between Pindell and Lippard is palpable in the correspondence between the two, in which Lippard remarked she was "getting pretty damn sick of all this" as she sought to defend the Center and correct what she cast as misinformation about the circumstances of the show.[93] These textual ephemera suggest that Pindell's multipronged activism against art world racism strained relationships with her own allies. And her antagonism was a precursor to an even peskier mode of discord.

PESTS, an anonymous arts organization whose formation was inspired by "Art World Racism," debuted in 1986 with a mission that extended Pindell's rebuke against racism and tokenism. In Lowery Stokes Sims's words, PESTS was a "short-lived 'minority' corollary to the Guerrilla Girls," the latter a small group of feminist artists-turned-activists that formed the year before PESTS's arrival.[94] PESTS, though largely forgotten today, is featured as the very last entry in artist Julie Ault's chronology of selected alternative spaces and artists' groups in New York from 1965 to 1985. This genealogy reads like a road map of Pindell's artistic and activist career, from PESTS to the Studio Museum of Harlem and A.I.R., and from provocateurs like the Art Workers' Coalition to Action against Racism in the Arts (AARA), an ad hoc organization formed in 1979 in response to the Artists Space controversy. In addition to creating and distributing posters, Ault writes, PESTS "published a newsletter that listed exhibitions of work by artists of color, relevant events and panels, notices, and reproductions of PESTS posters."[95] The latter, in particular, were important visual sites (and dialogues) directed toward the public. In fact, as Coco Fusco remarked in 1993, the public actions of PESTS— and those of ACT UP, the Guerrilla Girls, and Women's Action Coalition (WAC)—"constitute[d] some of the most interactive public engagements with the media and the arts" that had emerged in the preceding decade, as each sought to "redress inequities by taking its concerns to the street and other public spaces, merging activism with spectacle."[96]

While the presence of PESTS in contemporary art discourses is scant—as if its anonymity ensured its swift erasure—its tethering to the also-anonymous Guerrilla Girls offers an important clue. The Guerrilla Girls formed in 1985 in response to the paucity of women (thirteen out of 169 artists) included in *An International Survey of Recent Painting and Sculpture*, an exhibition of contemporary art at MoMA. In a "desire to do something more creative than holding a press conference or handing out leaflets," they donned gorilla masks, took on names of famous women artists, and created bravura posters.[97] One of the latter

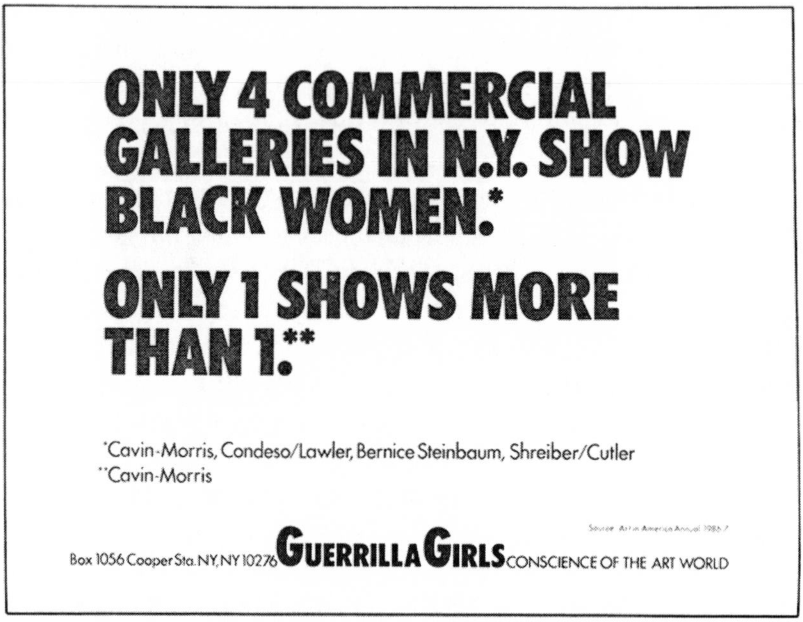

ONLY 4 COMMERCIAL GALLERIES IN N.Y. SHOW BLACK WOMEN.*

ONLY 1 SHOWS MORE THAN 1.**

*Cavin-Morris, Condeso/Lawler, Bernice Steinbaum, Shreiber/Cutler
**Cavin-Morris

Box 1056 Cooper Sta. NY, NY 10276 **GUERRILLA GIRLS** CONSCIENCE OF THE ART WORLD

Source: Art in America Annual 1986-7

Figure 4.6. Guerrilla Girls, advertisement, 1986. Courtesy of the Getty Research Institute, Los Angeles (2008.M.14). © New Observations Ltd and the authors.

ran in the *Art in America* annual for 1986–87; it read, "Only 4 Commercial Galleries in N.Y. show Black Women. Only 1 Shows More than 1."[98] Though members of the group have recently filed lawsuits against each other, the Guerrilla Girls' visual interventions and guerrilla tactics are noteworthy, and its position in cultural histories (and art history) is secure. Class, as earlier in Pindell's critique of A.I.R., played a role; the Guerrilla Girls' financial and cultural capital seems to have insured the preservation of their memory, while the meager resources of PESTS, conversely, has perpetuated its obsolescence.[99] Nevertheless, in one testament to the Guerrilla Girls' archival permanence—an oral history conducted for the Smithsonian Archives of American Art with two of the group's members, using the names "Frida Kahlo" and "Kathe Kollwitz"—the link between the Guerrilla Girls and PESTS was made explicit. When the interviewer asked about a rumor of "a splintering off of African American women artists" from the Guerrilla Girls, "Ms. Kahlo" replied, "PESTS. One of our members started PESTS. She did that simultaneously and got more involved with it and left Guerrilla

Girls to do her own thing with PESTS. I remember her asking me for advice about some of the projects they did."[100] This anonymous member of both organizations—quite possibly Pindell herself—served, temporarily, as an embodied link between them. Just as this illustrates the coalition building across multiple identities that occurred at the intersection of art and activism, it suggests the sharing of insurrectionist visual strategies as well.

If "what becomes history is to some degree determined by what is archived," the paucity of PESTS's visual and textual remains make them all the more important.[101] The archival memory of the group is limited mainly to its publication of just two newsletters, themselves difficult to locate. The residues of these ephemera are directly tethered to Pindell. In her file at the Hatch-Billops Collection in New York, she left copies of PESTS memorabilia alongside other materials. When I asked about her involvement in the organization, she hesitated but then admitted her participation.[102] Her elusive touch haunts, for instance, a typed press release prominently featuring PESTS's address (a P.O. box at the Canal Street Station in lower Manhattan) and an image of a large insect resembling a wasp, PESTS's stinging visual insignia. "Presaging contemporary street art," Gill Saunders writes, "PESTS devised a distinctive logo—a wasp-like insect whose armoury was enhanced by a pair of serrated pincers and a scorpion's tail—that featured not only on their flyers, but also on a series of stickers."[103]

Dated December 6, 1986, the press release asked in bold print, "How often do you see a one-person show by an artist of color?" In smaller print below, the questions continued: "Have you ever wished that the art world was more informed and knowledgeable about works created by artists of color?" Finally, the press release declared that "it is time to reverse art world apartheid."[104] PESTS's stated aims were to publicize the "myopia of the art establishment," increase "positive interest in artists of color," and highlight the "serious omission and de facto censorship practiced by galleries, museums and art publications. As a person of conscience, you must have reflected on these issues and wished you had been presented with a broader and more accurate view." Along with a request for donations, the release offered what would become the group's trademark humorous proclamation: "We plan to bug the art world!"[105]

December 6, 1986

How often do you see
a one-person show
by an artist of color?

PESTS
P.O. BOX 1996
CANAL ST. STATION
N.Y.C. 10013-0873

Have you ever wished that the art world was
more informed and knowledgeable about works created by artists
of color? Observations have led us to feel that it is time to
reverse art world apartheid, which misrepresents a multiethnic
and multiracial culture.

PESTS, an anonymous artists organization aims to publicize
the myopia of the art establishment. Through our future activities
we plan to generate positive interest in artists of color, overriding
past neglect and misrepresentation.

Our immediate goals are to publicize the serious ommission and
de facto censorship practiced by galleries, museums and art
publications. As a person of conscience, you must have reflected on
these issues and wished you had been presented with a broader and
more accurate view.

Support your local
PESTS activities!

We need your help now,
no matter how small
the contribution!

We plan to bug the art world!

Please send check or money order to:

PESTS
P.O.Box 1996
Canal Street Station
New York, N.Y. 10013-0873

Thank you for your support!

Figure 4.7. PESTS, press release, 1986. Courtesy of the Getty Research Institute, Los Angeles (2008.M.14). © PESTS.

The flyer's iconic buzzing insect, as well as Pindell's critique of token-ism, carried over to what appears to be the first issue of the newsletter (though it is identified as "no. 2").[106] The seven-page printed newsletter profiled an alternative version of the standard late-1980s art scene, one composed entirely of performances, lectures, and exhibitions by artists of color. Readers of the listings, or the "PESTS STRIP," could self-direct their aesthetic experience by genre and even region. They could, for instance, catch a show of James Van Der Zee's photographs on Avenue B in the East Village, see Juan Sanchez's show at Exit Art in SoHo, or venture uptown to the Harlem School of the Arts and attend a gallery talk by Kellie Jones for *9 Uptown*, an exhibition of nine artists including Pindell. Or they could visit the Asian Arts Institute, see Emma Amos's *The Water Series*, or hear a panel discussion on "Cultural Chauvinism" in SoHo featuring Pindell and artist Fred Wilson. Meanwhile, readers who wanted to help "Post-a-Pest," could be sent posters and "pest strips kits." Two of those posters were pictured within the newsletter as examples. The "latest" one, with two adjoining panels, read: "WE'RE HERE. ¿WHY WON'T YOU SEE US? THERE ARE AT LEAST 11,009 ARTISTS OF COLOR IN NEW YORK. ¿WHY DON'T YOU SEE US?"[107] While "next month's posters" read: "WHAT IS TOKENISM? WHEN YOU'VE SEEN ONE ARTIST OF COLOR BUT THINK YOU'VE SEEN TEN. WE ARE NOT EXOTIC. WE ARE NOT PRIMITIVE. WE ARE NOT INVISIBLE." "WE ARE NOT FEW IN NUMBER. WE ARE ARTISTS . . . JUST LIKE YOUR GIFTED WHITE BOYS." A coterie of PESTS's maverick insects buzzed along the bottom of the page, as if signaling their disapproval of tokenism and its effects.[108]

In the second newsletter—identified as "no. 3," and dated "fall/winter 1987"—the list of galleries, exhibitions, and lectures filled ten pages. Its rich contents included a retrospective of Ana Mendieta's work at the New Museum, a panel of Pindell and two other artists at Asian CineVision, and a panel on "Sex, Race, and Performance Art" at Columbia University featuring Jessica Hagedorn, Robbie McCauley, and others. In an expansion of the newsletter's geographical reach, the "PESTS STRIP" also listed exhibitions outside of New York. These events included Benny Andrews's and Vivian Browne's respective shows at Shifflet Gallery in Los Angeles, a exhibition of Pindell's work at the N'Namdi Gallery in Detroit, and—in a leap across the Pacific Ocean—*Afro American Modernism: 1937-1987* in Tokyo. While not a physical space like the A.I.R. Gallery, the extensive newsletter was an important analogous one, if space is considered, in Martin Beck's terms, "primarily as a contested political arena. In this viewpoint, the physical condition of that space is less important than the social inclusion and exclusion processes that regulate access to and representation within it."[109] And, ever on the cutting edge, the newsletter

Figure 4.8. PESTS newsletter, vol. 1, no. 2, "PESTS STRIP," 1987. Courtesy of the Getty Research Institute, Los Angeles (2008.M.14). © PESTS.

Figure 4.9. PESTS newsletter, vol. 1, no. 2, "PESTS STRIP," 1987. Courtesy of the Getty Research Institute, Los Angeles (2008.M.14). © PESTS.

made plain those stakes of visibility, exclusion, and tokenism in its other quirky features and often biting asides. The "Pest-a-cide," for instance, listed nineteen galleries and the percentage of white artists in their shows, based on "printed announcements, posters and press releases" in 1986–87, similar to the statistics collected for "Art World Racism." It included the aforementioned *Law and Order Show*, identified as 94 percent white. And, in the "Pest-a-watch," PESTS members remarked, "Would someone tell the kind ladies at the National Museum of Women in the Arts in Washington, D.C that not every female artist of color answer to the name EDMONIA or LOIS even if you put MS in front of it." Thus, while the "relationship between artwork and space" in the newsletter was one, symbolically, of "foreground to background—the space is there as a venue for the artwork," PESTS's newsletters also acted as insurgent political agents interrupting the status quo.[110]

This sentiment was perhaps most apparent in the images that appeared on the front and back pages of the newsletter, which packed a stark visual punch. In the first, a seemingly innocuous place setting—complete with polished silver utensils, a porcelain plate, and glass, ashtray, and cylindrical vase on top of a pristine white tablecloth—sat beneath a caption: "We Serve Whites Only." On the plate, instead of food, was an open pamphlet reading, "The following New York City galleries are 100% white." Beneath the pamphlet was a list of thirty-eight galleries, several of them prominent and still in existence, such as Metro Pictures and Mary Boone, and alternative sites such as Gracie Mansion. The statistics were credited to the *Art in America* annual for 1987–88, a comprehensive guide that listed the artists represented in galleries and museums in cites across the United States (Pindell used the previous year's issue for "Art World Racism"). This incendiary visual statement was echoed on the back cover. The image there showed a silver buffet and the headline "Artists Du Jour," followed by a list of twenty-five galleries organized by share of white representation, from 69 percent to 95 percent. If the statistical shaming of galleries via the metaphor of restaurants and tastes suggested that artists of color were simply not de rigueur, its class commentary pointed to the elitist, closed circle of an increasingly corporatized art world. The two images served as pesky visual bookends to PESTS's second and seemingly final newsletter, cloaked

Figure 4.10. PESTS newsletter, vol. 1, no. 3, "We Serve Whites Only," 1987. Courtesy of the Getty Research Institute, Los Angeles (2008.M.14). © PESTS.

in anonymity while New York City's persistent infestation of "art world racism" was on full display.

Both the flyer and newsletters continued articulations of Pindell's antiracist urgings in "Art World Racism," while also animating what Nancy Fraser terms "subaltern counterpublics."[111] In these textual remains, we perceive hints of how they served as "new spheres of possibility" for the anonymous dissident member(s) of PESTS—Pindell and, presumably, other artists of color—and readers of its newsletter. The vociferous visual refrains of its posters, moreover, acted in opposition to the "dominant public sphere," in this case the New York art world writ large.[112]

Figure 4.11. PESTS newsletter, vol. 1, no. 3, "Artists du Jour," 1987. Courtesy of the Getty Research Institute, Los Angeles (2008.M.14). © PESTS.

"Organized not by a place or an institution but by the circulation of discourse," the newsletters, flyers, and posters of PESTS addressed and united this counterpublic's potential members. Meanwhile, the listing of what Pindell has elsewhere called "alternative venues" was also important to the "poetic world making" of this counterpublic.[113] Despite their operation within a "fragile financial margin," alternative art sites—like Exit Art, the Jamaica Arts Center, and the Native American Community House Gallery—were "fertile training grounds for future curators" and key locales for "art students to learn about a diverse arts community," promoting the work of artists such as Martin Wong and David Hammons at pivotal points in their careers.[114] Furthermore, as Brian Wallis describes, while the impetus for these alternative spaces was "economic, an effort to break the commercial galleries' stranglehold on exhibition opportunities," especially (as Pindell noted) for artists of color, the experimental work they made often "seemed to require the sort of raw, quirky contexts that alternative spaces provided."[115] This printed matter, finally, buttressed Pindell's larger project against tokenism, exemplified eight years earlier by *Free, White, and 21*. Here again we witness cross-pollination across genres, as Pindell's video art and visual paraphernalia both furthered her art activism against racism in the art world.

Coda

The goal of my work is knowledge. I do not see life and art
as separate.
—Howardena Pindell

While Howardena Pindell, as an art activist in the 1970s, confronted art institutions' elitism and egregious lack of support for artists of color and their work, her example makes painfully clear the laborious task of being a black woman artist in New York during this period. She, like other black women artists, had to debunk the perception that "artist" and "black woman" were incompatible terms. Moreover, Pindell's work itself—classified as not "black art" and excluded from the white avant-garde altogether—presented its own challenges, particularly concerning where it could be shown. Despite her eventual clashes with the A.I.R. Gallery and MoMA colleague Lucy Lippard, the heady mix of art, feminism, and activism espoused by the latter sharpened Pindell's political consciousness, while A.I.R. gave her the first opportunity to exhibit her work.

Free, White and 21, in spite of its recent critical recognition, is still often reduced to its biting rebuke of white feminists; yet, as I have shown above, its components—particularly its imaginative uses of avatars—warrant a closer look. As versions of Pindell, these digital doppelgangers deliver powerful forms of testimony; these unapologetic likenesses calmly and thoroughly explain what has happened to her. They refuse to stop talking even when their haughty counterpart—White Woman—contests the veracity of what's said and claims that these experiences fail to manifest in Pindell's art. In Margo Crawford's words, "Terror hides behind black sunglasses and a blond wig."[116] Through avatar production, Pindell bears witness to this terror and to herself, bruised but alive. And the avatars in *Free, White, and 21* are also silent creatures enabling Pindell's painterly play with surface, texture, and skin; they render the black female body as a pliable canvas. Finally, Pindell's exploration of family ancestry, identity formation, and skin color politics through these avatars shares themes with performance artist Robbie McCauley's *Sally's Rape* (1991); in both, black women performers utilized art and performance as conduits for sustained confrontation and profound reflection.[117]

As the final panel in this chapter's triptych, "Art World Racism" and the ephemera of PESTS also serve as bookends to Pindell's convergence of art and activism. They circle back, in fact, to the artistic experimentation and political activism she participated in soon after her 1967 arrival in New York, with an MFA from Yale but with no place to show her art. If Pindell's art activism through PESTS seems ancillary to our larger focus on performance and avatar production, it is not. Instead, it is an idiosyncratic extension of the versions of herself produced in *Free, White, and 21*, trading in the plaintive rage of her televisual personas for the irritation of the two-dimensional buzzing insect. In the video, Pindell was in plain sight—albeit, as one critic described, temporarily "whited out" in the "Barbie-doll blond wig, sunglasses, and pale makeup" of her white feminist avatar.[118] In the textual works, while Pindell was in/visible (present in "Art World Racism," camouflaged in PESTS), both were stages for the dramatization of her "rhetorical personae"; in that regard, these "texts *are* performances," in the words of Cherise Smith.[119] In "Art World Racism," we witness Pindell as Art Critic Activist, while in PESTS, we observe her (perhaps collaborative, maybe singular) performance of Invisible Art World Instigator.

While the visual ephemera of PESTS paraphernalia, moreover, are particularly fleeting—due both to the passage of time and our partial reliance on the archives of others, e.g., the Guerrilla Girls—that does not deny their aesthetic and political efficacy. If, as José Esteban Muñoz reminds us, "queering evidence" is partly about suturing it to the concept of ephemera itself, PESTS's potent ideological force also "partially (re) lives in its documentation."[120] Finally, PESTS and "Art World Racism" as a pair, and a particularly stinging one at that, serve a crucial role in cultural histories of alternative New York in the late 1980s. Not only did they—like *Free, White, and 21* in 1980—loudly challenge the status quo in this aesthetic milieu, but their continued erasure from many of these histories may not be accidental, since as Pindell herself noted, omission itself was one of "the artworld's arsenal of tactics."[121] Here on our stage, however, they are alive. And unlike the echoes of an off-script outburst, whispers of escape, and ponderous silence of black conceptual art that have so far formed the symphonic arc of this book, our ending refrains here are the ominous and monosyllabic sounds of an irate insect, descending along a discarded blond wig, and pricking the art world. Buzz buzz buzz!

Conclusion

"I've Been Performing My Whole Life"

The title of this conclusion, taken from sculptor and visual artist Simone Leigh's *Breakdown*, is a soaring and recurring lyric articulated by the star of that performance piece, opera singer Alicia Hall Moran. We watch her in the midst of a fitful, and mournful, psychological breakdown. The line is expressed as a brief moment of triumph by the unnamed protagonist, amid her otherwise plaintive melodies, as we witness her spectacular coming undone. I return to the elegant sorrow of *Breakdown* momentarily, but I start here in order to emphasize a by-now obvious point: that the blunt poetic truth implicit in this mantra-like phrase could just as easily be expressed by any one of the tenacious performers I have discussed thus far. We can imagine Ellen Craft whispering this phrase *sotto voce* to her husband and coconspirator William, as it embodies the endurance art she made as her disabled white male avatar, Mr. William Johnson, as well as her post-escape career as a living theatrical exhibit for the British abolitionist movement—serving as embodied visual proof of chattel slavery's tenuous and inept one-drop rule.[1] Shouted with exasperation by Joice Heth, it could attest to the ever-evolving scripted narratives—be they of national heritage or later accusations of her nonhumanness—her fragile morphology was repeatedly made to sustain, with and against her will. Spoken in the erudite cadences of a trained philosopher, it would reflect Adrian Piper's maneuverability across seemingly disparate fields— Minimalism, Conceptualism, and performance art—as she repeatedly, and at her own risk, presented herself as a paradoxical presence and, more recently, as a glaring public absence. And finally, calmly confessed by Howardena Pindell, it would be a fitting rebuttal to the multitude of refusals hurled her way, and painstakingly detailed by her in *Free, White, and 21*, due to her inability to adequately perform her roles as a "token," a woman, and a black artist.

This assemblage of performers eluded the cleavages between art and life—and occupied the fuzzy nether realms between objecthood and subjectivity—continually disrupting the protocols of art making and proper comportment, wielding the instrumentality of the black female body as an artistic and public flashpoint. They designed and staged performance works in venues far beyond the proscenium arch and before a vast variety of audiences: audiences who refused to listen, let alone believe, its content (Pindell); who failed to recognize its efficacy or appearance as "art" (Piper); who ravenously documented the performer's bravery, pulchritude, and shocking *whiteness* (Craft); and who utilized the performer's ersatz black maternal memories as an explicit occasion to indulge in a truly American nostalgia (Heth). Performing their whole lives, this quartet of black female performers, whose seditious acts and aesthetic breakthroughs have filled these pages, caution us about the stakes of black performance art as they artfully and magnificently rendered themselves the subject—and object—of art.

Throughout this book, I have emphasized the triumvirate of objecthood, black performance art, and avatar production as a set of interlaced analytics, critical to interpreting the aesthetic provocations and ontological labor executed by black women performers. While this methodology has revealed self-objectification as a recurring strategy in black women's performance work, there are still further questions to be explored. Central to these intrepid acts of self-staging have been the dense ligatures between agency, self-objectification, and black female subjectivity. As I emphasized at the outset, performing objecthood does not always, or necessarily, point toward an emancipated subjectivity. Joice Heth's black maternal dramas of memory are a haunting reminder of this very predicament. Made manifest before rapturous nineteenth-century audiences eager for an embodied link to a primeval America, her performances as George Washington's nursemaid reflect the contingencies of objecthood, if not its limits, as a technique of self-making. Principally, Heth's ultimate debasement in her very last performance—her public autopsy, staged in a saloon in New York City on February 25, 1836—sought to exhaust all the possible meanings her inanimate corpse could provoke, all in the name of popular entertainment. Her freedom, already a dubious matter when alive, was, in this last gruesome scene, bluntly foreclosed; the display of her dissected flesh echoed, as Amber

Jamilla Musser writes, the "particularly fraught space" black women have occupied in "configurations of power, agency, and subjectivity."[2] Invoking Hortense Spillers's distinction between the body and the flesh, postmortem Heth was irrevocably denied the self-possession and legal personhood symbolized by the body, and instead forcibly reduced to the zero degree of ruptured, dismembered flesh.[3] In short, Heth's final act, rather than the seemingly innocuous medical theater it purported to be, was a purposeful and didactic staging of the very conditions of what, and *who*, constituted the human. It fortified the *full* humanity of white nineteenth-century audiences as it resolidified Heth's less-than-equal membership, her not-quite-human status, suggesting, in Alexander G. Weheliye words, how "the banning of black subjects from the domain of the human occur in and through gender and sexuality."[4] Often reduced to freak show legerdemain and mere historical footnote, the tattered remnants of Heth's brief but illustrious acts have been overlooked in historiographies of performance art, let alone performance writ large.

I have attempted to counter such scholarly neglect by resituating Heth—as well as Ellen Craft—as emblematic of the *longue durée* of black cultural subjects performing objecthood. In doing so, I have sought to reposition Heth and Craft not only as key figures who undergird and extend the historical arc of performance art, but also as historical forebears to the wide expanse of black performance art, as designed and practiced by black women across the second half of the twentieth century. Specifically, their conceptual foils—Adrian Piper and Howardena Pindell—wedded artistic praxis with deft experiments in self-estrangement amid the New York–based art scenes of the late 1960s and 1970s, in Piper's case, and the 1970s and 1980s, in Pindell's. As such, the multiple ontological hoaxes of Heth and unlawful role-plays of Craft gave way to the extreme self-alienating acts of Piper and her Mythic Being, and the satiric whiteface avatar and anonymous art-world activism of Pindell. Both involved, to varying degrees, in the heady duo of art and politics, Piper and Pindell's ardent (and ongoing) desires for artistic freedom would anticipate the politicized debates around censorship and artistic expression characteristic of the "culture wars" of the late 1980s and early 1990s. And their shared manipulation of their physicality as raw material echoed the consequential wielding of performance art in this period as an especially potent means for "debating the relationship between art, artists, and the state."[5]

Nonetheless, in situating these four performers together I do not mean to imply clear lines of descent. After all, as Paul Gilroy asserts, such an approach is unrealistic when confronting the crisscrossing currents inherent in genealogies of black performance. Specifically, he reminds us, linear frameworks assuming an "unbroken continuity or essential connectedness between today's mongrel dynamics and past purities" ignore how black performance culture is "propagated by unpredictable means in non-linear patterns. Promiscuity is the key principle of its continuance."[6] Concurring with this, I have positioned Heth and Craft as proto-figures whose clandestine acts and quotidian self-stagings set precedents that—following the logic of avatars—morph and resurface in Pindell's and Piper's ingenious and trenchant performance works more than a century later. Their legacies as recognized performers in the nineteenth century, moreover, make striking counterpoints to the less recognized careers and works of these later artists in the twentieth century. In short, it is not insignificant that all four of these black women embraced the dynamic nexus of black performance art, objecthood, and avatars as they sought an urgent means of resculpting their bodies into supple matter and rendering themselves as art.

In what follows, I urge us to consider the present-day appeal of this vital linkage as I further interrogate the perils and possibilities of performing objecthood via an electrifying pair: hip-hop and pop star Nicki Minaj and aforementioned sculptor Simone Leigh. While in the first half of this book I sought to elongate the category of performance art, to include politically resistant self-displays by nineteenth-century black cultural subjects, I now seek to stretch the putative borders of performance art in the opposite direction—by encompassing the heavily mediated and exoteric performances of the twenty-first century. Conjoined to the self-conscious and often esoteric artworks I described in the previous two chapters, I continue to vigorously pursue a more panoramic vision of black performance art, augmenting the range and depth of materials included under its banner while continuing to question received histories of *what* counts as performance art and *who* counts as a performance artist.

Borrowing Shannon Jackson's language, while the two "cross-disciplinary art performance[s]"[7] I primarily discuss here seem wildly dissimilar—the former (Minaj's) the seemingly fleeting product of mass cultures, the latter (Leigh's) granted the cultural privilege ascribed to high art—both are forms of digital media that pivot between the real and the virtual. As Nicole R. Fleetwood suggests, while the audiences for fine art, black popular culture, and mass culture are distinct, they also overlap, as do the audiences for the art objects discussed here.[8] Leigh's *Breakdown* is a case study for these slippages. Filmed in Harlem, *Breakdown* is a single-channel video artwork that debuted at the Studio Museum of Harlem exhibition *Evidence of Accumulation* in July 2011, while Leigh was part of the prestigious Artist-in-Residence program there, and hence was viewed primarily by culturally elite museum-going audiences. At the time of this writing, it can also be accessed as a streaming video file at Leigh's website (www.simoneleigh.com). In its multiplicity, it is very similar to the music video for Kanye West's "Monster," featuring Minaj; originally produced for television channels like MTV (where it was banned upon release), "Monster" can be viewed as a streaming file via YouTube, and downloaded as a QuickTime movie file from the Vimeo website. Both "Monster" and *Breakdown*, in their digital reincarnations, evince what new media scholar Lisa Nakamura identifies as the Internet's ability to swiftly convert and encapsulate *all* forms of media. This process is emblematic, she writes, of its rapid transformation since 1995, from a textual into an increasingly graphical space that progressively incorporates more and more types of media under its purview.[9]

In our present era of escalated mediation, the constant engagement with user-created avatars and other forms of media stimulation has rendered distinctions between the real and virtual, online and offline, nearly moot.[10] As such, the increasing interplay between digitally manipulated forms of cultural production and the racial meanings and identifications created alongside them—or, in Nakamura's terms, "digital racial formation"—becomes increasingly important.[11] The black women performers and alternate selves I analyze below are situated at different positions on the continuum between the repertoire of embodied acts more prototypical of black performance art and the "graphical humanesque figures" of digitized black female avatars.[12] And they fluidly travel between the streaming (video), the live (performance), and the still (photographs, video stills). In what follows, I direct us to how these performers mold themselves into sui generis and self-effacing performances that often alter further into pixelated digital assemblages; in so *the transform him into pixels*

doing, they nimbly construct ephemeral acts staged and viewed by live audiences offline *and* interactive significations communicated to networked viewers online.

In unpacking this sly shearing across art objects, genres, and academic disciplines, I employ a loose triptych structure to continually make plain the stakes of black performance art, objecthood, and avatar production in the contemporary moment. I begin with the mercurial Nicki Minaj, zeroing in on her vocal calisthenics in "Monster," before dissecting her deployment of grotesque aesthetics in its controversial and morbid visual counterpart. In dialogue with art historian Kobena Mercer's analysis of the savvy aesthetic strategies wielded by black artists, I also briefly loop back to Joice Heth, ruminating on her as another tricky figure whose performances—though historically and aesthetically divergent—trafficked in the hybrid meanings attached to the grotesque as well. Switching gears, I then turn toward Simone Leigh's *Breakdown*, in which mezzo-soprano Alicia Hall Moran performs as an anonymous woman undergoing a crippling, if mellifluous, mental breakdown. Reading the piece alongside José Esteban Muñoz's scholarship, I consider its skilled aesthetics of failure and solemn suggestion of the psychological toll role-playing has on black diasporic women. In the last few pages, I very briefly discuss performance artist Narcissister, digital avatar Kismet Nuñez, and the android Cindi Mayweather, portrayed by musician Janelle Monáe, before the final discussion that closes the book. While it may seem counterintuitive to continue enlarging our cast of characters—performers as well as their synthetic figurations—at the denouement of *Embodied Avatars*, the members of this fiery trio perfectly epitomize, as we will soon see, the recurring risks of these experimental performances as well as their acute capacity for righteous self-transformations.

the grotesque as visual cultural mimicry

A Planet Yet Undiscovered: The Grotesque Aesthetics of Nicki Minaj

Nicki Minaj—former *American Idol* judge and three-time Grammy nominee (including for Best New Artist)—continues to defy expectations of what a black female rapper should be, and in the process has single-handedly stretched the roles that someone like her can inhabit and perform. She has adeptly transformed herself into a frequent Twitter

Figure C.1. Nicki Minaj, Hot 97 Summer Jam XX, New York, June 2, 2013. Photo credit: Mel D. Cole.

topic (she has over sixteen million followers), a wacky fashion maverick (who has graced the covers of *Elle, Teen Vogue, W,* and *Marie Claire*), and a magnetic (and inescapable) pop star. Her ascent, to quote the *New York Times,* has been "breathtakingly swift, even by Warholian standards."[13] Raised in Queens, New York—by way of Port of Spain, Trinidad—Minaj, neé Onika Tanya Maraj, graduated from the drama division of New York's prestigious LaGuardia High School for the Arts. Prior to her eventual record deal, Minaj released three mixtapes in rapid succession—*Playtime Is Over* (2007), *Sucka Free* (2008), and *Beam Me Up Scotty* (2009). The last one—which featured Minaj dressed as Wonder Woman on the cover and included the playful boast "You know they say who, who is Nicki Minaj?/You know I'm like a multiple personality bitch"—led the *New York Times* to presciently dub her the "Cindy Sherman of rap."[14] Amid delivering a blistering amount of cameos on singles by prominent artists—so much so that "Nicki Minaj verses" were listed, ironically, as one of the top ten songs of 2010 by *Entertainment Weekly*—her big break was her first studio album, *Pink Friday.* Released in November 2010 on the heels of a prominent MTV-produced

Figure C.2. Nicki Minaj, Hot 97's VIP Lounge, SIR Studio, New York, November 18, 2010. Photo credit: Mel D. Cole.

documentary about Minaj, *My Time Now*, it was certified platinum a month after its release. Her second studio album, *Roman Reloaded*, was released in April 2012 and its first single, "Starships," peaked at number 2 in the United Kingdom and number 5 in the United States. The same year, she was tapped to endorse Pepsi in a campaign that used her 2010 single "Moment for Life" (featuring Canadian rapper Drake) and performed on the Super Bowl halftime show with American pop icon Madonna and Sri Lankan rapper M.I.A. In April 2013, she became the most-charted female rapper in the history of the *Billboard* Hot 100 (forty-four singles). And in August 2014, she set not one but two records, becoming the first female rapper to have two of her singles place at number 1 and number 2 simultaneously on iTunes' digital tally and the first female rapper to top the iTunes chart with a solo single.[15]

I conceive of Minaj's prolific oeuvre as a vibrant form of black performance art, centered on her excessive body as the provocative, and often explosive, objet d'art. Akin to the other performers in this book, Minaj deftly wields self-objectification as an artistic strategy; in doing so, she renders herself a disruptive agent able, with varying degrees of success, to thwart limits placed on black women's bodies in the public sphere while challenging, and in some cases rescripting, perceptions of the black female body. Performance art's axiomatic interest, moreover, in the proliferation of artistic personas—where "the distinction between the personality of the artists and the work presented is blurred"[16]—is particularly well-suited for a performer like Minaj, whose oft-remarked métier is character itself, vocally (and visually) transmuting herself with dizzying speed into a dazzling array of avatars. Her cultural work thus mirrors the often-assaultive stance of performance art, albeit on the sonic register—such as the swift verbal shifts in her vertiginous cameo on "Monster." In addition, she performs this abrasiveness at the level of the visual, where she often manipulates the highly charged and sexualized meanings of her black diasporic body as an apparatus to trouble discourses of respectability, taste, and femininity. The most salient qualities of Minaj's performances—her pleasure in self-objectification, revelry in racial and gender stereotypes, strategic enactment of self-fragmentation and alterity, and (especially earlier in her career) keen use of artifice and black camp[17]—are also the most paradoxical and, at times, controversial. Indeed, they prove a particular challenge to black feminist theories of the visual, discourses that often emphasize wholeness and positive self-representation as part of the recovery process to salvage the black female body from the historical violence of the visual sphere.[18] Instead, as I argue below, the grotesque is a more suitable interpretive frame for Minaj's slippery performance work, since it helps us locate her devastating play and continual (and gleeful) violation of tidy boundaries squarely within evolving discourses on the "cultural politics of 'race' and aesthetics"[19] and, in this book, within genealogies of art and performance staged by black women.

In doing so, I anticipate the manifold hesitations in recognizing Nicki Minaj's performance work as such—specifically, its adamant nonrelationship to fine art, its collusion with capitalism, and the quandary of intentionality. While this anxiety is valuable, and understandable as we move into the less venerated realm of popular music, it is revealing that several of these critiques can (and have) also been levied against the other performers in this book. For instance, while little in Minaj's corpus bears the indicia of high art, it is important to recall not only that neither Joice Heth nor Ellen Craft were interpreted as performance artists (let alone artists), but that even the rarefied performances of Adrian Piper—easily the most culturally elite of the artists in this book and the one most canonized in art history—were often not recognized as art until *after* she wrote about them much later; as we've seen, the inability of street audiences to recognize Piper's anomalous actions as "art" often put her in extremely uncomfortable situations that bordered on dangerous. Moreover, Minaj's performances certainly do not aspire to the anticapitalist logic that is usually perceived as synonymous with performance art, emblematized by its mantra-like inability to be bought or sold. On the contrary, she is situated as (and expertly marketed as) a highly consumable product in the convergence of corporate interests and transnational flows of capital that imbue mass cultures. In this milieu, to quote Stuart Hall, "the scene, *par excellence*, of commodification, of the industries where culture enters directly into the circuits of a dominant technology—the circuits of power and capital,"[20] Minaj is judged less by the tenets of beauty, taste, and art historical allusion that characterize formalist aesthetics, and more by contemporary metrics that measure cultural relevance: percentage gains in Twitter mentions, for instance, or sharp increases in Instagram followers. While such metrics may certainly complicate definitions of performance art, I caution that market imperatives affected iterations of nineteenth-century black performance art as well. In fact, the sales of Ellen Craft's engraving (meant to, among other things, purchase her sister-in-law out of chattel slavery) or the admission fees charged at Joice Heth's freak show exhibitions (and post mortem autopsy) are not simply indicators of the brute historical legacy that undergirds black women's performance work. Rather, they also suggest that capital was a necessary component (if not a foundational principle) of black performance art from the very beginning, especially when its practitioners were so often fungible commodities themselves.

Finally, Nicki Minaj's intentions for any given performance are, admittedly, exceptionally hard to pinpoint; this is particularly true when it comes to the question of whether or not she is always aware of the loaded historical narratives she appropriates,[21] as well as the vexed cultural meanings her presence, especially her callipygian corporeality, induces.[22] The ambiguities inherent in Minaj's performances, however, are symptomatic of black popular culture itself, an electric force field of meanings where contradictions, counternarratives, fantasies, and aesthetic contestations flourish. The late Stuart Hall, writing in 1992, characterized black popular cultures in exactly this way. If, as Hall argues, there are no pure forms in black popular cultures (but instead only hybridized ones), black popular cultures are also highly charged, mixed, and clashing spaces where cultural identities are imagined, stylized, theatricalized, and rendered "mythic." In his words,

> The first [thought] is to remind you that popular culture, commodified and stereotyped as it often is, is not at all, as we sometimes think of it, the arena where we find who we really are, the truth of our experience. It is an arena that is *profoundly* mythic. It is a theatre of popular desires, a theatre of popular fantasies. It is where we discover and play with the identifications of ourselves, where we are imagined, where we are represented, not only to the audiences out there who do not get the message, but to ourselves for the first time.[23]

Hall's primer for comprehending popular cultures also serves as a critical template for interpreting Minaj, a deviant figure working at the plexus of performance and visuality. Contrary to popular belief, popular cultures are not mirrors that reflect back the truth of who we are. Instead, they are a shifting collision of forces, fabulations, and yearnings. If fantasy itself is a part of identity formation, as Anne Anlin Cheng argues,[24] then Minaj's often-hyperbolic performances can be understood as an aggressive and imaginative form of self making. And in Minaj's case, this has often taken the form of her transubstantiation into mythic-like selves—a process I have been terming *avatar production*—that rises to a feverish pitch in her audacious, *monstrous* appearance with Kanye West.

Minaj's bewildering vocality—likened to a pastiche of "feminine New York bark, lilting British brogue, valley girl gangsta, and occasional wild tones that come from who knows where, but sound like the dialect of a planet yet discovered"[25]—is on full kooky display in her brief but incendiary cameo on West's single "Monster," from his 2010 album *My Beautiful Dark Twisted Fantasy*. In the lineup of the single, slightly over six minutes in length, Minaj is positioned as the last rapper—and the only woman—after an ominous distorted introduction by Justin Vernon of indie group Bon Iver, followed by verses from rappers Rick Ross, West, and Jay-Z. Yet her vocal eruptions—clocking in at just under a minute and a half—make the lyrical boasts of these veterans look lackadaisical in comparison. Minaj's careening sonic abrasion in "Monster" is a significant, distinct (and heretofore unexamined) presence in the pulsating networks of black performance art flowing throughout these pages.

Minaj's verses in "Monster" stage an aural tour de force featuring at least three vocal personas, alternating between her normal, but swift, register, a rumbling beast-like roar, and a breathy adolescent whisper. While she opens her verse with the low register, this athletic vocal shift begins when she announces, a few lines in, that "I'm all up, all up, all up in the bank with the funny face/And if I'm fake, I ain't notice, cause my money ain't!" It is at the phrase "cause my money ain't" that Minaj's voice unexpectedly erupts in an animalistic growl before transforming, just as quickly, to a girly lilt for the verse immediately after it. This elasticity continues throughout her vocal acrobatics, some phrases rapped in a girlish tone ("But really really, I don't give a F-U-C-K/ Forget Barbie, fuck Nicki, she-she's fake"), while others sonically explode, like her maniacal boast "Fifty K for a verse/No album out!"

Minaj's jarring declarations, at once primal and prim, are an example of her zany aesthetic. An "aesthetic of action pushed to physically strenuous extremes," in Sianne Ngai's description, "zany works of language tend to be filled with performative utterances and to bristle with markers of affective insistence: italics, dashes, exclamation points, full capitals." Situated in the mise-en-scène of the recorded song, rather than the printed page, Minaj skillfully performs this affective surplus, lacing her pugnacious, no-holds-barred verses with bursts of caps-locked emphases and fiery exclamation points. For listeners, the experience of hearing the relentless force of her brash verses in "Monster" is to be subject to a blistering array of accents, personalities, and cultural references, echoing how "the experience of zaniness is one of physical bombardment."[26]

Minaj's labor-intensive vocal mechanics here are a form of avatar production, albeit in the now hypertheatricalized sphere of a hip-hop single. Similar to Howardena Pindell in *Free, White, and 21*, she stages versions of herself whose borders bleed into each other mid-verse, even mid-syllable. Moreover, as the content of the lyrics above imply, wealth—hip-hop's hallmark—is paradoxically linked to Barbies, Willy Wonka, and discourses of fakeness. Forsaking authenticity, respectability, and even reality, Minaj and her mouthy avatars instead embrace (even boast about) their pointed failure to properly perform any of these attributes,[27] suturing hip-hop's typically masculine braggadocio to frenetic, if oddly juvenile, paeans to a plastic artificiality.

Minaj's verse (and the entirety of "Monster") crests at her concluding lines, as she raps rapid-fire: "Pink wig, thick ass, give 'em whiplash/I think big, get cash, make 'em blink fast/Now, look at what you just saw; This is what you live for/[screams] I'm a muthafuckin' monster!" Amid Minaj's skilled wielding of her "aural aesthetic," this brief, ecstatic, and improvisational scream stands out.[28] While an item of studio manipulation, partly manufactured by West's production, it is nonetheless "in the break" (to borrow Fred Moten's words) of this explosive eruption that some intriguing black performance work is occurring. Moreover, in light of its sounding toward the end of this book, this sonic rapture circles us back to another verbal outburst, in 1835, which revealed a very different type of objectification in the field of black performance art.

How do we connect Nicki Minaj's dissonant scream in "Monster," merging art and pop, to Joice Heth's shattering cri de coeur at the scene of her subjection recorded in a dubious medical journal, published in 1850? Is there any traction between the forcible disciplining of Heth in the field of performance and Minaj's, to borrow Adrian Piper's idiom, "voluntary self-objectification" in the aural sensorium?[29] Though markedly different, in tone and context, Heth's off-script shriek to white spectators that "dey make me say dat all the time: gimme drink!" or what I called a sonic of dissent, shares resonances with Minaj's climactic scream-verse. Counterintuitively, though, it is the aural residue of Heth's propulsive shouts in the nineteenth century, ones we cannot hear, that aid us in sorting through Minaj's vociferous "sonic text."[30]

In "Monster," we witness Nicki Minaj's return to and extension of an experimental grotesque aesthetic, one first perceived in Joice Heth's antebellum performance art. Art historian Kobena Mercer's scholarship on black avant-garde artists is utile as we begin to think through what such an aesthetic might both look and sound like. In his essay "Tropes of the Grotesque in the Black Avant-Garde," he discusses a trio of black American artists between the late 1960s and mid-1980s who, despite their dissimilarities, shared "a disruptive edge to the aesthetic strategies" they employed. These artists' works acted to "'de-familarise' or 'estrange' the visual text of blackness" through, among other tactics, "'shock' effects of perceptual disturbance and optical double take that reveal blackness as a polyvocal signifier."[31] If this purposeful estrangement from standard visual tropes of blackness could also describe Howardena Pindell's obstinately abstract art, the perceptual disturbance Mercer delineates is resonant in the aims of Adrian Piper's provocative performances as well. I would like to conceive of Minaj's vocal hyperexpressivity and Heth's corporeal spectacularity in a similar aesthetic register, both moving outside of prototypical and parochial notions of blackness via performances of black monstrosity. In both cases, moreover, this black grotesque aesthetic was not simply vocal but visually performed as well. Rejecting formalist notions of beauty as the aesthetic ideal, these black objects-cum-performers instead linger (forcibly or not) in the space of the abject.

The genre of the grotesque is buttressed by cultural anomalies that refuse to stay within the boundaries of tautly delimited categories and, instead, in Leonard Cassuto's words, consistently "resist integration. "It consequently questions the basis on which knowledge rests."[32] The category of the grotesque is socially constructed and constantly shifting, disrupting order while pivoting away from the normal, and even from the "human" altogether. However, when the difference that is perceived becomes *racial* difference, the disorder posed by the grotesque is amplified and, as history has shown, dealt with more severely. The racial grotesque in the United States has historically depended on a willful objectification of human beings, efforts to render people (especially those of darker, non-European descent) not simply as inferior, but also not fully human—or, in Alexander G. Weheliye's terms, as not-quite-humans and nonhumans.[33] This "thingification"[34] of humans is itself an impossibility that, as Cassuto notes, never fully succeeds. Regardless, those proponents of human subjection continued to manipulate the grotesque—most especially its abilities to challenge cultural perceptions and subvert classificatory systems—for sordid uses; this is emblematized most nefariously by the dramaturgical enactment of the freak show. Freak shows repositioned "figures at the borders of citizenship," such as the piebald bodies of "white negroes," not simply as cultural deviations ripe for exhibition on the basis of their nonmembership and divergent appearance but as lesser bodies—freaks—in the so-called natural order, and hence grotesque.[35]

These trends, recall, surfaced in this book's very beginnings, in the exhibitions of Joice Heth as George Washington's ostensible nursemaid; the designation of Heth as both biological aberration *and* national maternal icon solidified the simultaneous current of desire and repulsion that bolsters the grotesque. P. T. Barnum's savvy manipulation of grotesque aesthetics surfaced in his assiduous scripting of Heth as a relic from a faraway land (see her faux biography); in the purposeful distortion of Heth's visual likenesses in his autobiographies and her publicity materials—increasingly rendering her more bestial and cartoonish; and most notoriously, in his vicious removal of Heth's teeth, a heinous act designed to render her older—and, disturbingly, *more* grotesque—for curious mid-nineteenth-century white spectators-turned-scientists.

In contrast, a wildly different black grotesque aesthetic is on display in Kanye West's 2011 video for "Monster," in which tropes of monstrosity are resituated in postmillennial pop to bizarre, and misogynistic, effect. The Jake Nava–directed video, when partly leaked before its official release, was sharply criticized for its sexist representation of often seminude female bodies in compromising positions that, at worst, strongly suggested sexual violence toward women. Seemingly in response, the official video (which, as mentioned, was promptly banned by MTV) begins with an unusual and forcibly worded disclaimer: "The following content is in no way to be interpreted as misogynistic or negative towards any groups of people. It is an art piece and it shall be taken as such." This rather hollow statement does little to mitigate the sensational content that follows, let alone render it as "art." This is especially true of the video's first, and most disturbing, images: close-up shots of two scantily clad, lifeless women in mauve lingerie and high heels hanging from chain-link nooses, as wisps of smoke slowly rise around them. Especially lurid, these disturbing opening images, undeniably invoking charged histories of lynching, render the exceptionally violent objectification of women as mere erotic fashionable tableaux, setting the stage for the ghastly, and male chauvinistic, imagery that follows. A wider shot soon reveals a trio of hanging women that encircle and frame an opulently dressed Rick Ross, seated in a heavily gilded chair, smoking a cigar. Kanye West's verse that follows extends this gendered and unabashedly sexualized imagery. The camera toggles between shots of a shirtless West being frantically pawed at from behind by zombie-like women held back by an iron grate—zooming in on the contrast between the blood-red fingernails of the mostly white female hands and the bare, brown chest of West—and shots of him in a royal-blue satin bed, rearranging the limbs of two glassy-eyed and listless women in undergarments, who recline like attractive corpses.

These images hint at the fraught aesthetic dilemma of "Monster." On the one hand, the haunting visual vocabulary that pervades the video—cannibalistic zombies, werewolf-like beings, the elegant castle setting, and the overall macabre style—treads heavily in the gothic imagery of horror films, and is clearly designed to literalize the multiple allusions to monsters in the song's lyrical content. Its fleeting image of a set of computer-generated black female conjoined twins, moreover, traffics in the racial grotesque I described above; it recalls the so-called monstrous hybrids—such as piano prodigies Millie and Christine McKoy, the "Two-Headed Nightingale"—whose bodies rendered indistinct otherwise tightly guarded borders between the human and the mechanical, the real and the fake, the normal and the monstrous.[36] On the other hand, its sadistic visual depiction of women is unrelenting. An inexplicable shot of a nude woman in red heels, frozen as if by rigor mortis, sandwiched inside a couch during the verse by a tuxedoed Jay-Z, and a later shot of West, in a camel-colored coat, holding a dismembered female head are particularly salacious and egregious examples of this visual dynamic. If the single "Monster" is, in some ways, a revealing expression of West's expansive id, its sleek and yet crude visual accompaniment is especially alarming. It leads one to ask: is the imagined subjection of white women, rendered transparent in "Monster," an intrinsic part of the "beautiful and dark twisted fantasy" that is West's raison d'être?

In contrast, Nicki Minaj's brief appearance offers a muscular, and monstrous, performance of an altogether different order. She stages herself as dueling personas, yoking her vocal shock effects to a vivid visual representation of avatar production. Her aforementioned skill at character is put to apt use as she performs as two avatars simultaneously—both recognizable as Minaj. The first, a black-wigged and gold-teethed dominatrix-like figure with thigh-high patent leather boots brandishing a flogger, prances menacingly around a second figure, with a black hood obscuring her face, who is tied down to a chair. Eventually, the first figure takes off the black hood, to reveal the second persona: a very

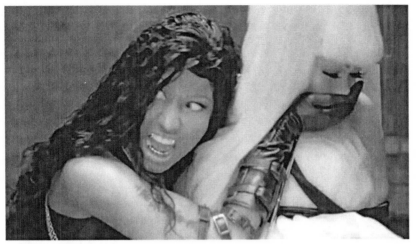

Figure C.3. Nicki Minaj, "Monster" (video still), 2012. Music video, 6 min. (dir. Jake Nava; comp. Kanye West, feat. Jay-Z, Rick Ross, Nicki Minaj, and Bon Iver).

feminine version of Minaj in a long hot pink wig dressed in a frothy white tulle dress and white platform heels. The personas trade barbs at each other, aggressively and ultimately humorously, the former embodying the ferocious monster-like persona in Minaj's verses, the latter performing the breathy voice of the girlish persona in her cameo. The volatile dominatrix avatar, seemingly exasperated by the taunts of her comely captive, attempts to silence her, cupping her leather gloved hands over her mouth before eventually placing the black hood back over her head and attempting to strangle her as Minaj's short yet vivid appearance ends.

Nicki Minaj's histrionics, far from ineffectual, reconfigure the grotesque as a vantage point through which to recast herself as a dynamic visual subject. Until her appearance, "Monster" trades in a blatant reification (and glamorization) of a grisly objectification; the members of its female supporting cast are reduced to docile, decorative, and variously compromised visual objects situated in its shadowy backgrounds. Firmly positioned in the foreground, Minaj disrupts and temporarily upends these scripted visual logics. She wields grotesque aesthetics as a skillful strategy of self-estrangement. In doing so, while Minaj is in accord with the polyglot meanings the grotesque suggests—its disruption of order, challenge to notions of the normal, and strange ability to evoke both fear and desire from audiences—her performance work in "Monster," I argue, goes further. Seemingly rupturing herself into a set of unruly black female avatars, a ferocious fanged creature and a persona elsewhere described as the Harajuku Barbie,[37] she enacts the disruptive aesthetic techniques—principally, defamiliarization and optical double-take—that Kobena Mercer describes as signature characteristics of black avant-garde praxis. Her multiplicity of selves, rather than simply self-fragmentation, elucidate how objecthood is harnessed here for self-actualizing effect, producing a fecund expansion of roles, especially those available to women in this fantastic fantasy. In that vein, her digital polymorphous selves recall how black performers, historically, have devised clever methods to create meanings from within problematic representational structures. Frame by frame, to borrow Michael Fried's language, Minaj is a "vexing stage presence"[38] that gets in our way, refusing—like minimalist sculptures—to cede space and hang silently on a museum wall, or abide by gendered and racialized preconceptions of her body's limits. Overtly theatrical and otherworldly, Minaj's verbal pyrotechnics and simulated doppelgangers propel us toward planets, and personas, yet undiscovered.

The Tipping Point: Performing Failure in Simone Leigh's *Breakdown*

If Simone Leigh—sculptor, video artist, and in her words, "preacher's daughter"—evades facile categorization, so too do her art objects. Leigh's oeuvre is a study in contradictions. Her ceramics employ strikingly beautiful materials—terra cotta, gold, graphite, platinum, and porcelain—often positioned with (or even sutured to) utterly banal forms such as toilet plunger handles, steel clamps, and brightly colored plastic buckets. They juxtapose the merely disposable with the purely ornamental, high art with the brutally utilitarian, and quotidian objects with surrealist fantasy. Her enlarged (and engorged) cowrie shell–like sculptures, with jagged ridges meant to resemble vagina dentata, are an example of this; their pointed antennae suggest their ontology as living things, receiving and transmitting information whether from an ancestral past, or conversely, a mythic future.[39] Similar themes were on display in her 2012 single-channel video projection *Uhura (Tanka)*, starring author Sharifa Rhodes-Pitts as a playful modern-day version of *Star Trek*'s Lieutenant Uhura. These sci-fi themes and Leigh's adroit praxis across video and ceramics prompted the *New Yorker*, on the occasion of her solo show at The Kitchen, to provocatively declare that if "Leigh's polyvalent approach had a label, it might be Afrofuturist Formalist Feminism."[40] This apt descriptor alludes to Leigh's widely disparate influences (*Mad Max*, AfriCobra, Gilbert and Sullivan, and punk icon Poly Styrene), her meticulous craftsmanship, and her broader interests in women's work, a theme certainly flickering around *Breakdown*'s coloraturas.

Through these lenses, we approach *Breakdown*. Just under ten minutes in length, the video was shot in the austere surroundings of New Covenant Temple, a church (where Leigh's mother worships) in the Manhattan neighborhood of Hamilton Heights. In the opening scene, we hear our protagonist, brought to life by mezzo-soprano Alicia Hall Moran, before we see her. Peering at the backlit surroundings of the church's upper balcony, we hear the sound of high heels before we espy a black woman in a sleeveless black dress descend halfway down the stairs before stopping. The camera zooms in and the subject, looking down, shrieks, "Oh my God!" raising her hand to the side of her face and cupping her mouth, as she says, mid-sob, "I'm so sorry." Anguished, she pleads, "Please. Strike that. Please don't. Please don't," before looking directly into the camera and urging, "Please don't look. Erase. Erase. Erase." While a specific allusion to the television character Mary Hartman's excruciating Technicolor meltdown in 1976,[41] the anonymous black woman's ache in *Breakdown* reads differently in these quiet sacrosanct surroundings with neither clues as to the source of her unnamed grief nor spectators to witness it.

In a rambling soliloquy, *Breakdown*'s main character speak-sings clusters of phrases—"It's just everything," "It's just too much"—alternating between utter dismay and flickers of joy. Traces of a smile occasionally surface, amid her usual scowl. She points at the camera accusingly, staring for an extended period, as she says quietly, "It's just," and then, in an extended riff that suggests a temper tantrum, belts repeatedly, "How am I going to go to the ballgame?!" and "I don't want to go!" After a series of vocal leaps and frenzied gestures, she takes an audible deep breath before singing what will become *Breakdown*'s climactic phrase: "Because

Figure C.4. Liz Magic Laser and Simone Leigh in collaboration with Alicia Hall Moran, *Breakdown* (video still), 2011. High-definition video, 6 min. Courtesy of Simone Leigh.

I've always done it. I've always done it. And I've been performing my whole life. Performing my whole life." As she sings these provocative confessions, Hall Moran eventually folds her outstretched arms across her chest as she peers at the camera to haltingly proclaim her perpetual self-performance. While singing the last phrase, she closes her eyes, tilts her head back, and lets her hands rapturously flutter behind her. Only five and half minutes into the video, Hall Moran's dexterous, emotionally and physically exhausting performance, in turn, leaves us as viewers equally drained by its intensity, its sheer volume, and its affective weight. As Jennifer Doyle suggests, in art that uses emotion as a form of "social engagement," "difficulty itself" is an "integral part of its emotional landscape."[42]

"There is a whole history of black performance," Leigh has remarked elsewhere, in Hall Moran's movements, specifically those "jazz hands," and her repeated refrain "I've been performing my whole life."[43] In *Breakdown*, we witness an archetypal black female subject's vexing despair. Her vocal virtuosity and her solitary performance echo the scripts of everyday life. In a counterintuitive move, Hall Moran's technical savvy is the instrument through which the meltdown of her avatar, a representational stand-in for diasporic black women, is conveyed. Vocally careening off course, reminiscent of Minaj and her sonic eruptions in "Monster," this persona conveys her downward spiral through her highly skilled vocality.

José Esteban Muñoz has discussed such a twinning, or "an aesthetic of simultaneous failure and virtuosity," as a central strategy in queer performance art.[44] "This is a modality of being off script, off page, which is not so much a failure to succeed as it is a failure to participate in a system of valuation that is predicated on exploitation and conformity."[45] Here, the refusal to obey logics of respectability and psychological stability is palpable in the character's almost blithe hysteria.[46] The character's operatic misbehaving is a rupture that punctures the tautly scripted understandings of proper behavior, particularly for black women. In addition, her going off the deep end, in all its beautiful incoherence, restages the defamiliarizing and estrangement techniques Kobena Mercer describes as a leitmotif of certain black avant-garde aesthetic practice. Suturing the "elegant and the grotesque in the act," like the eccentric black children performers in fin-de-siècle Europe described in Jayna Brown's scholarship, there is indeed a technique to the protagonist's social alienation redeployed through song, a method to *Breakdown*'s madness.[47]

Her lament—"I've been performing my whole life"—contains multiple layers and serves myriad functions. Returning to Muñoz, its declaration attests to a break in, even an escape from, normativity and, specifically, the roles imposed on black women. Indeed, as I noted earlier, it is a statement that could very well be spoken by any of the performers in this book. Though in an altogether different historical register than the Crafts' durational art of escape or Joice Heth's scripted act, Hall Moran's arias of despair nonetheless suggest the high stakes of black performance work.

In the final half of Leigh and video/performance artist Liz Magic Laser's sonic opus, this vocal laboring temporarily breaks down into nonsensical speech, and then ends with a final allusion to social deviance. Hall Moran, speak-singing now against the background of the church's intricate and gargantuan chandelier (New Covenant Temple was a theater before it was a church), sings "Because," extending the note, has a quick fitful aside (again, about not wanting to go to the ballgame), and then explodes in song about how she has always done it, but yet does not want to go. Even on screen, Hall Moran's voice reverberates off of the walls of the church and saturates the film with its propulsive force. Then, perhaps in a pantomime of instability, she hums to herself, murmuring and stuttering, sloshing sounds around her mouth, as if her breakdown has temporarily robbed her of speech itself. The screen goes dark and it seems that *Breakdown* will end here. But it does not. The camera pans back to Hall Moran on the balcony, disheveled and slightly hunched over, as she sings, "No metaphors. No grunts. No wiggles in the darkness of her soul. No grunts. No metaphors. No wiggles in the darkness of her soul." She repeats the line, then turns and slowly walks up the stairs. A stunning silence—except for the rhythmic clunk of her heels—envelops the sacred space as the screen slowly fades to black. These repurposed final lines are extracted from Anthony Harvey's 1967 film adaptation of LeRoi Jones's incendiary 1964 play *The Dutchman*.[48] There, the lines are part of a long, irate soliloquy on a subway car delivered by a character named Clay (Al Freeman Jr.) who, undergoing his own breakdown, drops his studied politeness and formal speech. Rage filled, at the end of his tirade, he announces, "Murder. Just murder! Would make us all sane."[49] Here, out of the mouth of *Breakdown*'s anonymous protagonist, Clay's vituperative remarks sound more resigned, suggesting that she has no words left to say (or sing) about her madness. She has, after all, been performing her entire life and will probably continue to. Those are the stunning conditions of being who she is.

Coda

I begin this final section with very brief considerations of three new figures— Brooklyn-based visual and performance artist Narcissister, Kismet Nuñez and her digital likenesses, and the infectious Cindi Mayweather, musician Janelle Monáe's dapper android double—to make evident the continued persistence of avatar production in three very different twenty-first-century creative projects that, in this ode to black performance art staged across two centuries, hint at its generative future iterations. If Minaj and Leigh execute daring, improvisational, and boundary-breaking artistic statements that demonstrate, with theatrical flair and exquisite technique, the aesthetic capabilities inherent

Figure C.5. Liz Magic Laser and Simone Leigh in collaboration with Alicia Hall Moran, *Breakdown* (video still), 2011. High-definition video, 6 min. Courtesy of Simone Leigh.

Figure C.6. Liz Magic Laser and Simone Leigh in collaboration with Alicia Hall Moran, *Breakdown* (video still), 2011. High-definition video, 6 min. Courtesy of Simone Leigh.

alternative modalities of being

in using the black female body as an insurgent instrument, these three mavericks stretch even further toward alternative modalities of being. Despite their divergent approaches, Narcissister and Nuñez—both of black and Puerto Rican descent—wield avatars to perform fierce alternatives for black diasporic women; their aggressive transubstantiations into many-masked personas and digital simulations are defiant, even narcissistic, acts of profound self-love. If love, meanwhile, is Cindi Mayweather's aspiration and also her deadly downfall, Monáe uses her doppelganger to evoke cross-temporal analogies between fungible objects, fugitivity, and forbidden love in her afrofuturist parable. In doing so, she suggests, akin to the late novelist Octavia Butler, that the shattering subjugation of yore does not dissolve and disappear in the future, but only gets reproduced, making avatars an attractive option when one's freedom is in a bind.

Narcissister is a still-anonymous artist, a former dancer with the Alvin Ailey American Dance Theater who majored in Afro-American studies at Brown University, who debuted her "avant-porn" at the Galapagos Art Space in Brooklyn in 2007.[50] Since then, she has performed at various New York City museums and experimental art spaces—several of them sites of the epochal performance works I have described—including the New Museum, MoMA PS1, The Kitchen, and the Studio Museum of Harlem, where she was featured in the exhibition *FORE* and its accompanying series of performance art, *perFOREmance*. In 2011, she was even featured on the television program *America's Got Talent*, briefly bringing her quirky abilities to a mainstream stage. In her acrobatic performances, she wears her signature double-faced mask—eerily resembling a lifeless Barbie—on her head as well as over her nether regions, repeatedly contorting her body to reveal all four mask faces; in swirling petticoats, she resembles a modern-day topsy-turvy doll come to life. In the humorous and mesmerizing performance I witnessed at Los Angeles's Human Resources Gallery in July 2013, she executed this art-dance-striptease to Diana Ross's "Upside Down" and Bill Withers' "Just the Two of Us." Meanwhile, in her crisp and colorful photography, Narcissister poses with a cornucopia of wigs and prosthetic breasts, while in her darkly comic video art she pulls flowers, clothes, and fruit out of fake orifices.[51] As Cesar Garcia writes, Narcissister's work confronts us with "bodies that urge, desire, pleasure, expose, consume, and

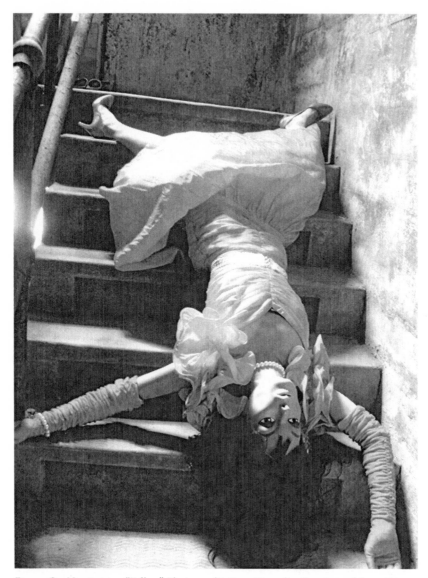

Figure C.7. Narcissister, "Fallen." Photo credit: Tony Stamolis. Courtesy of the artist and envoy enterprises, 2007.

indulge, and excrete, bodies that through the act of performance reclaim their agency while simultaneously liberating themselves from confining visual paradigms."[52]

In contrast, Kismet Nuñez exists entirely in virtual space on Tumblr, a microblogging platform and social networking website, and other digital universes. Nuñez is the creation of historian Jessica Marie Johnson, a self-described "black feminist/radical woman of color digital humanist and media maker."[53] Johnson writes as Nuñez and also operates, in her words, as a "'Fleshy Professional Avatar'—the person in the real world who is seen and heard and must pay bills and keep her clothes on."[54] Johnson manipulates a total of four digital beings—three alters (Pretty Magnolia, Zora Walker, and the Sable Fan Gyrl) who together contribute to the more substantive ego, Kismet Nuñez—across a collection of seven Tumblr pages, two Twitter accounts, and two Facebook pages. Nuñez is creator and founder of I Wanna Live Productions, a "social media collective, specializing in radical black gyrl media" and "utter disruption of the archive, academy and hu-MAN-ity as we know and understand it."[55] In a dynamic merging of new media and black feminist politics, Nuñez and her erudite reincarnations (or #AntiJemimas, to use her term) attend to the preservation of black female subjectivity, urging sex positivity and self-care.[56] The performance of these digital avatars, Nuñez emphasizes, is about "multiple selves, not about being fractured."[57] Fiona M. Barnett concurs, arguing that the "multimodal AntiJemimas universe" is "an archive of notes, images, quotations, documents, media files, and images, but it is also the imagination of a self and a radical community of selves coming together to be both archived and imagined into being at the same time."[58] This project also demonstrates, as Lisa Nakamura writes, how women of color, long the objects of interactivity, are using the abundance of new media possibilities to "negotiate their identities as digital objects and in incremental ways move them toward digital subjecthood."[59]

Finally (and fittingly), musician Janelle Monáe manipulates avatar production for the future. Her conceptual opus *Metropolis: Suite I (The Chase)*, an afrofuturist parable set in the year 2719, positions the avatar Cindi Mayweather—pictured on the cover as a white-faced android version of Monáe missing her entire right arm—as a modern-day "runaway fugitive," fleeing her "immediate disassembly" by the Wolf-

NUÑEZ DAUGHTER

Figure C.8. Kismet Nuñez, 2008. Courtesy of Jessica Marie Johnson.

masters for breaking "the rules" and falling in love with a human named Anthony Greendown.[60] In the short film for the single "Many Moons," Mayweather sings her own "freedom dreams" (to borrow Robin D. G. Kelley's phrase) at the annual android auction. The song asks if we, the audience, are bold enough to reach for love despite the consequences; for her, the stakes are high. Mayweather's cross-species love imperils her freedom and, hence, her life. The conclusion of the video, after her surreal murder in the midst of a performance, are words attributed to her: "I imagined many moons in the sky lighting my way to freedom."[61] Janelle Monáe's Cindi Mayweather character has striking parallels to all the figures in this book: like Craft, Mayweather seeks an escape from slavery; following Heth, Pindell, and Minaj, Monáe creates female-to-female avatars; social alienation figures prominently in Mayweather's performance, similar to those of Piper, Pindell, and Leigh; her image mirrors portraits with missing/camouflaged limbs, such as Craft's, or Minaj's cover for *Pink Friday*, in which she appears as an armless Barbie; finally, "Many Moons" is a provocative merging of music and video art, echoing the works of Minaj and Leigh. In the staging of Mayweather's imperiled bid for freedom, Monáe's performance suggests, performing objecthood is an ever-tenuous process that, even in its failures, dramatizes both the conditions necessary for the emergence of black female subjectivity and the stultifying constrictions that threaten its extinguishment.

* * *

Ultimately, my aim is that the densely layered discussions embedded in *Embodied Avatars* create a robust infrastructure for pondering the unique and recurring relationship between objecthood, black performance art, and avatar production in the construction and deformation of black female subjectivities. Both overtly political and, at other moments, less obviously so, this agile assemblage of expressive self-stagings recasts, if only temporarily, the highly charged terms by which audiences—be they nineteenth-century abolitionists or twentieth-century art world cognoscenti—viewed and interpreted these women's singular bodies. If these polymorphous, and paradoxical, performances confounded and even harshly rebuked spectators, they also reoriented the movements of those who brazenly put their bodies on the line for the sake of art and freedom. In their risky physical and artistic wanderings, these black female flâneuses provocatively remapped the ever-precarious pathways their liminal bodies traveled and acted in while also rerouting their access to, and mobility across, distinct and seemingly entrenched aesthetic categories. In addition, I have revealed how these artists and performers have often acted in concert with male counterparts, in ways both ameliorative and corrosive, such as the late Sol LeWitt's early tutelage of and financial assistance to Adrian Piper, William Craft's role as a supporting actor in his wife's perilous escape acts, and, of course, the sinister and sadistic dealings of Joice Heth's Svengali, P. T. Barnum.

In closing, I am conscious of an altogether more pressing theme: historical erasure. If the artists in the second half of this book seem all too aware of this predicament—hence, Piper's voluminous writings and Pindell's extensive records—the performers in the first half of the book were neither able to ensure, nor closely protect, their obsolescence. Joice Heth, reduced to an index card–sized gallery tag in the New-York Historical Society's popular *Slavery in New York* exhibition, is but one example of this distressing dilemma. Still, as I learned on a return visit to Fales Library at NYU, the storing of memorabilia, on the precondition of archival permanence, does not guarantee historical accuracy. As I leafed through the miscellaneous photo negatives, newspaper printings, and other esoterica collected in the numerous files of the A.I.R. Gallery, I was repeatedly struck by *how* Howardena Pindell was represented. Barely visible in the dusky edges of several black-and-white photographs, she is sometimes recognizable mostly by her professorial glasses and the static mass of her Afro, while in others, the barely discernable features of her visage are almost indistinguishable from the recesses of the doorway she is standing by. This presence via absence, though, is most explicit in another photograph, where Pindell, her back turned to the viewer, is flanked by five women—all fellow members of A.I.R, all white. Written on a Post-it note, affixed on top of the photograph, are the last names of each member above arrows pointing down toward the hastily drawn inky outlines of each corresponding figure in the photograph. All the women are named, all except Pindell; she remains unmarked and unidentifiable, almost invisible, except if one knows to look for her.[62]

Eerily similar to Pindell's shadowy appearances in the A.I.R. Gallery's visual ephemera, the multitudinous selves of the black female performers I amass here are hiding in plain view. Intermittently visible in the far corners of our perception, they are positioned just outside the visual frame, whether by design or historical circumstance. In their sly reincarnations, these polymaths, ever attuned to their marginality, utilize the tools of performance art to partially defy it, becoming obdurate and obstreperous objects. In their shape-shifting qualities, they collectively forsake ontological certitude for the variously embodied.

NOTES

INTRODUCTION

1 Lorraine O'Grady, "Mlle Bourgeoise Noire: Performance Synopsis," 2007. Unless otherwise noted, all quotations from this performance are from this source. http://www.lorraineogrady.com/mlle-bourgeoise-noire (accessed February 14, 2014).

2 Founded by filmmaker Linda Goode Bryant in 1974 on West 57th Street (known as New York's venerable gallery row), Just Above Midtown was a key site in the late 1970s and 1980s New York arts scene, supporting an eclectic group of artists—many of them video and performance artists—including David Hammons, Lawrence Weiner, Joan Jonas, Linda Nishio, Howardena Pindell, and Performance Space 122 cofounder Peter Rose. By 1985, in addition to publishing a quarterly journal, *B Culture*, JAM sponsored a laboratory program for artists and a dance series for choreographers (*Retakes*) to develop new works. A year later, JAM hosted a four-week series exploring the "rap esthetic." Downtown Flyers and Invitations Collection, ca. 1980–1990, MSS 119, Fales Library and Special Collections, New York University, Box 2, Folder 234. Historically, JAM also is particularly important in introducing black West Coast artists to the New York art scene, several of whom participated in its inaugural exhibition, *Synthesis*. Kellie Jones, "Now Dig This! An Introduction," in Kellie Jones, ed., *Now Dig This! Art and Black Los Angeles, 1960–1980* (Los Angeles: Hammer Museum; New York: Delmonico Books, 2011), 27.

3 Linda M. Montano, "Lorraine O'Grady," *Performance Artists Talking in the Eighties* (Berkeley and Los Angeles: University of California Press, 2000), 403, 404.

4 *Personae*, which ran September 19–November 12, 1981, was dedicated to exploring how artists "in making or presenting their work, assume specific alter-egos or personae (human or animal, fictitious or historical) that serve as vehicles for greater freedom of expression. 'Persona' explores the territory of the surrogate self, alter ego, disguise or alias." Mlle. Bourgeoise Noire derisively termed it the "Nine White Personae show." Exhibition details available at http://archive. newmuseum.org/index.php/Detail/Occurrence/Show/occurrence_id/43 (accessed February 14, 2014).

5 Coco Fusco, "Performance and the Power of the Popular," in Catherine Ugwu, ed., *Let's Get It On: The Politics of Black Performance* (London: Institute of Contemporary Arts; Seattle: Bay Press, 1995), 158; Paul Schimmel, *Out of Actions:*

Between Performance and the Object, 1949–1979 (Los Angeles: Museum of
Contemporary Art; New York: Thames & Hudson, 1998), 11.

6 The erasure of black women artists within rapidly calcifying historiographies of
feminist art briefly took center stage in the late 2000s. The occasion was "The
Feminist Future: Theory and Practice in the Visual Arts," a sold-out two-day
symposium at the Museum of Modern Art (MoMA) in New York City, held in late
January 2007. It coincided with the debut, two months later, of not one but two
museum surveys of feminist art, *WACK! Art and the Feminist Revolution* at the Los
Angeles County Museum of Art (LACMA) and *Global Feminisms* at the Brooklyn
Museum. In an audience that was "almost entirely white," only one of the promi-
nent artists, critics, and art historians chosen to speak, Kenyan-born artist
Wangechi Mutu, was black. Holland Carter, "Feminist Art Finally Takes Center
Stage," *New York Times*, January 29, 2007. "I feel like I'm gatecrashing a reunion,"
Mutu mused during her opening remarks. At the end of her presentation, in a
stinging reproof to the "inequity" of both MoMA and the feminist movement writ
large, Mutu staged a performative rejoinder of her own: she read a list of thirty-two
prominent professors, curators, artists, and graduate students—all black diasporic
women—who had not been invited to speak. "Invite them next time; I can't be the
only one here," she sternly admonished the crowd at the conclusion of her talk.
Mutu's speech can be viewed in its entirety at the MoMA website: http://www.
moma.org/explore/multimedia/videos/16/179 (accessed February 3, 2014).

7 *Embodied Avatars* builds on the groundwork laid by two important museum
publications on black performance art—in the United Kingdom and the United
States, respectively—while expanding upon the primary focus of both (late-
twentieth-century contemporary art). The first, *Let's Get It On: The Politics of Black
Performance*, focuses on black British and American live art in the decade prior to
1995. The provocative use of "black" to describe a broad coalition of African, South
Asian, Caribbean, and other immigrant groups mirrors the term's charged use by
artists in 1980s Britain to describe not simply identity, but an oppositional aesthetic
approach. See Coco Fusco, "A Black Avant-Garde? Notes on Black Audio Film
Collective and Sankofa," in *English Is Broken Here: Notes on Cultural Fusion in the
Americas* (New York: New Press, 1995). For more on black Britain, the cultural
politics of diaspora, and its relationship to black expressive cultures, see Paul
Gilroy, *There Ain't No Black in the Union Jack: The Cultural Politics of Race and
Nation* (1987; Chicago: University of Chicago Press, 1991), especially chap. 5; Stuart
Hall, "Cultural Identity and Diaspora," reprinted in Nicholas Mirzoeff, ed.
Diaspora and Visual Culture: Representing Africans and Jews (London and New
York: Routledge, 2000), 21–33. *Let's Get It On* situates an artistic form "without a
historical context or critical framework" that is "often perceived as operating at the
margins of society," while also insisting that this form, as Fusco argued, is far more
than the misbegotten product of multiculturalism and the concomitant death of
traditional "high art." Ugwu, "Introduction," *Let's Get It On*, 10; Fusco,
"Performance and the Power of the Popular," *Let's Get It On*, 158.

The second, *Radical Presence: Black Performance in Contemporary Art*, is the first comprehensive survey of black performance from the 1960s to 2012. Using the musical scores of underrecognized Fluxus artist Benjamin Patterson as a point of departure, the exhibition and collection of essays centers on "black visual artists working in, with, and around performance." Valerie Cassel Oliver, "Acknowledgments," *Radical Presence: Black Performance in Contemporary Art* (Houston: Contemporary Arts Museum; New York: Distributed Arts Publishers, 2013), 8. *Radical Presence* was first shown November 17, 2012–February 16, 2013, at the Contemporary Arts Museum Houston. The show's extensive tour included the Grey Art Gallery at New York University, New York; Studio Museum of Harlem, New York; and Walker Art Center, Minneapolis. *Radical Presence* highlights the risks of black performance work, specifically, its physically laborious intensity and the potential danger of staging bodily acts not recognized by the public as art; these works, the contributors reiterate, receive scant attention in art history. This last point is directly relevant to the artists I reckon with here, though I diverge in casting this discussion backward in time—while narrowing its focus to black women performers—to interrogate the limits these cultural subjects encountered and pushed against in becoming art objects.

8 RoseLee Goldberg, *Performance Art: From Futurism to the Present* (1979; New York: Thames & Hudson, 2001), 14, 16.

9 The contours of this book are indebted, of course, to the abundant scholarship on feminist art and feminist performance art. These include Lynda Hart and Peggy Phelan, eds., *Acting Out: Feminist Performances* (Ann Arbor: University of Michigan Press, 1993); Lisa Gabrielle Mack, ed., *WACK! Art and the Feminist Revolution* (Cambridge, MA: MIT Press; Los Angeles: Museum of Contemporary Art, 2007); Helena Rickett, ed., *Art and Feminism* (2001; New York: Phaidon, 2012); and Josephine Withers, "Feminist Performance Art: Performing, Discovering, Transforming Ourselves," in Norma Broude and Mary D. Garrard, eds., *The Power of Feminist Art: The American Movement of the 1970s, History and Impact* (New York: Harry N. Abrams, 1994), 158–73. For a very brief overview, see Sue-Ellen Case, *Feminism and Theater* (New York: Methuen, 1988), 56–61.

10 Coco Fusco, "The Other History of Intercultural Performance," *TDR: The Drama Review* 38, no. 1 (Spring 1994): 143–67; Amelia Jones, *Body Art/Performing the Subject* (Minneapolis: University of Minnesota Press, 1998), 8. For discussion of "body art" versus "performance art," see pgs. 12–14.

11 Toni Cade Bambara, *The Black Woman: An Anthology* (New York: New American Library, 1970), 7; Hazel V. Carby, "White Woman Listen! Black Feminism and the Boundaries of Sisterhood," in Houston A. Baker, Manthia Diawara, and Ruth H. Lindeborg, eds., *Black British Cultural Studies: A Reader* (1982; Chicago: University of Chicago Press, 1996); Bibi Bakare-Yusuf, "The Economy of Violence: Black Bodies and the Unspeakable Terror," in Janet Price and Margit Shildrick, eds., *Feminist Theory and the Body: A Reader* (New York: Routledge, 1999), 313.

12 Lowery Stokes Sims, "Aspects of Performance in the Work of Black American Women Artists," in Arlene Raven, Cassandra Langer, and Joanna Frueh, eds., *Feminist Art Criticism: An Anthology* (Ann Arbor: University of Michigan Research Press, 1988), 207, 208.

13 Harry J. Elam Jr., "The Black Performer and the Performance of Blackness: *The Escape; or, A Leap to Freedom* by William Wells Brown and *No Place to Be Somebody* by Charles Gordone," in Harry Elam Jr. and David Krasner, eds., *African American Performance and Theater History* (Oxford: Oxford University Press, 2001), 289.

14 Goldberg, *Performance Art*, 7.

15 Part of the work lies, as James Harding suggests, in forcing avant-garde histories to rethink themselves along gendered lines, focusing less on how women fit into an already existing avant-garde than in how they shift our understandings of it. See James M. Harding, *Cutting Performances: Collage Events, Feminist Artists, and the American Avant-Garde* (Ann Arbor: University of Michigan Press, 2012). The recognition of a black avant-garde, Fred Moten argues, depends on a similar conceptual shift, challenging the presumption that the very term itself is an oxymoron. See Fred Moten, *In the Break: The Aesthetics of the Black Radical Tradition* (Minneapolis: University of Minnesota Press, 2003), 32.

16 Sally Banes, *Greenwich Village 1963: Avant-Garde Performance and the Effervescent Body* (Durham, NC: Duke University Press, 1993), 111. Fred Moten's *In the Break*, in its exploration of the black avant-garde in music and literature of the 1950s and 1960s, is in many ways a corrective to the focus on white avant-garde artists that dominate Banes's text.

17 Heresies Collective, a feminist art collective, published a journal, *Heresies: A Feminist Publication on Art and Politics*, from 1977 to 1992. Ironically, while leafing through an old copy of the journal—*Heresies #8 (Third World Women)*—O'Grady reencountered Adrian Piper's work and was shocked to "discover she was black, and that her socio-cultural experience was a duplicate of my own—I can't tell you what an effect that had on me! From that moment, my acquaintance with Adrian Piper and her brilliantly provocative art helped me stop feeling alone." Grassroots art publications like *Heresies*, thus, served an important role, even if they were not without their own tensions and biases. Quoted above from Lorraine O'Grady, "Thinking Out Loud: Performance Art and My Place in It" (unpublished essay, 1983).

18 Judith Butler, "Performative Acts and Gender Constitution: An Essay in Phenomenology and Feminist Theory," *Theatre Journal* 40, no. 4 (Dec. 1988): 520.

19 Specifically, I am indexing colonization's ability to render the native a mere "instrument of production" for the colonizer, a process that results in his tragic *thingification*. See Aimé Césaire, *Discourse on Colonialism* (1955; New York: Monthly Review Press, 2000), 42. Similarly, the white gaze's reduction of the black man into a negative sign in the field of vision renders him, in Frantz Fanon's words, "an object among objects." See Frantz Fanon, *Black Skin, White Masks* (1952; New York: Grove Press, 2008), 89.

20 Saidiya V. Hartman, *Scenes of Subjection: Terror, Slavery, and Self-Making in Nineteenth-Century America* (New York: Oxford University Press, 1997), 56. Hartman's phrase "performing blackness" is of particular use here in articulating the difficulties in imagining blackness, performance, and agency together alongside a history of abjection and social dominance. In her words, "'performing blackness' conveys both the cross-purposes and the circulation of various modes of performance and performativity that concern the production of racial meaning and subjectivity, the nexus of race, subjection, and spectacle, the forms of racial and race(d) pleasure, enactments of white dominance and power, and the reiteration and/or rearticulation of the conditions of enslavement. It is hoped that 'performing blackness' is not too unwieldy and, at the same time, that this unruliness captures the scope and magnitude of the performative as a strategy of power and tactic of resistance" (57).

21 This notion of agency is paraphrased from Jane Bennett. See her brief but illuminating discussion of agency—both human and her attempt to stretch it to nonhuman materialities—in her *Vibrant Matter: A Political Ecology of Things* (Durham, NC: Duke University Press, 2010), 28–31.

22 Tavia Nyong'o, "Between the Body and the Flesh: Sex and Gender in Black Performance Art," in *Radical Presence*, 26; Coco Fusco, "The Bodies That Were Not Ours," in *The Bodies That Were Not Ours: And Other Writings* (New York: Routledge, 2001), 3–17.

23 Hortense J. Spillers, "Mama's Baby, Papa's Maybe: An American Grammar Book," *Diacritics* 17, no. 2 (Summer 1987): 67. Spillers's scholarship is particularly important, since as others have argued, black women are conspicuously absent in *Black Skin, White Masks*; Fanon infamously stated, "I know nothing about her." See Lola Young, "Missing Persons: Fantasizing black women in *Black Skin, White Masks*," in Alan Read, ed., *The Fact of Blackness: Frantz Fanon and Visual Representation* (Seattle: Bay Press; London: Institute of Contemporary Arts, 1996), 86–101; Nicole R. Fleetwood, *Troubling Vision: Performance, Visuality, and Blackness* (Chicago: University of Chicago Press, 2011), 224.

24 Mel Y. Chen, *Animacies: Biopolitics, Racial Mattering, and Queer Affect* (Durham, NC: Duke University Press, 2012), 40.

25 Darieck Scott, *Extravagant Abjection: Blackness, Power, and Sexuality in the African American Literary Imagination* (New York: New York University Press, 2010).

26 I borrow the wording of this now-rote binary from the title of the third chapter, "Objectified Bodies or Embodied Subjects?" in Gen Doy, *Black Visual Culture: Modernity and Postmodernity* (London and New York: I.B. Tauris, 2000). This dialectic also surfaces in literary discourses, particularly around slave narratives. Print literatures, especially in the form of slave narratives written in the first person, offer the promise of the formerly enslaved (i.e., abject *objects*) transforming into full-fledged citizens (i.e., liberated *subjects*). See Henry Louis Gates, *The Signifying Monkey: A Theory of African-American Literary Criticism* (New York: Oxford University Press, 1989), 129.

27 Scott, *Extravagant Abjection*, 13. Similarly, other recent work has argued for more complicated understandings of abjection, pleasure, power, shame, and subjectivity's intertwining as well as what constitutes agency, resistance, and subversion. See Nguyen Tan Hoang, *A View from the Bottom: Asian American Masculinity and Sexual Representation* (Durham, NC: Duke University Press, 2014), 20; Amber Jamilla Musser, *Sensational Flesh: Race, Power, and Masochism* (New York: New York University Press, 2014); Juana María Rodríguez, *Sexual Futures, Queer Gestures, and Other Latina Longings* (New York: New York University Press, 2014); Christina Sharpe, *Monstrous Intimacies: Making Post-Slavery Subjects* (Durham, NC: Duke University Press, 2010); Alexander G. Weheliye, *Habeas Viscus: Racializing Assemblages, Biopolitics, and Black Feminist Theories of the Human* (Durham, NC: Duke University Press, 2014), 2.

28 Michael Fried, "Art and Objecthood," in Gregory Battcock, ed., *Minimal Art: A Critical Anthology* (1968; Berkeley and Los Angeles: University of California Press, 1995), 128. For a brief gloss of Fried's objecthood alongside Adrian Piper's notion of objecthood in her *Food for the Spirit* performance, within the frame of consumption and aesthetic exchange, see Patrick Anderson, *So Much Wasted: Hunger, Performance, and the Morbidity of Resistance* (Durham, NC: Duke University Press, 2010), 85–91. For a different take on objecthood and consumption—routed through the deviant object relations inherent in the vexed figure of the hoarder—see Scott Herring, *The Hoarders: Material Deviance in American Culture* (Chicago: University of Chicago Press, 2014).

29 Bruno Latour, *We Have Never Been Modern*, trans. Catherine Porter (1991; Cambridge, MA: Harvard University Press, 1993), 10; Bill Brown, "Reification, Reanimation, and the American Uncanny," *Critical Inquiry* 32, no. 2 (2006): 207, 179. See also Bill Brown, *A Sense of Things: The Object Matter of American Literature* (Chicago: University of Chicago Press, 2004).

30 Mel Y. Chen uses this evocative phrase to describe the focus of new materialisms, or the ways scholars are working through "posthumanist understandings of the significance of stuff, objects, commodities, and things, creating a fertile terrain of thought about object life." I redeploy it here for its obvious resonances with my own project. See Chen, *Animacies*, 5.

31 For more on the term *actuant*, see Bruno Latour, "On Actor-Network Theory: A Few Clarifications," *Soziale Welt* 47, no. 4 (1996): 369–81; *Politics of Nature: How to Bring the Sciences into Democracy*, trans. Catherine Porter (Cambridge, MA: Harvard University Press, 2004); Bennett, *Vibrant Matter*, 119.

32 In 1985, the video game *Ultima IV: Quest of the Avatar* was released, in which the player's quest was to become an "Avatar." The same year, Chip Morningstar, a designer of Lucasfilms's *Habitat*, a role-playing game released a year later, first used "avatar" to describe a virtual representation of a player.

33 B. Coleman, *Hello Avatar: Rise of the Networked Generation* (Cambridge, MA: MIT Press, 2011), 46, 12.

34 Carla L. Peterson, *Doers of the Word: African-American Women Speakers and Writers in the North, 1830–1880* (New Brunswick, NJ: Rutgers University Press, 1995), 18; Hazel V. Carby, *Reconstructing Womanhood: The Emergence of the Afro-American Woman Novelist* (New York: Oxford University Press, 1987), 6.

35 Jayna Brown, *Babylon Girls: Black Women Performers and the Shaping of the Modern* (Durham, NC: Duke University Press, 2008), 129, 227.

36 Sianne Ngai, *Ugly Feelings* (Cambridge, MA: Harvard University Press, 2005), 117.

37 Stuart Hall, "What Is This 'Black' in Black Popular Culture?" in Gina Dent, ed., *Black Popular Cultures* (Seattle: Bay Press, 1992), 27.

38 Adrian Piper, "Preparatory Notes for *The Mythic Being*," in *Out of Order, Out of Sight*, Vol. 1: *Selected Writings in Meta-Art, 1968–1992* (Cambridge, MA: MIT Press, 1996), 109.

39 This term is Bruno Latour's. See Latour, *We Were Never Modern*, 75.

40 Ann Weinstone, *Avatar Bodies: A Tantra for Posthumanism* (Minneapolis: University of Minnesota, 2004), 24; Rebecca Schneider, *Performing Remains: Art and War in Times of Theatrical Reenactment* (New York: Routledge, 2011), 10.

41 Schneider, *Performing Remains*, 24.

42 Tavia Nyong'o, *The Amalgamation Waltz: Race, Performance, and the Ruses of Memory* (Minneapolis: University of Minnesota Press, 2009), 138.

43 Weinstone, *Avatar Bodies*, 41.

44 Peggy Phelan, *Unmarked: The Politics of Performance* (New York: Routledge, 1993), 146.

45 José Esteban Muñoz, *Cruising Utopia: The Then and There of Queer Futurity* (New York: New York University Press, 2009), 65; Joseph Roach, *Cities of the Dead: Circum-Atlantic Performance* (New York: Columbia University Press, 1996), xii; Schneider, *Performing Remains*, 102.

46 Roach, *Cities of the Dead*, 13. For more on restored behaviors, see Richard Schechner, *Between Theater and Anthropology* (Philadelphia: University of Pennsylvania Press, 1985), especially chap. 2.

47 Moten, *In the Break*, 5.

48 A focus on the "live" in performance art, Frazer Ward observes, overemphasizes the initial moment over its "temporally extended effects," ignoring how meaning and value accrue over time. He argues for a more complex view of performance art's duration, one that recognizes how performance art manifests not just one time, but rather occupies a "temporality of double experience," which would acknowledge the extended time of its reception beyond the actual event. Put simply, "performance (with its documentation) projects a virtual audience (or public, or community) across time." See his *No Innocent Bystanders: Performance Art and the Audience* (Hanover, NH: Dartmouth College Press, 2012), 153, 13, 12. Meiling Cheng makes a similar argument. In her words, "To be remembered, a performance has to live at least twice. For the first time, a performance lives an ephemeral life in actuality, its mortality consumed by the performing artists and their spectators for a designated duration." A performance "ensures its possible

resurrection by leaving multimedia traces" that can be reassembled, thus ensuring its "potential to live again, posthumously, in virtuality." See her *In Other Los Angeles: Multicentric Performance Art* (Berkeley and Los Angeles: University of California Press, 2002), xxv–xxvi.

49 Amelia Jones, "'Presence' in Absentia: Experiencing Performance as Documentation," *Art Journal* 56, no. 4 (Winter 1997): 13.

50 This language is Barbara Kirshenblatt-Gimblett's. The full quote is as follows: "The field of Performance Studies takes performance as an organizing concept for the study of a wide range of behavior. A postdiscipline of inclusions, Performance Studies sets no limit on what can be studied in terms of medium and culture. Nor does it limit the range of approaches that can be taken. A provisional coalescence on the move, Performance Studies is more than the sum of its inclusions." See her "Performance Studies," Rockefeller Foundation, Culture and Creativity, September 1999. This report is available at http://www.nyu.edu/classes/bkg/issues/rock2.htm (accessed March 16, 2014).

51 Sianne Ngai, *Our Aesthetic Categories: Zany, Cute, Interesting* (Cambridge, MA: Harvard University Press, 2012), 18.

52 Darby English, *How to See a Work of Art in Total Darkness* (Cambridge, MA: MIT Press, 2007), 18.

53 E. Patrick Johnson, *Appropriating Blackness: Performance and the Politics of Authenticity* (Durham, NC: Duke University Press, 2003), 9; Stephanie Leigh Batiste, *Darkening Mirrors: Imperial Representation in Depression-Era African American Performance* (Durham, NC: Duke University Press, 2011), 233. For an early articulation of black performance studies as a site of intellectual inquiry, see E. Patrick Johnson, "Black Performance Studies: Genealogies, Politics, Futures," in D. Soyini Madison and Judith Hamera, eds., *The Sage Handbook of Performance Studies* (Thousand Oaks, CA: Sage Publications, 2006), 446–63. For more on black performance theory, see Thomas F. DeFrantz and Anita Gonzalez, eds., *Black Performance Theory* (Durham, NC: Duke University Press, 2014).

54 For more on fabulation in the archive, see Saidiya Hartman's "Venus in Two Acts," *Small Axe* 26 (June 2008): 1–14.

55 By "worlding," I mean to signal what José Esteban Muñoz has described, by way of Jack Smith and Carmelita Tropicana, as the world-making potential of queer performance art; in short, "performance art changes one's perception of the world." See José Esteban Muñoz, *Disidentifications: Queers of Color and the Performance of Politics* (Minneapolis: University of Minnesota Press), xiii.

CHAPTER 1. MAMMY MEMORY

1 According to Barnum, prior to his purchase of her, Heth was exhibited in Philadelphia's Masonic Hall by "R.W. Lindsay of Jefferson County, Kentucky." In a contract dated June 10th, 1835 (and reproduced inside his biography), Barnum purchased Heth for the reduced price of a thousand dollars from Lindsay and John S. Bowling "for the term of twelve months to participate equally in the gains

and losses in exhibiting the African woman, Joice Heth, in and amongst the cities of the United States." See Phineas T. Barnum, *The Life of P.T. Barnum Written by Himself* (1855; Chicago: University of Illinois Press, 2000), 148, 151.

2 For more on Heth's engagement at Niblo's, see Matthew Goodman, *The Sun and the Moon: The Remarkable True Account of Hoaxers, Showmen, Dueling Journalists, and Lunar Man-Bats in Nineteenth-Century America* (New York: Basic Books, 2008), 120–25.

3 "Joice Heth," *Salem Gazette*, September 8, 1835, 2.

4 A. H. Saxon, *P. T. Barnum: The Legend and the Man* (New York: Columbia University Press, 1989), 74.

5 "Joice Heth," *Baltimore and Gazette Daily Advertiser*, August 13, 1835, 2.

6 Beverly Guy-Shetfall, "The Body Politic: Black Female Sexuality and the Nineteenth-Century Euro-American Imagination," in *Skin Deep, Spirit Strong: The Black Female Body in American Culture*, ed. Kimberly Wallace-Sanders (Ann Arbor: University of Michigan Press, 2002), 18. On the continued legacy of Sarah Baartman, see Deborah Willis, ed., *Black Venus 2010: They Called Her "Hottentot"* (Philadelphia: Temple University Press, 2010). For a poetic linking of Heth, Baartman, and other spectacles of black womanhood, see Nikky Finney, "The Greatest Show on Earth," in *Black Venus*, 147–48. For a discussion of J. Marion Sims's experiments on black women, see Harriet A. Washington, *Medical Apartheid: The Dark History of Medical Experimentation on Black Americans from Colonial Times to Present* (New York: Doubleday, 2006).

7 Diana Taylor, *The Archive and the Repertoire: Performing Cultural Memory in the Americas* (Durham, NC: Duke University Press, 2003), 28. The "scenario," Taylor writes, includes "features well theorized in literary analysis, such as narrative and plot, but demands we also pay attention to millieux and corporeal behaviors such as gestures, attitudes, and tones not reducible to language."

8 Raymond Williams, *Marxism and Literature* (1977; New York: Oxford University Press, 2009), 134. My aim, in filtering mammy memory through Williams's "structures of feeling" is to draw our attention to the shifting ideologies under-girding mammy memory, particularly its ambivalent racial impulses. This ambiguity is akin to the paradoxical desire for and aversion to the "Africanist" subject that, according to Toni Morrison, was a foundational presence that haunts American literature writ large. See her *Playing in the Dark: Whiteness and the Literary Imagination* (New York: Vintage, 1992). Moreover, as an antebellum social formation in process as well as one tethered to morphologies of performance, mammy memory is also in dialogue with what Eric Lott terms an "antebellum structure of racial feeling"; he describes the blackface minstrel as a "social semantic figure highly responsive to the demands and troubled fantasies of its [white] audiences." See his *Love and Theft: Blackface Minstrelsy and the American Working Class* (Oxford: Oxford University Press, 1995), 6.

9 Williams, *Marxism and Literature*, 131. While Williams's argument against artificial distinctions in social and cultural analysis—such as thought versus

feeling or the social versus the cultural—is utile in cultural studies writ large, its particularly useful for the discussion in this chapter. Williams cautions us that these binaries are predicated on the notion of the past as "finished products" and hence, the swift conversion of protean, "active" and "flexible" cultural forms, like feelings, into "fixed, finite, receding forms" (128–29). Likewise, I grapple here with the constellation of protean cultural forms and haunting presences, or remains, of Joice Heth, embracing their obdurate refusal to become easily interpreted or categorized. As Heth's performances made so clear, even the past itself was (and continues to be) active, echoing José Esteban Muñoz's dictum that "the past *does* things." See his *Cruising Utopia: The Then and There of Queer Futurity* (New York: New York University Press, 2009), 28; emphasis added.

10 *New York Sun,* August 21, 1835. A full excerpt of the advertisement for her exhibit at Niblo's is quoted in Benjamin Reiss, "P. T. Barnum, Joice Heth, and Antebellum Spectacles of Race," *American Quarterly* 51, no. 1 (1999): 81.

11 Robin Bernstein, *Racial Innocence: Performing American Childhood from Slavery to Civil Rights* (New York: New York University Press, 2011), 6, 8.

12 Douglas A. Jones Jr., for instance, situates Heth's exhibits within a larger "fantasy of proslavery domesticity," one that specifically "tapped into a desire for a form of domestic harmony that aligned audiences with Washington" while affirming "magnanimous white mastery as an ideal of Americanness." See his *The Captive Stage: Performance and the Proslavery Imagination of the Antebellum North* (Ann Arbor: University of Michigan Press, 2014), 88, 95.

13 Diana Fuss, *Identification Papers* (New York: Routledge, 1995), 1.

14 Ibid., 22–24. Maternity and psychoanalysis's interplay gestures toward the latter's historical basis in the concept of the former, albeit an imaginary birth.

15 Anne Anlin Cheng, *The Melancholy of Race: Psychoanalysis, Assimilation, and Hidden Grief* (New York: Oxford University Press, 2000), 10.

16 Fuss, *Identification Papers,* 34.

17 Deborah Willis and Carla Williams, *The Black Female Body: A Photographic History* (Philadelphia: Temple University Press, 2002), 128.

18 Shawn Michelle Smith, *American Archives: Gender, Race, and Class in Visual Culture* (Princeton, NJ: Princeton University Press, 1999), 117.

19 See Harryette Mullen, "'Indelicate Subjects': African American Women's Subjugated Subjectivity," in *Sub/versions: Feminist Studies* (Santa Cruz: University of California Press, 1991); quoted in Laura Wexler, "Seeing Sentiment: Photography, Race, and the Innocent Eye," in Elizabeth Abel, Barbara Christian, and Helene Moglen, eds., *Female Subjects in Black and White: Race, Psychoanalysis, Feminism* (Berkeley: University of California Press, 1997), 174.

20 John Tagg, *The Burden of Representation: Essays on Photographs and Histories* (Amherst: University of Massachusetts Press, 1988), 37.

21 Wexler, "Seeing Sentiment," 178, 181, 180.

22 Raymond Williams, *Keywords: A Vocabulary of Culture and Society* (New York: Oxford University Press, 1976), 156.

23 Muñoz, *Cruising Utopia*, 65.

24 "Joice Heth's Grandmother," *Eastern Argus*, March 7, 1837, 3.

25 "Joice Heth's Grandmother," *Portsmouth and Great-Falls Journal of Literature and Politics*, March 11, 1837, 4.

26 "Grandmother to Joice Heth," *Barre Gazette*, March 10, 1837, 2.

27 Taylor, *The Archive and the Repertoire*, 28.

28 Joseph Roach, *Cities of the Dead: Circum-Atlantic Performance* (New York: Columbia University Press, 1996), 36.

29 Susan J. Pearson, "Infantile Specimens: Showing Babies in Nineteenth-Century America," *Journal of Social History* 42, no. 2 (Winter 2008): 350, 348.

30 Quoted in "An Old Character," *Liberator*, October 12, 1855, 161.

31 For an extended discussion of this, see the third chapter, "Circus Africanus: The Popular Display of Black Bodies," in Washington, *Medical Apartheid*, 75–100.

32 "Joice Heth," *Chicago Daily Tribune*, July 29, 1878, 7.

33 Barnaby Diddleum, "The Adventures of an Adventurer, Being Some Passages in the Life of Barnaby Diddleum," *Atlas*, April 11, 1841.

34 Barnum, *The Life of P. T. Barnum*, 149.

35 Diddleum, "The Adventures of an Adventurer."

36 *Portsmouth Journal of Literature and Politics*, September 5, 1835.

37 Rosemarie Garland Thomson, ed., "Introduction: From Wonder to Error—An Genealogy of Freak Discourses in Modernity," in *Freakery: Spectacles of the Extraordinary Body* (New York: New York University Press, 1996), 4.

38 Robert Bogdan, *Freak Show: Presenting Human Oddities for Amusement and Profit* (Chicago: University of Chicago Press, 1998), 30–1.

39 Thomson, *Freakery*, 5.

40 Washington, *Medical Apartheid*, 79. These discourses, as Mel Y. Chen describes, were "tied to colonialist strategy and pedagogy that superimposed phylogenetic maps onto synchronic human racial typologies, yielding simplistic promulgating equations of 'primitive' peoples with prehuman stages of evolution." It is no accident that this was particularly evident with Joice Heth's exhibits, since African slaves first carried what Chen calls the "epistemological weight of animalization" through their animalized visual depiction by slave owners and political cartoonists. Mel Y. Chen, *Animacies: Biopolitics, Racial Mattering, and Queer Affect* (Durham, NC: Duke University Press), 101–2, 111.

41 William Henry Johnson was arguably one of most famous freak show performers, besides Millie and Christine McKoy, his career spanning the late nineteenth and early twentieth centuries. Johnson, assumed to be a mentally underdeveloped microcephalic—or, pejoratively, a "pinhead"—was displayed inside P. T. Barnum's American Museum in 1860 as "Zip the Pinhead" and the "What-Is-It?" as an ostensible "missing link" between civilization and barbarity, reportedly discovered in Africa. Johnson's costume of a fur suit, captured in an image by photographer Matthew Brady around 1872, was presumably designed to further emphasize his exoticism. See Bogdan, *Freak Show*, esp. 134–42. William Johnson and Joice Heth's

performances direct us to a distinct phenomenon in genealogies of black performance of African American actors and actresses who made careers out of "going native," or portraying versions of Africans, for white audiences. This striking phenomenon was perhaps most acutely (and infamously) evident in thespians George Walker and Bert Williams's hired impersonation as Dahomians in San Francisco in 1894.

42 William Ragan Stanton, *The Leopard's Spots: Scientific Attitudes toward Race in America, 1815–59* (Chicago: University of Chicago Press, 1960), 5, 13.

43 Quoted in ibid., 66. This letter, and others, were manipulated to substantiate the claim that the South provided a better climate for slaves to live longer, since their temperament, build, and skin were more accustomed to the temperate weather of the Southern states. These ideological intentions are salient in this letter's claim that free blacks had a lower life expectancy than slaves and hence "the welfare of the Negro was dependent upon the protective mantel of slavery." Interestingly, Joice Heth's performances led to her association with other cases of black longevity, evinced by this mention in a newspaper: "We received details yesterday of another case of longevity, which if it does not corroborate the case of 'Joice Heth' [. . .] is nevertheless worthy of passing notice." The subject of this brief article—an elderly black woman named Phillis Walke—was said to be 115 years old. See "Joice Heth; London; New Monthly Magazine; Phillis Walke; Strawberry Plains; Princess Anne County," *New London Gazette and General Advertiser,* October 14, 1835, 2.

44 Henry Moss, afflicted with the skin disorder vitiligo, self-exhibited himself in Philadelphia in the 1790s, charging twenty-five cents for admission. In a striking intersection with Heth, President George Washington himself was in the audience at an appearance Moss made at a tavern, the Sign of the Black Horse, in Philadelphia in 1796. See Washington, *Medical Apartheid,* 80–82. Conjoined twins Millie and Christine McKoy were born in 1851, the same year an engraving of fugitive slave Ellen Craft was made in England. They were exhibited in the United States (including at Barnum's American Museum) and Europe for most of their lives until their deaths in 1912. For more on the McKoys, see Joanne Martell, *Millie-Christine: Fearfully and Wonderfully Made* (New York: John F. Blair, 1999). Moy is briefly mentioned in Benjamin Reiss, *The Showman and the Slave: Race, Death, and Memory in Barnum's America* (Cambridge, MA: Harvard University Press, 2001), 38, 95, 101.

45 Nicholas Mirzoeff, "The Shadow and the Substance: Race, Photography and the Index," in Coco Fusco and Brian Wallis, eds., *Only Skin Deep: Changing Visions of the American Self* (New York: Harry N. Abrams and International Center of Photography), 118.

46 Washington, *Medical Apartheid,* 86.

47 Thomson, "Introduction," *Freakery,* 7.

48 Saxon, *P. T. Barnum,* 114; Barnum, *The Life of P. T. Barnum,* 152.

49 Saxon, *P. T. Barnum,* 114.

50 David M. Henkin, *City Reading: Written Words and Public Spaces in Antebellum New York* (New York: Columbia University Press, 1998), 105, 106. The radical effect of the rise of penny presses on readership and urban landscapes cannot be overemphasized. Daily newspapers, "attuned to the life of the city, addressed impersonally to unprecedented numbers of people, and circulated visibly in the streets" connected denizens both to the local attractions in the city in which they lived as well as to each other (124). "Hawked, posted, traded, and read in public view," Henkin writes, "they had a palpable material presence in the streets" and in their shape emphasized a particularly special "symbiotic relationship" between printed matter and the spaces of the metropolis, the "rectilinear print columns" mirroring the "rectilinear city blocks" urban dwellers negotiated (104).

51 Goodman, *The Sun and the Moon*, 124. This fee was charged as an additional admittance fee to the general fifty-cent admission charged at Niblo's Garden in New York, a nineteenth-century "pleasure garden" where Heth's exhibitions, administered by Barnum, made their debut in the Diorama Room upstairs in August 1835 (9). Children, meanwhile, were charged a reduced admission of twelve and a half cents.

52 Edward H. Dixon, M.D., ed. "Barnum and Joice Heth." *The Scalpel: A Journal of Health, Adapted to Popular and Professional Reading, and the Exposure of Quackery* 3, no. 1 (November 1850): 58.

53 "Gen. Washington; Niblo; Capt. Riley," *Vermont Phoenix*, September 4, 1835, 3.

54 "Joice Heth," *Portsmouth Journal of Literature and Politics*, September 5, 1835.

55 "Joice Heth," *Chicago Daily Tribune*, July 29, 1878, 7. Newspaper accounts differ as to the exact amount Barnum made. "The ingenious gentleman made $20,000 out of this hoax of Joice Heth," reported one, while according to another, the "'Joice Heth' humbug, it is now said, cleared the proprietor $13,000." *Patriot and Democrat*, September 17, 1836; *New Hampshire Sentinel*, February 16, 1837.

56 Fuss, *Identification Papers*, 152.

57 Anonymous, *The Life of Joice Heth, the Nurse of George Washington (The Father of Our Country), Now Living at the Astonishing Age of 161 Years, and Weighs only 46 Pounds* (New York: Printed for the Publisher, 1835), 9–10.

58 Bernstein, *Racial Innocence*, 11.

59 Terrance Whalen, "Introduction," *The Life of P .T. Barnum*, xvi.

60 Muñoz, *Cruising Utopia*, 27.

61 Tavia Nyong'o, *The Amalgamation Waltz: Race, Performance, and the Ruses of Memory* (Minneapolis: University of Minnesota Press, 2009), 35.

62 Barnum, *The Life of P. T. Barnum*, 150.

63 Roach, *Cities of the Dead*, 2.

64 P. T. Barnum, *Struggles and Triumphs, or Forty Years Recollections of P.T. Barnum. Written by Himself* (Buffalo, NY: Warren, Johnson, and Co., 1872), 74.

65 *Salem Gazette*, September 8, 1835.

66 For more on this distinction between impairment as a physical lack and disability as a social category, see Lennard J. Davis, "The End of Identity Politics: On

Disability as an Unstable Category," in Lennard J. Davis, ed., *The Disability Studies Reader*, third ed. (New York: Routledge, 1997), 303.

67 Rachel Adams, *Sideshow U.S.A.: Freaks and the American Cultural Imagination* (Chicago: University of Chicago Press, 2001), 11.

68 Chen, *Animacies*, 111.

69 Reiss, *The Showman and the Slave*, 38.

70 Daphne A. Brooks, *Bodies in Dissent: Spectacular Performances of Race and Freedom, 1850–1910* (Durham, NC: Duke University Press, 2006), 156.

71 Diddleum, "The Adventures of an Adventurer."

72 Davis, "The End of Identity Politics," 309.

73 Thomson, "Introduction," 4.

74 Reiss, *The Showman and the Slave*, 6–47, 56.

75 Jennifer DeVere Brody, *Impossible Purities: Blackness, Femininity, and Victorian Culture* (Durham, NC: Duke University Press, 1998), 73.

76 Reiss, *The Showman and the Slave*, 55.

77 Terence Whalen, "Introduction: P.T. Barnum and the Birth of Capitalist Irony," in Barnum, *The Life of P. T. Barnum*, xiv.

78 Barnum, *The Life of P. T. Barnum*, 152, 148, 154.

79 Ibid., 156, 157.

80 Reiss, *The Showman and the Slave*, 116. For more discussion of this incident, see 115–22.

81 Derek J. de Solla Price, "Automata and the Origins of Mechanism and Mechanistic Philosophy," *Technology and Culture* 5, no. 1 (Winter 1964): 2, 19; Silvio A. Bedini, "Automata in the History of Technology," *Technology and Culture* 5, no. 1 (Winter 1964): 31. Reprints available at Charles E. Young Research Library, Special Collections, University of California, Los Angeles.

82 Vera Brodsky Lawrence, *Strong on Music: The New York Music Scene in the Days of George Templeton Strong, 1836–1875*, Vol. 1: *Resonances, 1836–1850* (New York: Oxford University Press, 1988), 35.

83 Ibid., 35, 104, 284. P.T. Barnum himself participated in this contagious trend: in 1840 alone, he shifted the entertainment to blackface when he took over management of Vauxhall Garden, and in his own repertoire, featured a child prodigy/ blackface entertainer named "Master John Diamond" (106, 104).

84 Ibid., 232.

85 Zora Neale Hurston, "Characteristics of Negro Expression" (1931), in Cheryl Wall, ed. *Zora Neale Hurston: Folkore, Memoirs, and Other Writings* (New York: Literary Classics of the United States, 1995), 835. To quote Hurston: "After adornment, the most striking manifestation of the Negro is angularity. Everything he touches becomes angular. In all African sculpture and doctrine we find the same thing. Anyone watching Negro dancers will be struck be the same phenomenon. Every posture is another angle. Pleasing, yes. But an effect achieved be the very means which an European strives to avoid" (834).

86 Jane Bennett, *Vibrant Matter: A Political Ecology of Things* (Durham, NC: Duke University Press, 2010), 7

87 Sianne Ngai, *Ugly Feelings* (Cambridge, MA: Harvard University Press, 2005), 94.

88 Ibid., 91, 97, 101.

89 Barnum, *The Life and Times of P. T. Barnum*, 155.

90 De Solla Price, "Automata and the Origins of Mechanism and Mechanistic Philosophy," 16.

91 Barnum, *The Life of P. T. Barnum*, pp. 157–159.

92 Roland Barthes, *Camera Lucida: Reflections on Photography* (1980; New York: Hill and Wang, 1981), 27.

93 Petite Bunkum [P. T. Barnum], *The Autobiography of Petite Bunkum, the Showman Showing His Birth, Education, and Bringing Up; His Astounding Adventures by Sea and Land; His Connection with Tom Thumb, Judy Heath, the Woolly Horse, the Fudge Mermaid, and the Swedish Nightingale; Together with Many Other Strange and Startling Matters in His Eventful Career; All of Which Are Illustrated with Numerous Engravings* (New York: P.F. Harris, 1856), 24.

94 Ibid., 26.

95 Muñoz, *Cruising Utopia*, 28.

96 Judith Halberstam, *The Queer Art of Failure* (Durham, NC: Duke University Press, 2011), 15.

97 Dixon, "Barnum and Joice Heth," *The Scalpel*, 58.

98 Ibid., 59.

99 Alexandra Vazquez, "Salon Philosophers: Ivy Queen and Surprise Guests Take Reggaetón Aside," in Deborah Pacini-Hernandez, Wayne Marshall, and Raquel Z. Rivera, eds., *Reggaeton* (Durham, NC: Duke University Press, 2009), 306.

100 I borrow this wording from Ramón H. Rivera-Servera's "Exhibiting Voice/Narrating Migration: Performance-Based Curatorial Practice in ¡Azucar! The Life and Music of Celia Cruz," *Text and Performance Quarterly* 29, no. 2 (2009): 140.

101 Fred Moten, *In the Break: The Aesthetics of the Black Radical Tradition* (Minneapolis: University of Minnesota Press, 2003), 20–21, 7.

102 Feminist scholar Ellen Samuels's astute discussion of the legacy of conjoined African American twins and freak show performers Millie and Christine McKoy is a wonderful example of just how to do this sort of work; she uses Evelynn Hammonds's "black holes" analogy as a method to reposition the McKoys within what she calls an "intersectional feminist disability analysis." See her "Examining Millie and Christine McKoy: Where Enslavement and Enfreakment Meet," *Signs* 37, no. 1 (Autumn 2011): 53–81. Equally compelling is Hershini Bhana Young's plea to move away from questions of "agency" and "resistance," and instead toward the *illegibility* of will, in coercive performances like Heth's. In lieu of empirical fact, she advocates different methods of narration when approaching these slippery archives, including what she calls a "queer imaginative conjuring." See her *Illegible*

Will: Coercive Performances in Southern African Spectacles of Labor (Durham, NC: Duke University Press, forthcoming). For more on consent theory in freak shows, see David Gerber, "The 'Careers' of People Exhibited in Freak Shows: The Problem of Volition and Valorization," in Thomson, *Freakery*, 38–54. For more on Heth's agency (or lack thereof) see Reiss, *The Showman and the Slave*.

103 Roach, *Cities of the Dead*, 26.

104 Dixon, "Barnum and Joice Heth," *The Scalpel*, 58.

105 Saidiya V. Hartman, *Scenes of Subjection: Terror, Slavery, and Self-Making in Nineteenth-Century America* (Oxford: Oxford University Press, 1997), 56.

106 See Coco Fusco, "The Other History of Intercultural Performance," *Drama Review* 38, no. 1 (Spring 1994): 143–67.

107 Lauren Berlant and Elizabeth Freeman, "Queer Nationality," in Michael Warner, ed., *Fear of a Queer Planet: Queer Politics and Social Theory* (Minneapolis: University of Minnesota Press, 1993), 218.

108 See Lott, *Love and Theft*; Brian Currid, "'We Are Family': House Music and Queer Performativity," in Sue-Ellen Case, Phillip Brett, and Susan Leigh Foster, eds., *Cruising the Performative: Interventions into the Representation of Ethnicity, Nationality, and Sexuality* (Bloomington: Indiana University Press, 1995), 188.

109 Daphne Brooks, "Fraudulent Bodies/Fraught Methodologies," *Legacy* 24, no. 2 (2007): 310.

110 See Peggy Phelan, *Unmarked: The Politics of Performance* (New York: Routledge, 1993), especially chapter 7.

111 Reiss, *The Showman and the Slave*, 5.

112 Saidiya Hartman, *Lose Your Mother: A Journey along the Atlantic Slave Trade* (New York: Farrar, Straus and Giroux, 2007), 137. I face a similar historical challenge to Hartman here in her attempted reconstruction of a narrative of a murdered slave woman out of a void of information. To quote her fully, "I am too trying to save the girl, not from death but from oblivion. Yet I am unsure if it is possible to salvage an existence from a handful of words: *the supposed murder of a Negro girl.* Hers is a life impossible to reconstruct, not even her name survived."

113 Brooks, "Fraudulent Bodies/Fraught Methodologies," 307.

114 Guy-Shetfall, "The Body Politic," 18.

115 There are numerous contemporary examples of this phenomenon, both fictional and real. For instance, the main character in August Wilson's play *Gem of the Ocean*—the first in his ten-play cycle of the African American experience that ran on Broadway between 2004 and 2005—is Aunt Esther, a former slave who claims to be 285 years old. Likewise, in popular music, rapper Talib Kweli's song "For Women"—a reinterpretation of Nina Simone's searing "Four Women"—transformed the character Aunt Sarah into a 107-year-old black woman in Brooklyn who had "lived from nigger to colored to negro to black/To afro then African-American and right back to nigger." The archetype of the elderly black woman as the embodiment of triumph over a tragic American history resurfaced, most potently, in the news coverage of 106-year-old Georgia resident Ann Nixon

Cooper voting for Barack Obama in the 2008 presidential election and Obama's mention of her in his televised acceptance speech in Chicago's Grant Park the night of November 4, 2008.

116 Rebecca Schneider, *Performing Remains: Art and War in Times of Theatrical Reenactment* (New York: Routledge, 2013), 14.

CHAPTER 2. PASSING PERFORMANCES

1 William and Ellen Craft, *Running a Thousand Miles to Freedom: The Escape of William and Ellen Craft from Slavery* (1860; Athens: University of Georgia Press, 1999), 20–21. *Running a Thousand Miles to Freedom* was published by the eponymous London publishing house of British abolitionist William Tweedie. His press also distributed the *Anti-Slavery Advocate* for the Anglo-American Anti-Slavery Association.

2 Ibid., 21–24.

3 Lindon Barrett, "Hand-Writing: Legibility and the White Body in Running a Thousand Miles to Freedom," *American Literature* 69, no. 2 (June 1997): 324.

4 Craft and Craft, *Running a Thousand Miles to Freedom*, 24, 28, 49, 51, 54.

5 Brown wrote a letter to William Lloyd Garrison, the editor of the abolitionist *Boston Liberator* newspaper, regarding the appearance of the Crafts, or the "Georgia Fugitives," in New England. See "The Georgia Fugitives," *Boston Liberator*, January 12, 1849. In the letter, Brown retold the story of the Crafts' escape and assured Garrison that the Crafts would be present "at a meeting of the Massachusetts Anti-Slavery Society, in Boston" later that month, where "I know the history of their escape will be listened to with great interest." "They are very intelligent," he continued, and very young, "Ellen 22, and William 24 years of age." The letter's closing paragraph revealed Brown's ambitions to link his own career to that of the Crafts. He wrote,
P.S. They are now hid away within 25 miles of Philadelphia, where they will remain until the 6th, when they will leave with me for New England. Will you please say in the *Liberator* that I will lecture, in connection, with them as follows:
At Norwich, Conn., Thursday evening, Jan. 18
At Worcester, Mass., Friday evening, January 19
At Pawtucket, Mass., Saturday evening, January 20
At New Bedford, Mass, Sunday afternoon and evening, Jan. 28

6 Dorothy Sterling, "Ellen Craft: The Valiant Journey," in *Black Foremothers: Three Lives* (Old Westbury, NY: The Feminist Press, 1979), 22.

7 Historian R.J.M. Blackett describes the order of events as follows: "First, Brown spoke against American slavery, then William described their escape, and finally, in a tear-jerking scene, Ellen was invited onstage. This careful orchestration was guaranteed to provoke strong antislavery sentiments. What sort of country, newspaper reports asked, could enslave such articulate and obviously intelligent people? And, more important, if they were a sample of the sort of persons who

were slaves, what a destruction of talent! Ellen's appearance on the stage increased
the audience's dismay, for a black slave was one thing but a 'white' woman
enslaved was unconscionable." See R.J.M. Blackett, "The Odyssey of William and
Ellen Craft," in *Beating against the Barriers: Bibliographic Essays in Nineteenth-
Century America* (Baton Rouge: Louisiana State University Press, 1986), 98. Later,
when the Crafts were in England, Ellen's limited role in the lectures was questioned by a British abolitionist, Dr. John Estlin, who hosted the Crafts in his home
in Bristol. In a letter to another abolitionist, he noted his desire "to improve the
tone of Brown and Craft's exhibition, altering their too showmanlike handbills
and securing a higher position for Ellen." See Sterling, "Ellen Craft," 40.

8 Blackett, "The Odyssey of William and Ellen Craft," 90.

9 The Fugitive Slave Law, signed into law September 18, 1850, by President
Millard Fillmore, threatened that "any black—fugitive or freeborn—could be
seized and taken to the South on the word of any white" (Sterling, "Ellen Craft,"
28–29). Ellen's former owner, Robert Collins, wrote a personal appeal to
Fillmore for federal aid to assist in Ellen's capture. Days after an abolitionist
meeting held in Boston's Faneuil Hall in opposition to the law was attended by
thirty-five hundred people, two slave catchers—"Hughes and Knight"—arrived
in Boston claiming the Crafts, prompting their flight from the United States.
See Sterling, "Ellen Craft," 36; Blackett, "The Odyssey of William and Ellen
Craft," 91–93.

10 *Boston Liberator*, July 11, 1851. This article also made note of lecturer Henry Box
Brown's exploits abroad. For an analysis of Brown's performances in America and
the British Isles, see Daphne A. Brooks, *Bodies in Dissent: Spectacular
Performances of Race and Freedom, 1850–1910* (Durham, NC: Duke University
Press, 2006), 66–130.

11 For more on the Crafts' educational training in Surrey, see "William and Ellen
Craft," *Boston Liberator*, September 26, 1851.

12 Blackett, "The Odyssey of William and Ellen Craft," 128.

13 Richard Schechner, *Performance Studies: An Introduction* (New York: Routledge,
2002), 24.

14 Kevin Young, *The Grey Album: On the Blackness of Blackness* (Minneapolis:
Greywolf Press, 2012), esp. 21–63.

15 See William Wells Brown, *The Narrative of William W. Brown, a Fugitive Slave,
Written by Himself* (Boston: Anti-Slavery Office, 1847).

16 E. Patrick Johnson, "Black Performance Studies: Genealogies, Politics, Futures," in
D. Soyini Madison and Judith Hamera, eds., *The Sage Handbook of Performance
Studies* (Thousand Oaks, CA: Sage Publications, 2006), 453.

17 Paul Gilroy, "'. . . To Be Real': The Dissident Forms of Black Expressive Culture,"
in Catherine Ugwu, ed., *Let's Get It On: The Politics of Black Performance*
(London: Institute of Contemporary Arts; Seattle: Bay Press, 1995), 14, 15.

18 Richard Bauman, "Performance," in Erik Barnouw, ed. *International Encyclopedia
of Communications* (New York: Oxford University Press, 1989), 262.

19 RoseLee Goldberg, *Performance Art: From Futurism to the Present* (1979; New York: Thames & Hudson, 2001), 138.

20 Michel de Certeau, *The Practice of Everyday Life* (Berkeley and Los Angeles: University of California Press, 1984), xv.

21 Charles H. Rowell, "'Words Don't Go There': An Interview with Fred Moten," *Callaloo* 27, no. 4 (2004): 965.

22 De Certeau, *The Practice of Everyday Life*, xix.

23 The Crafts were not the only fugitive slaves to enact passing performances; strikingly, after the their escape, abolitionist newspapers referenced the Crafts when reporting on other successful escapes via racial (and gender) impersonations. According to one such account, "a couple of fugitives—husband and wife—arrived here this morning from Alabama, by this route [the Ohio River], a la William and Ellen Craft, with this difference; the husband being quite dark and of small stature, was disguised in female apparel, and passed as the servant of his wife, who is white, and withal very beautiful." "Another Remarkable Escape," *Frederick Douglass Paper*, February 25, 1853. Another such story relied on a correspondent who described "a recent case that goes ahead of even the Crafts for craftiness." A mulatto man "whose complexion has been bleached by successive amalgamations, so as to approximate closely that of our own favored race," traveled from Georgia on "public conveyances" to Richmond, Virginia, and then Wilmington, Delaware, on foot before running out of funds. He then ingratiated himself with a slave owner, borrowed "several hundred dollars," and dined at the "best hotel at Havre de Grace, Maryland," before boarding a boat across the Susquehanna River and escaping via the Underground Railroad. The article ends by noting that "our correspondent shrewdly and cuttingly, remarks that the slaveholders should be careful not to whitewash their 'chattels' so much, seeing that it renders it so difficult to distinguish them from MEN!" "A Little Matter," *North Star*, March 1, 1850.

24 Monica L. Miller, *Slaves to Fashion: Black Dandyism and the Styling of Black Diasporic Identity* (Durham, NC: Duke University Press, 2009), 81.

25 Fred Moten, *In the Break: The Aesthetics of the Black Radical Tradition* (Minneapolis: University of Minnesota Press, 2003), 7.

26 Craft and Craft, *Running a Thousand Miles to Freedom*, 21, 24, 39, 24.

27 Miller, *Slaves to Fashion*, 83, 93.

28 Craft and Craft, *Running a Thousand Miles to Freedom*, 43.

29 "Persona-play" is a variation of Moira Roth's term "personae-play"; quoted in Cherise Smith, *Enacting Others: Politics of Identity in Eleanor Antin, Nikki S. Lee, Adrian Piper, and Anna Deavere Smith* (Durham, NC: Duke University Press, 2011), 12.

30 "The Fugitives at Kingston," *Boston Liberator*, February 4, 1849, 23.

31 Miller, *Slaves to Fashion*, 113.

32 Craft and Craft, *Running a Thousand Miles to Freedom*, 13, 14.

33 Ibid., 16, 17–18, 18, 19.

34 Stuart Hall, "The Afterlife of Frantz Fanon: Why Fanon? Why Now? Why Black Skin, White Masks?" in Alan Read, ed., *The Fact of Blackness: Frantz Fanon and Visual Representation* (London: Institute of Contemporary Arts; Seattle: Bay Press, 1996), 20.

35 By this turn of phrase, I mean to evoke performance artist and scholar Coco Fusco's essay (and book) of the same name. See her "The Bodies That Were Not Ours," in *The Bodies That Were Not Ours and Other Writings* (New York: Routledge, 2001), 8–17.

36 Carol Simpson Stern and Bruce Henderson, *Performance: Texts and Contexts* (White Plains, NY: Longmans, 1993), 382–405.

37 Marvin Carlson, *Performance: A Critical Introduction*, second ed. (1996; New York: Routledge, 2004), 85.

38 Ellen Samuels, "'A Complication of Complaints': Untangling Disability, Race, and Gender in William and Ellen Craft's *Running a Thousand Miles to Freedom*," *MELUS* 31, no. 3 (Fall 2006): 43, 15.

39 Julie Clarke, "pros+thesis," in Adrian Heathfield, ed., *Live: Art and Performance* (New York: Routledge, 2004), 208.

40 Joseph R. Roach, *Cities of the Dead: Circum-Atlantic Performance* (New York: Columbia University Press, 1996), 3.

41 Clarke, "pros+thesis," 208.

42 Jennifer Devere Brody, *Punctuation: Art, Politics, and Play* (Durham, NC: Duke University Press, 2008), 65.

43 Craft and Craft, *Running a Thousand Miles to Freedom*, 24.

44 Ibid., 30.

45 Ibid., 34–35.

46 Samuels, "'A Complication of Complaints,'" 17.

47 Craft and Craft, *Running a Thousand Miles to Freedom*, 34.

48 In this way, Craft's prosthetic performances also disturbed what Robert McRuer has termed "compulsory able-bodiedness." See his *Crip Theory: Cultural Signs of Queerness and Disability* (New York: New York University Press, 2006).

49 Craft and Craft, *Running a Thousand Miles to Freedom*, 36.

50 Ibid., 37.

51 Samuels, "'A Complication of Complaints,'" 18.

52 Barrett, "Hand-Writing," 327.

53 Uri McMillan, "Crimes of Performance," *SOULS* 13, no. 1 (2011): 42.

54 In this scene, narrated by William, a gentleman traveling with his two daughters presented Mr. William Johnson with a "recipe, which he said was a perfect cure for the inflammatory rheumatism. But the invalid not being able to read it, and fearing he should hold it upside down in pretending to do so, thanked the donor kindly, and placed it in his waistcoat pocket." Craft and Craft, *Running a Thousand Miles to Freedom*, 39. Other instances in the escape narrative emphasizing this joint illiteracy include an earlier one remarking on the inability of the Crafts to read each other's passes from their respective master's granting a few

days off (22), as well as their later remark in Part II that "we had, by stratagem, learned the alphabet while in slavery, but not the writing characters" (53).

55 Ibid., 23–24.

56 Robin Bernstein, *Racial Innocence: Performing American Childhood from Slavery to Civil Rights* (New York: New York University Press, 2011), 11.

57 Craft and Craft, *Running a Thousand Miles to Freedom*, 44, 46, 47.

58 Ibid., 47; emphasis added.

59 Carlson, *Performance*, 110; Brooks, *Bodies in Dissent*, 19.

60 Carlson, *Performance*, 111, 105.

61 Wilbur H. Siebert, *The Underground Railroad from Slavery to Freedom* (New York: MacMillan, 1898), 374–75.

62 Ibid., 376.

63 Barbara McCaskill, "Introduction: William and Ellen Craft in Transatlantic Literature and Life," in Craft and Craft, *Running a Thousand Miles to Freedom*, 525.

64 Jennifer DeVere Brody, *Impossible Purities: Blackness, Femininity, and Victorian Culture* (Durham, NC: Duke University Press, 1998), 67.

65 Tavia Nyong'o, *The Amalgamation Waltz: Race, Performance, and the Ruses of Memory*, (Minneapolis: University of Minnesota Press, 2009), 55.

66 The centerpiece of the American exhibition was Hiram Power's marble sculpture *The Greek Slave*. A portrayal of a nude white woman with chains on her wrists, it was displayed in twelve cities in the 1840s. The sculpture's idealized figure of the "female slave as the pinnacle of female purity," Jennifer Brody remarks, sutured "connections between whiteness, beauty, and purity" to its ostensible "perfect hardness." See Brody, *Impossible Purities*, 67, 68. Brown, refusing the ideological motivations behind it, wryly remarked that the sculpture was "the only production of art which the United States has sent. And it would have been more to their credit to keep that at home." Brown attempted to boldly disrupt this warped scripting of the nation by depositing a representation of *The Virginia Slave*—a depiction of a black female slave published in the British weekly satirical magazine *Punch*—in the enclosure of *The Greek Slave*, declaring ,"As an American fugitive slave, I place this 'Virginia Slave' by the side of the 'Greek Slave,' as its most fitting companion." William Wells Brown, *The American Fugitive in Europe; Sketches of Places and People Abroad. With a Memoir of the Author* (1855; New York: Negro Universities Press, 1969), 196; William Still, *The Underground Railroad* (1872; Chicago: Johnson Publishing, 1970), 376.

67 For more discussion of both the image and the article that accompanied it, see Sterling, "Ellen Craft," 34–35.

68 For instance, in 1857, the Leeds Anti-Slavery Society sold an "illustrated youth edition of *Uncle Tom's Cabin* on the same page as a notice for a shilling portrait of Ellen wearing masculine garments." McCaskill, "Introduction" in Craft and Craft, *Running a Thousand Miles to Freedom*, xvii.

69 Phillis Wheatley's engraving accompanied her 1773 book *Poems on Various Subjects Religious and Moral*, the first by a colonial American woman to

accompany her writings. For more on the history and construction of this image, see Gwendolyn DuBois Shaw, "'On Deathless Glories Fix Thine Ardent View': Scipio Moorhead, Phillis Wheatley, and the Mythic Origins of Anglo-Africa Portraiture in New England," *Portraits of a People: Picturing African Americans in the Nineteenth-Century* (Seattle: University of Washington Press; Andover, MA: Addison Gallery of American Art, 2006), 26–43.

70 By "representational work," I mean to refer to Stuart Hall's discussion of representation as the active production of meaning into language (or as I stress in this section, *visual* languages), a labor often performed by racially marked bodies. See Stuart Hall, "The Work of Representation," in Stuart Hall, ed., *Representation: Cultural Representations and Signifying Practices* (London: Sage Publications/ Open University, 1997), 13–74.

71 Nyong'o, *Amalgamation Waltz*, 65.

72 For more on James Presley Ball, see Deborah Willis, *J. P. Ball, Daguerrean and Studio Photographer* (New York and London: Garland, 1993); Carla L. Peterson, *Doers of the Word: African-American Women Speakers and Writers in the North, 1830–1880* (New Brunswick, NJ: Rutgers University Press, 1995), 40.

73 Brooks, *Bodies in Dissent*, 85.

74 In the case of the two black women represented—Delia and Drana—their state of undress, breasts exposed, conveyed what Deborah Willis and Carla Williams call "a different sort of pornography, the pornography of their forced labor and of their inability to determine whether or how their bodies would be displayed." Deborah Willis and Carla Williams, *The Black Female Body: A Photographic History* (Philadelphia: Temple University Press, 2002), 23. Zealy's daguerreotypes, art historian Lisa Gail Collins asserts, illustrate that the medium of photography is not "inherently democratic, as all do not have equal access to the camera or the ability to deny its gaze." Lisa Gail Collins, "Historic Retrievals: Confronting Visual Evidence and the Imaging of Truth," in Deborah Willis, ed., *Black Venus 2010: They Called Her "Hottentot"* (Philadelphia: Temple University Press, 2010), 77.

75 Nicholas Mirzoeff, "The Shadow and the Substance: Race, Photography, and the Index," in Coco Fusco and Brian Wallis, eds., *Only Skin Deep: Changing Visions of the American Self* (New York: Harry N. Abrams and International Center of Photography), 111.

76 Roland Barthes, *Camera Lucida: Reflections on Photography*, trans. Richard Howard (1980; New York: Hill and Wang, 1981), 26, 27. If the tassel and tartan of his sash were signs of his upper-class privilege, Barbara McCaskill argues, so too were the elegant top hat, pristine white shirt, and dark suit accompanying them. See McCaskill, "Yours Very Truly," 518.

77 Samuels, "'A Complication of Complaints,'" 21. In this portrait, Samuels notes, disability—usually perceived as a "fixed bodily condition"—was as "easily removed as a bandage" (22).

78 Sterling Lecater Bland Jr., *Voices of the Fugitive: Runaway Slave Stories and Their Fictions of Self-Creation* (Westport, CT: Praeger, 2000), 150; Ellen M. Weinauer,

"'A Most Respectable Gentleman': Passing, Possession, and Transgression in *Running a Thousand Miles to Freedom*," in Elaine K. Ginsberg, ed., *Passing and the Fictions of Identity* (Durham, NC: Duke University Press, 1996), 50, 53; Samuels, "'A Complication of Complaints,'" 22.

79 Peggy Phelan, *Unmarked: The Politics of Performance* (New York: Routledge, 1996), 35, 36.

80 Deborah Willis, "The Sociologist's Eye: W.E.B. Du Bois and the Paris Exposition," in David Levering Lewis and Deborah Willis, *A Small Nation of People: W.E.B. Du Bois and African-American Portraits of Progress* (Washington, DC: Library of Congress, 2003), 66, 53.

81 In this context, Butler is specifically discussing gender identity. See Judith Butler, "Performative Acts and Gender Constitution: An Essay in Phenomenology and Feminist Theory," *Theatre Journal* 40, no. 4 (December 1988): 519.

82 Young, *Embodying Black Experience*, 27.

83 Phelan, *Unmarked*, 36.

84 Barthes, *Camera Lucida*, 10.

85 Rebecca Schneider, *Performing Remains: Art and War in Times of Theatrical Reenactment* (New York: Routledge, 2011), 141, 157. "The conviction that photography captures 'this here now' to become 'that there then,'" she further remarks, "assumes that the 'here now' is non-recurrent, not cross-temporal, and not of multiple or variable duration" (222).

86 Suzette Min, "Aesthetics," *Social Text* 100 (Fall 2009): 27; Craft and Craft, *Running a Thousand Miles to Freedom*, 9–10.

87 Robert Reid-Pharr, *Conjugal Union: The Body, The House, and the Black American* (New York: Oxford University Press, 1999), 41.

88 Cheryl Harris, "Whiteness as Property," *Harvard Law Review* 106, no. 8 (1993): 1709–95; Still, *The Underground Railroad*, 371.

89 Michael Ralph, "Commodity," *Social Text* 100 (Fall 2009): 78.

90 Henry Louis Gates, "The Trope of the Talking Book," in *The Signifying Monkey: A Theory of Afro-American Literary Criticism* (New York: Oxford University Press, 1988), 127–69.

91 McCaskill, "Yours Very Truly," 516, 519, 520.

92 Hazel V. Carby, *Reconstructing Womanhood: The Emergence of the Afro-American Woman Novelist* (New York: Oxford University Press, 1989), 30.

93 Brooks, *Bodies in Dissent*, 156.

94 Still, *The Underground Railroad*, 377.

95 P. Gabrielle Foreman, "Who's Your Mama?: 'White' Mulatta Genealogies, Early Photography, and Anti-Passing Narratives of Slavery and Freedom," *American Literary History* 14, no. 3 (Fall 2002): 534, 525, 507.

96 Reid-Pharr, *Conjugal Union*, 39.

97 For more on "beside" as a method of cultural analysis, see Eve Kosofsky Sedgwick, *Touching Feeling: Affect, Pedagogy, Performativity* (Durham, NC: Duke University Press, 2003), 8–9.

CHAPTER 3. PLASTIC POSSIBILITIES

1 This "mantra" is from cycle one of Piper's "dispersion" of the Mythic Being's utterances in the *Village Voice*, listed as her journal entry for "12-12-64." See Adrian Piper, "Preparatory Notes for *The Mythic Being*," in *Out of Order, Out of Sight*, Vol. 1: *Selected Writings in Meta-Art, 1968–1992* (Cambridge, MA: MIT Press, 1996), 103–11.

2 Adrian Piper, "The Mythic Being: Getting Back," in *Out of Order, Out of Sight*, Vol. 1, 147.

3 Piper earned a Ph.D. in philosophy at Harvard in 1981 and became the first black American woman in the United States tenured in the field of philosophy in 1987. In 2008, in a striking parallel to the ontological dangers confronted by her mythic avatar, Piper's refusal to return to the United States after being listed as a "suspicious traveler" on the U.S. Transportation Security Administration's watch list, resulted in her full professorship in philosophy at Wellesley College being revoked. She currently resides in Berlin, where she founded the Adrian Piper Research Archive (APRA). Most biographical material, unless otherwise cited, has been paraphrased from Adrian Piper's website. See http://www.adrianpiper. com/biography.shtml (accessed July 16, 2013).

4 Cherise Smith, *Enacting Others: Politics of Identity in Eleanor Antin, Nikki S. Lee, Adrian Piper, and Anna Deavere Smith* (Durham, NC: Duke University Press, 2011), 52.

5 See Piper, "The Mythic Being: Getting Back," 147.

6 Adrian Piper, "Notes on the Mythic Being I–III," in *Out of Order, Out of Sight*, Vol. 1, 117.

7 Ibid.

8 Cherise Smith, "Re-member the Audience: Adrian Piper's Mythic Being Advertisements," *Art Journal* 66, no. 1 (Spring 2007): 52.

9 Adrian Piper, "Xenophobia and the Indexical Present II: Lecture," in *Out of Order, Out of Sight*, Vol. 1, 263.

10 Richard Bauman, "Performance," in Erik Barnouw, ed., *International Encyclopedia of Communication* (New York: Oxford University Press, 1989), 262.

11 Fred Moten, *In the Break: The Aesthetics of the Black Radical Tradition* (Minneapolis: University of Minnesota Press, 1993), 7.

12 Smith, "Re-member the Audience," 49.

13 Piper, "Preparatory Notes for *The Mythic Being*," 101.

14 Adrian Piper, "Flying," in *Out of Order, Out of Sight*, Vol. 1, 224.

15 Sarah Jane Cervenak, "Against Traffic: De/formations of Race and Freedom in the Art of Adrian Piper," *Discourse* 28, nos. 2 and 3 (Spring/Fall 2006): 116.

16 Moten, *In the Break*, 241.

17 Daphne A. Brooks, *Bodies in Dissent: Spectacular Performances of Race and Freedom, 1850–1910* (Durham, NC: Duke University Press, 2006), 4, 3, 5.

18 Adrian Piper, "Introduction: Some Very FORWARD Remarks," in *Out of Order, Out of Sight*, Vol. 1, xxxi.

19 Maurice Berger, *Minimal Politics: Performativity and Minimalism in Recent American Art*, Issues in Cultural Theory 1 (Baltimore: Center for Art and Culture, University of Maryland Baltimore County, 1997), 21–22.

20 See Michael Fried, "Art and Objecthood," *Artforum* 5, no. 10 (June 1967): 12–23.

21 John P. Bowles, *Adrian Piper: Race, Gender, and Embodiment* (Durham, NC: Duke University Press, 2011), 23.

22 Valerie Cassel Oliver, "Through the Conceptual Lens: The Rise, Fall, and Resurrection of Blackness," in Valerie Cassel Oliver, ed., *Double Consciousness: Black Conceptual Art since 1970* (Houston: Contemporary Arts Museum Houston; New York: Distributed Art Publishers, 2005), 17, 18; Franklin Sirmans, "An American Art Job," in Oliver, ed., *Double Consciousness*, 12; Bowles, *Adrian Piper*, 53–56.

23 Gwen Allen and Cherise Smith, "Publishing Art: Alternative Distribution in Print," *Art Journal* 66, no. 1 (Spring 2007): 41.

24 Adrian Piper, "Artist's Statement," in Maurice Berger, ed., *Adrian Piper: A Retrospective*, Issues in Cultural Theory 3 (Baltimore: Fine Arts Gallery, University of Maryland Baltimore County, 1999), 174.

25 Piper, "Introduction: Some Very FORWARD Remarks," xxxiv, xxxv.

26 Bowles, *Adrian Piper*, 110.

27 Kobena Mercer, "Decentering and Recentering: Adrian Piper's Spheres of Influence," in Berger, ed., *Adrian Piper: A Retrospective*, 47.

28 Bowles, *Adrian Piper*, 108; Piper, "Personal Chronology," in Berger, ed., *Adrian Piper: A Retrospective*, 188.

29 "Adrian Piper" in Linda M. Montana, *Performance Artists Talking in the Eighties* (Berkeley and Los Angeles: University of California Press, 2000), 419–20.

30 In April 1974, Piper participated in a series of four performances titled "PersonA," staged at Artists Space, an alternative art space located at 155 Wooster Street that quickly established itself as a venue for SoHo nightlife. Piper, sharing the closing night bill with Jack Smith and Dennis Oppenheim, distributed written texts from her *Talking to Myself: The Ongoing Autobiography of an Art Object*. It appears Piper was the sole black American performance artist to participate. J. Hoberman, "'Like Canyons and Rivers': Performance for Its Own Sake," in Jay Sanders and J. Hoberman, *Rituals of Rented Island: Object Theater, Loft Performance, and the New Psychodrama—Manhattan, 1970–1980* (New York: Whitney Museum of American Art; New Haven, CT: Yale University Press, 2013), 14.

31 Adrian Piper, "Talking to Myself: The Ongoing Autobiography of an Art Object," in *Out of Order, Out of Sight*, Vol. 1, 30, 31, 30.

32 Adrian Piper, "Personal Chronology," in Berger, ed., *Adrian Piper: A Retrospective*, 188.

33 Kellie Jones, "It's Not Enough to Say 'Black Is Beautiful': Abstraction at the Whitney, 1969–1974," in Kellie Jones, *Eyeminded: Living and Writing Contemporary Art* (Durham, NC: Duke University Press, 2011), 417. It is worth noting, however, that black artists were not the only ones who used withdrawal as a political tactic. In a letter to Kynaston McShine, an associate curator at MoMA,

dated May 16, 1970, minimalist artist Robert Mangold confirmed his and painter Jo Baer's desire to have their work removed from view at MoMA until May 30, 1970. "The works' removal symbolize[s]," he wrote, "my repulsion for the United States actions in Southeast Asia and it's recent repressive domestic measures." In a press release, dated the day before, he also asked the Whitney Museum to close his one-man show of sculpture for similar reasons. John B. Hightower Papers, III.1.13. Museum of Modern Art Archives, New York. Hereafter cited as JBH. MoMA Archives, NY.

34 A letter addressed to John Hightower the day of the strike—and signed by sculptor Robert Morris and performance/installation artist Poppy Johnson, temporary chairmen of New York Art Strike—asked, as an extension of this symbolic act, that museums perform a series of additional actions, including a "statement of position with regard to racism, war, and repression," the suspension of normal operations for two weeks, the allocation of their main floors to the public, free of charge, for information gathering and discussion, and—perhaps most contentiously—the immediate inclusion of "artist-representatives on policy-making bodies within the institutions themselves." JBH, III.1.13. MoMA Archives, NY.

35 Ibid.

36 "Manifesto for the Guerrilla Art Action Group," JBH, III.1.11.b. MoMA Archives, NY. Art Workers' Coalition (AWC) demanded, for instance, that one third of the board of trustees be made up of artists and, in their words, "Artists should retain a disposition over the destiny of their work, whether or not it is owned by them, to ensure that it cannot be altered, destroyed, exhibited or reproduced without their consent." "The Demands of Art Workers Coalition," JBH, III.1.11.b. MoMA Archives, NY.

37 Piper, "Personal Chronology," 188; Sirmans "An American Art Job," in *Double Consciousness*, 13.

38 Piper, "Talking to Myself," 35.

39 Montana, *Performance Artists Talking in the Eighties*, 416.

40 Piper, "Talking to Myself," 42.

41 Ibid., 42–44.

42 Adrian Piper, "Untitled Performance for Max's Kansas City," in *Out of Order, Out of Sight*, Vol. 1, 27. Unless otherwise noted, all future citations from this performance are from this source.

43 "Howardena Pindell," Paul Cummings interview, July 10, 1972, Howardena Pindell Papers, Archives of American Art, Smithsonian Institution, Washington, DC, 57.

44 Judith Wilson, "In Memory of the News and of Our Selves: The Art of Adrian Piper," *Third Text* 16/17 (Autumn–Winter 1991): 44.

45 Quoted in Bowles, *Adrian Piper*, 135.

46 Goldberg, *Performance Art*, 152. Piper's thoughts on the negation of the commercial art object and the art world that fetishizes it is most explicit in these words: "All around me I see galleries and museums faltering or closing as the capitalist

structure on which they are based crumbles. This makes me realize that art as a commodity really isn't a good idea after all. That the value of an artwork has somehow become subject to monetary rather than aesthetic interest. That inconceivable amounts of money are lavished on objects, while artists expend their energy in plumbing and secretarial work in order to support themselves and their art. That by depending on a gallery to package and sell his product, the artist becomes a parasite who produces works tailored to sell rather than innovate. That the artist as parasite necessarily dies when the host dies." See Piper, "Talking to Myself," 40. Peggy Phelan argues that while Piper's assessment of the crumbling art market now seems "almost quaint," her "connection between the parasite and the host, however, has only gained in power" due to the ever-tighter enmeshment of art and capital. See Peggy Phelan, "Marina Abramovic: Witnessing Shadows" *Theatre Journal* 56, no. 4 (December 2004): 570.

47 Lucy Lippard, *Six Years: The Dematerialization of the Art Object from 1966 to 1972* (Berkeley: University of California Press, 1997). For an earlier discussion of this, see Lucy Lippard and John Chandler, "The Dematerialization of Art," *Art International* 12 (February 20, 1968): 31–36.

48 Adrian Piper, "Performance: The Problematic Solution," in *Out of Order, Out of Sight*, Vol. 2: *Selected Writings in Art Criticism, 1967–1992* (Cambridge, MA: MIT Press, 1996), 104. Originally written in 1984, this essay was previously unpublished. See also her essay "Performance and the Fetishism of the Art Object," in *Out of Order, Out of Sight*, Vol. 2, 51–61.

49 Piper, "Xenophobia and the Indexical Present II," 248, 249.

50 In February 1976, "performance" (swiftly after called "performance art") arrived uptown at the Whitney Museum of American Art with *Performances: Four Evenings, Four Days*—perhaps the first performance art series organized by a New York museum. Piper was one of the artists, most of whom were staging performances in a museum for the first time, performing *Some Reflective Surfaces* on February 28. "This was the first performance," she remarked later in one of her essays, "I gave in front of an art audience, and one that recognized what I was doing as art." Jay Sanders, "Love Is an Object," in Sanders and Hoberman, *Rituals of Rented Island*, 34, 35; Adrian Piper, "Some Reflective Surfaces I," in *Out of Order, Out of Sight*, Vol. 1, 151.

51 Mercer, "Recentering and Decentering," in Berger, ed., *Adrian Piper: A Retrospective*, 55.

52 Bowles, *Adrian Piper*, 25, 163; Lucy Lippard and Adrian Piper, "Catalysis: An Interview with Adrian Piper," *Drama Review* 16, no. 1 (March 1972): 78; Lucy R. Lippard, "Transformation Art," *Ms.* (October 1975): 33–39. Reprinted in Martha Wilson, ed., *Martha Wilson Sourcebook: 40 Years of Reconsidering Performance, Feminism, Alternative Spaces* (New York: Independent Curators International, 2011), 81–85. In addition, in 1974, Piper's work was included in the group show *In Her Own Image* at the Philadelphia Museum of Art, and, in an interview with Effie Serlin in 1976, she discussed much of her work in terms that were distinctly

feminist, detailing the misogynistic reactions she received from men during her *Catalysis* pieces. See Jenni Sorkin and Linda Theung, "Selected Chronology of All-Women Group Exhibitions, 1943–83," in Cornelia Butler and Lisa Gabrielle Mark, eds., *WACK! Art and the Feminist Revolution* (Los Angeles: Museum of Contemporary Art; Cambridge, MA: MIT Press, 2007), 479; Effie Serlis, "Adrian Piper," in *Interviews with Women in the Arts: Part 2* (New York: School of Visual Arts, 1976), 24–27.

53 Kellie Jones, "Now Dig This! An Introduction," in Kellie Jones, ed., *Now Dig This!: Art and Black Los Angeles 1960–1980* (Los Angeles: Hammer Museum, 2011), 15, 19.

54 Bowles, *Adrian Piper*, 27, 189. For 1972, see Lippard and Piper, "Catalysis: An Interview with Adrian Piper"; for 1973, see Adrian Piper, "Talking to Myself: The Autobiography of an Art Object," 6.

55 Naima Keith, "Artist Biographies," in Jones., ed., *Now Dig This!*, 260; Valerie Smith, "Abundant Evidence: Black Women Artists of the 1960s and 70s," in Butler and Mark, eds., *WACK! Art and the Feminist Revolution*, 400–13; Sorkin and Theung, "Selected Chronology," 473.

56 Furthermore, if practitioners of black conceptual art, or art that fused conceptual art practices with a black sensibility, refused such dictates, so too did the works of black abstractionists, such as Los Angeles–based Fred Eversley's cast polyester resin sculptures, exhibited at the Whitney Museum in 1970. Cassel Oliver, "Through the Conceptual Lens," 26; Kellie Jones, "To the Max: Energy and Experimentation," in Jones, ed., *Energy/Experimentation*, 14–34.

57 See Darby English, *How to See a Work of Art in Total Darkness* (Cambridge, MA: MIT Press, 2010).

58 Piper, "Personal Chronology," 189. She describes starting a group with several women, including Rosemary Mayer, who took most, if not all, of the photographs of the *Catalysis* series.

59 Mercer, "Decentering and Recentering," 50. On a related note, Frazer Ward argues that while performance artists borrow ideas from protest culture—the "activation of the viewer" and performance art's deployment of the body in a manner analogous to protest culture's use of the body in demonstrations in the 1960s—they are also critical of the very ideas of "community" and "public space" (as well as like-mindedness) that protest culture draws on, instead making work that seems to "invoke community-as-limit." See his *No Innocent Bystanders: Performance Art and Audience* (Hanover, NH: Dartmouth College Press, 2012), 9.

60 Bowles, *Adrian Piper*, 113.

61 Ibid., 114.

62 Piper, "Talking to Myself," 48.

63 Montana, *Performance Artists Talking in the Eighties*, 420, 416.

64 Serlis, "Adrian Piper," 24.

65 Michel de Certeau, *The Practice of Everyday Life* (Berkeley and Los Angeles: University of California Press, 1984), xv.

66 Bowles, *Adrian Piper*, 261.

67 Adrian Piper, "Notes on Funk, I–IV," in *Out of Order, Out of Sight*, Vol. 1, 198.

68 Quoted in Goldberg, *Performance Art*, 141.

69 Thus, while Banes tells us that in Greenwich Village, as a hub for art activities, we witness the "roots of postmodernism in the revaluation and reworking of tradition, and in the aspiration to make 'new' traditions," racial equality (and access) was not a goal. Instead, while the white avant-garde "perceived an affinity between their situations and that of African-Americans" and "were sympathetic to black social movements and to black artists, as well as, in some cases, to African American forms of art," the "democratization of the avant-garde" they desired did not include race and ethnicity. Sally Banes, *Greenwich Village 1963: Avant-Garde Performance and the Effervescent Body* (Durham, NC: Duke University Press, 1993), 106, 111.

70 Piper, "Talking to Myself," 50–51.

71 Ibid.

72 This is an adaptation of Piper's line "Fuck it. Let's boogie." See Piper, "Notes on Funk, I–IV," 208.

73 Moten, *In the Break*, 239.

74 Piper, "Some Reflective Surfaces I," 154.

75 For instance, in an interview with Lucy Lippard, she remarked that performance art involves a type of "universal solipsism" that makes it hard to distinguish "whether what you are seeing is of your own making, or whether it is objectively true." She elaborated further, arguing that "you know you are in control, that you are a force acting on things, and it distorts your perception." See Lippard and Piper, "Catalysis: An Interview with Adrian Piper," 77.

76 Smith, *Enacting Others*, 22, 23.

77 Bowles, *Adrian Piper*, 164–67; Peter Osborne, ed., *Conceptual Art* (New York: Phaidon Press, Inc., 2002), 112.

78 Moten, *In the Break*, 26. This language is used by Moten to describe the "surplus lyricism" of Duke Ellington and, more generally, black performance itself; I redeploy it here for its resonance with how to categorize Piper's early work.

79 The funk music employed by Piper later was itself a sign of black working-class culture. "The funk idiom of black working class culture," according to Piper, "is an unbelievably rich and enriching art form that I disseminate in the performances not only to facilitate comprehension of my other work but also for the cultural benefit of my largely white, upper-middle-class audience. That is, it is black working-class culture that has invaluable gifts to offer that audience, and not just the other way around." Piper, "Notes on Funk I –IV," 203.

80 Moten, *In the Break*, 32–33.

81 Frederick Gross, *Diana Arbus's 1960s: Auguries of Experience* (Minneapolis: University of Minnesota Press, 2012), 114, 115. Jennifer Brody, in her discussion of Kusama's polka dots alongside Ralph Ellison's ellipsis in *Invisible Man* (1952), states that both "relied upon abstract concepts embodied in such material marks to convey their specific historical, philosophical, political, and aesthetic ideas."

Jennifer DeVere Brody, *Punctuation: Art, Politics, and Play* (Durham, NC: Duke University Press, 2008), 65.

82 Josephine Withers, "Feminist Performance Art: Performing, Discovering, Transforming Ourselves," in Norma Broude and Mary D. Garrard, eds., *The Power of Feminist Art: The American Movement of the 1970s, History and Impact* (New York: Harry N. Abrams, 1994), 160, 158, 160.

83 Cervenak, "Against Traffic," 121.

84 Piper, "Talking to Myself," 53.

85 Ibid., 47.

86 Piper, "Preparatory Notes for *The Mythic Being*," 100–1.

87 Ibid., 101–103.

88 Ibid., 112.

89 Karen Tongson, *Relocations: Queer Suburban Imaginaries* (New York: New York University Press, 2011), 180.

90 Piper, "Preparatory Notes for *The Mythic Being*," 103, 104.

91 Ibid., 103–4.

92 Paul Schimmel, "Leap into the Void: Performance and the Object," in Paul Schimmel, ed., *Out of Actions: Between Performance and the Object, 1949–1979* (New York: Thames & Hudson; Los Angeles: Museum of Contemporary Art, 1998), 17.

93 Mel Y. Chen, *Animacies: Biopolitics, Racial Mattering, and Queer Affect* (Durham, NC: Duke University Press), 11.

94 Bowles, *Adrian Piper*, 243.

95 Ibid., 124.

96 Ibid., 118.

97 Piper, "Preparatory Notes for *The Mythic Being*," 104.

98 Ibid., 108, 109.

99 Ibid., 109; Piper, "Notes on the Mythic Being I–III," 117.

100 Piper, "Notes on the Mythic Being I–III," 118.

101 Piper, "Preparatory Notes for *The Mythic Being*," 114; italics in original.

102 Alexander G. Weheliye, *Habeas Viscus: Racializing Assemblages, Biopolitics, and Black Feminist Theorizations of the Human* (Durham, NC: Duke University Press, 2014), 15.

103 Piper, "Preparatory Notes for *The Mythic Being*," 117.

104 Piper, "Talking to Myself," 52.

105 Smith, "Re-member the Audience," 54; Piper, "Notes on the Mythic Being I–III," 122.

106 Piper, "Preparatory Notes for *The Mythic Being*," 112.

107 Smith, *Enacting Others*, 70.

108 Anne Rorimer, "Reconfiguring Representation: Mechanical Reproduction and The Human Figure in Conceptual Art," in Matthew S. Witkovsky, ed., *Light Years: Conceptual Art and the Photograph, 1964–1977* (Chicago: Art Institute of Chicago, 2011), 208; Paul Schimmel, "Preface and Acknowledgements," in *Robert Rauschenberg: Combines* (Los Angeles: Museum of Contemporary Art, 2005),

8–9; Matthew S. Witkovsky, "The Unfixed Photograph," in Witkovsky, ed., *Light Years*, 16.

109 Abigail Solomon-Godeau, "The Woman Who Never Was: Self-Representation, Photography, and First-Wave Feminist Art," in Butler and Mark, eds., *WACK! Art and the Feminist Revolution*, 338.

110 Rorimer, "Reconfiguring Representation," 209.

111 Peggy Phelan, "The Returns of Touch: Feminist Performances, 1960–80," in Butler and Mark, eds., *WACK! Art and the Feminist Revolution*, 354.

112 Rorimer, "Reconfiguring Representation," 210; Gabriele Schor, "Cindy Sherman: The Early Years in Buffalo," in Gabriele Schor, ed., *Cindy Sherman: The Early Works 1975–1977* (New York: Hatje Cantz, 2012), 35.

113 Piper, "Notes on the Mythic Being I–III," 123, 124, 125, 137.

114 Ibid., 137-38.

115 Piper, "Talking to Myself," 43.

116 Cervenak, "Against Traffic," 118.

117 Ibid., 119.

118 Piper, "Flying," 228.

119 Piper, "Talking to Myself" 45; Piper, "Notes on the Mythic Being I–III," 138.

120 Piper, "Xenophobia and the Indexical Present II," 263, 264.

121 Smith, *Enacting Others*, 51.

122 Kobena Mercer, "Adrian Piper, 1970–1975: Exiled on Main Street," in Kobena Mercer, ed., *Exiles, Diasporas, and Strangers* (Cambridge, MA: MIT Press; London: Institute of International Visual Arts, 2008), 155.

123 Bowles, *Adrian Piper*, 235.

124 Piper, "The Mythic Being: Getting Back," 147; Piper, "Xenophobia and the Indexical Present II," 263.

125 Mercer, "Decentering and Recentering," 53.

126 Cherise Smith, "Re-member the Audience," 50; Smith, *Enacting Others*, 48.

127 Michael Omi and Howard Winant, *Racial Formation in the United States: From the 1960s to the 1990s*, second ed. (New York: Routledge, 1994), 13, 60.

128 Sara Ahmed, *Queer Phenomenology: Orientations, Objects, Others* (Durham, NC: Duke University Press, 2006), 111.

129 Mercer, "Decentering and Recentering," 52.

130 Piper, "Xenophobia and the Indexical Present II," 266.

131 Smith, *Enacting Others*, 97.

132 Piper, "Notes on the Mythic Being I–III," 124.

133 Ibid., 123.

134 Piper, "Xenophobia and the Indexical Present II," 267. Piper, John P. Bowles emphasizes, borrows from her critique of Kant's concept of the categorical imperative that she explored in her *Food for the Spirit* series. Piper's use of Kantian ethics—and their concomitant emphasis on individual responsibility—was designed, in part, to prompt audiences to take responsibility not only for their racism, but also for their role in creating the Mythic Being himself. This artistic

strategy was a risky one; confronting viewers with that responsibility could lead to violence. See Bowles, *Adrian Piper*, 208, 227, 11.

135 José Esteban Muñoz, *Disidentifications: Queers of Color and the Performance of Politics* (Minneapolis: University of Minnesota Press, 1999), 108; Bertolt Brecht, "Alienation Effects in Chinese Acting," in John Willett, ed., *Brecht on Theatre: The Development of an Aesthetic* (New York: Hill and Wang, 1964), 92; emphasis added.

136 Muñoz, *Disidentifications*, 100, 102, 100, 102.

137 Susan Sontag, *On Photography* (New York: Picador, 1973), 3.

138 Adrian Piper, "Goodbye to Easy Listening," in *Out of Order, Out of Sight*, Vol. 2, 177; Piper, "Xenophobia and the Indexical Present II," 255–56.

139 Michael Omi and Howard Winant, *Racial Formation in the United States: From the 1960s to the 1980s* (1986; New York: Routledge, 1990), 66.

140 Adrian Piper, "Xenophobia and the Indexical Present I: Essay," in *Out of Order, Out of Sight*, Vol. 1, 249.

141 Moten, *In the Break*, 249.

142 Bowles, *Adrian Piper*, 198, 196–97.

143 Adrian Piper, "Performance and the Fetishism of the Art Object," 51.

144 Piper, "Notes on the Mythic Being I–III," 125.

145 Bowles, *Adrian Piper*, 233.

146 Peggy Phelan, "Survey," in Helena Rickett, ed., *Art and Feminism* (2001; New York: Phaidon, 2012), 29.

147 Brooks, *Bodies in Dissent*, 5, 6.

148 Peggy Phelan, *Unmarked: The Politics of Performance* (New York: Routledge, 1993), 35.

149 See Henry Louis Gates, "The Trope of the Talking Book," in *The Signifying Monkey: A Theory of Afro-American Literary Criticism* (New York: Oxford University Press, 1988), 127–69.

150 Piper, "The Mythic Being: Getting Back," 147.

151 Phelan, "Survey," 29.

152 At the time of this writing, an eight-minute clip of the film continues to stream over Adrian Piper's website. See http://www.adrianpiper.com/vs/video_tmb.shtml (accessed September 5, 2012).

153 The full quote is as follows: "The intention here is to resist reductive conclusions about blackness: what it is or what it ain't. What is clear is that it exists and has shaped and been shaped by experiences. The artists in this exhibition have defied the 'shadow' of marginalization and have challenged both the establishment and at times their own communities."

154 Kevin Johnson, "Riffs on Race, Role, and Identity," *New York Times*, September 20, 2013, C29.

155 Debra Lennard, "The Radical Boundaries of African-American Performance," *Hyperallergic*, http://hyperallergic.com/95314/the-radical-boundaries-of-african-american-performance (accessed July 18, 2014).

CHAPTER 4. IS THIS PERFORMANCE ABOUT YOU?

1 Leslie King-Hammond and Lowery Stokes Sims, "Reflections on *Art as a Verb*: Twenty Years Later, in the New Millennium, Interview with Maren Hassinger, Senga Nengudi, and Howardena Pindell," in Andrea Barnwell Brownlee and Valerie Cassel Oliver, eds., *Cinema Remixed and Reloaded: Black Women Artists and the Moving Image since 1970* (Atlanta: Spelman College Museum of Fine Art; Houston: Contemporary Arts Museum Houston, 2008), 16.

2 Howardena Pindell, "Free, White, and 21," in *The Heart of the Question: The Writings and Paintings of Howardena Pindell* (New York: Midmarch Arts Press, 1997), 65, 65–66. In 1979, after Pindell quit her job at the Museum of Modern Art and was several months into her new job as a professor at SUNY Stony Brook, she was in a car accident with Donald Kuspit (her department chair) and two colleagues that left her with temporary amnesia. Eight months later, she made *Free, White, and 21*.

3 *Dialectics of Isolation* was exhibited at the A.I.R. Gallery, September 2–20, 1980. According to Kat Griefen, the director of the A.I.R. Gallery since 2006, artists Zarina designed the catalogue, Kazuko Miyamoto handled other aspects of the exhibition, and Mendieta wrote the introductory essay. In the latter, Mendieta described her own ambivalence to "A.I.R. itself—an organization that could be a vehicle for this radical exhibition, but also a group that was not as politically motivated or diverse as she would have liked." See Kat Griefen, "Ana Mendieta at A.I.R. Gallery, 1977–1982," *Women and Performance: A Journal of Feminist Theory* 21, no. 2 (July 2011): 175. The show also featured Senga Nengudi, Selena Whitefeather, Janet Henry, Judy Baca, and others. See Judith K. Brodsky, "Exhibitions, Galleries, and Alternative Spaces," in Norma Broude and Mary D. Garrard, eds., *The Power of Feminist Art: The American Movement of the 1970s, History, and Impact* (New York: Harry N. Abrams, Inc., 1994), 118. The following year, on February 26, 1981, *Free, White, and 21* was shown at Franklin Furnace, an avant-garde venue founded by performance artist Martha Wilson. See handwritten postmarked postcard, n.d., "Howardena Pindell" file, James Hatch-Camille Billops Collection, New York City (hereafter cited as HBC).

4 Griefen, "Ana Mendieta at A.I.R. Gallery," 171.

5 Kellie Jones, "To the Max: Energy and Experimentation," in Kellie Jones, ed., *Energy/Experimentation: Black Artists and Abstraction, 1964–1980* (New York: The Studio Museum of Harlem, 2006), 27.

6 Peggy Phelan, "Survey," in Helena Rickett, ed. *Art and Feminism* (2001; New York: Phaidon, 2012), 28.

7 Pindell, "Free, White, and 21," 66–7; Howardena Pindell, "An American Black Woman Artist in a Japanese Garden," in *The Heart of the Question*, 61.

8 These words are taken from the webpage for the exhibition; it was shown at the Geffen Contemporary at the Museum of Contemporary Art (MOCA) in Los Angeles, March 4–July 16, 2007. See www.moca.org/wack (accessed August 12, 2013).

9 The full title of the exhibition was *Art as a Verb—The Evolving Continuum: Installations, Performances, and Videos by 13 Afro-American Artists*. In addition to Piper and Pindell, it included Faith Ringgold, Betye Saar, Lorraine O'Grady, Maren Hassinger, and David Hammons, among others. For more on this exhibition, see King-Hammond and Sims, "Reflections on *Art as a Verb*," 15–21; Howardena Pindell, *Howardena Pindell: Paintings and Drawings* (New York: Roland Gibson Gallery at Potsdam College of the State University of New York, 1992), 22.

10 Cherise Smith, *Enacting Others: Politics of Identity in Eleanor Antin, Nikki S. Lee, Adrian Piper, and Anna Deavere Smith* (Durham, NC: Duke University Press, 2011), 12.

11 I thank one of the anonymous readers for New York University Press for prodding me to think more about this.

12 Piper, for instance, wrote a letter to Pindell dated August 7, 1989, when her essay "Open Letter from Adrian Piper" was omitted from the catalogue for the exhibition *Art of Conscience: The Last Decade*, curated by Donald Kuspit, coincidentally responsible for Pindell's earlier hire at SUNY. See Howardena Pindell, "Covenant of Silence: De Facto Censorship in the Visual Arts," in *The Heart of the Question*, 40. Infamously, two years earlier, Piper had lengthily responded to a similar omission by Kuspit from another exhibition. For a reprinting of the letter, see Adrian Piper, "An Open Letter to Donald Kuspit," in her *Out of Order, Out of Sight*, Vol. 2: *Selected Writings in Art Criticism, 1967–1992* (Cambridge, MA: MIT Press, 1996), 107–25. Also in 1989, both women's work was censored from the *Art as a Verb* exhibition (Piper's for using body fluids, Pindell's for political content), along with David Hammons's *How Do You Like Me Now?* and Joyce Scott's *Birthing Chair*. Pindell referenced both incidents in a later essay, writing that "Piper's words, as well as her bodily fluids in 'Art as a Verb,' were seen as a threat and were ripe for omission." See Pindell, "Covenant of Silence," 40. Conversely, Piper cited Pindell's controversial article "Art World Racism" in her 1990 article "The Triple Negation of Colored Women Artists," reprinted in Piper, *Out of Order, Out of Sight*, Vol. 2, 161–73. Finally, Pindell is one of the artists featured in Piper's *Colored Pictures*, a collaborative book project that is now out of print.

13 Artists Dan Flavin, Robert Ryman, and Robert Mangold were also employed at MoMA, mostly as guards. See Jones, "To the Max," 15.

14 In an interview conducted in 1972, Pindell stated she met Lippard in August or September of 1967. See "Howardena Pindell," Paul Cummings interview, July 10, 1972, Howardena Pindell Papers, Archives of American Art, Smithsonian Institution, Washington, DC.

15 "Abstraction or Essence," panel discussion (Maren Hassinger, Howardena Pindell, and William T. Williams), Museum of Modern Art, New York, June 17, 1997. Tape recording. Howardena Pindell Papers, Museum of Modern Art Archives, New York.

16 Thelma Golden, "My Brother," in Thelma Golden, ed., *Black Male: Representations of Masculinity in Contemporary American Art* (New York: Whitney Museum of American Art and Harry N. Abrams, 1994), 20.

17 Specifically, according to marginalia, BECC's demands for the Whitney were "a) black artists represented in the Whitney Annual, b) one-man shows for black artists, and c) "a 'quality' exhibition of black art in prime time." As noted, the results were the following: "Results: 1. The annual included 11 black artists in 1969, 2. The black show—Contemporary Black Artists in America—took place (1971); protested by BECC because no use of blacks on a curatorial level." Handwritten notes, n.d., "Howardena Pindell" file, HBC.

18 Quoted in Julie Ault, *Alternative Art New York, 1965–1985* (Minneapolis: University of Minnesota Press, 2002), 20; John Bowles, *Adrian Piper: Race, Gender, and Embodiment* (Durham, NC: Duke University Press, 2011), 114. BECC became a formal organization in late 1968—spearheaded by the efforts of cochair Benny Andrews (meetings were held in his studio) and Romare Bearden—in response to the Metropolitan Museum of Art's forthcoming exhibition *Harlem on My Mind* (1969). Its Art in Prison program, began in 1971, was operating thirty-seven programs for prisoners in fourteen states by 1980.

19 Kellie Jones, "Its Not Enough to Say 'Black is Beautiful': Abstraction at the Whitney 1969–1974," in her *EyeMinded: Living and Writing Contemporary Art* (Durham, NC: Duke University Press, 2011), 401. The exhibitions at the Whitney were as follows:
    Alvin Loving: Paintings, December 19, 1969–January 25, 1970
    Melvin Edwards: Works, March 2–29, 1970
    Fred Eversley: Recent Sculpture, May 18–June 7, 1970
    Marvin Harden, January 5–February 4, 1971
    Malcolm Bailey, March 16–April 25, 1971
    Contemporary Black Artists in America, April 6–May 16, 1971
    Frank Bowling, November 4–December 6, 1971
    Alma W. Thomas, April 25–May 28, 1972
    Jacob Lawrence, May 16–July 7,1974
    Jack Whitten, August 20–September 22, 1974
    Betye Saar, March 20–April 20, 1975
    Minnie Evans, July 3–August 3, 1975
       The lackluster curatorial efforts of the *Contemporary Black Artists in America* show, as Jones discusses, resulted in not only in an alternative show—*Rebuttal to the Whitney Museum*, staged at the black-owned Acts of Art Gallery in the West Village—but also in the withdrawal of many artists, several of whom signed a letter printed in *Artforum* (May 1971) critiquing the premises under which their work was shown. The letter's rebuke of the tokenism these artists faced was later echoed in Pindell's repeated references to tokenism in *Free, White, and 21* as well as her subsequent work with PESTS.

20 Dorothy C. Miller Papers, III.25. Museum of Modern Art Archives, New York. Hereafter cited as DCM, MoMA Archives, NY. See also Robert Windeler, "Modern Museum Protest Target," *New York Times*, March 31, 1969. Artist Tom Lloyd also wrote a letter to Bates Lowry on April 3, 1969, telling him that he and

two hundred black and Puerto Rican youth would be conducting a walking tour of MoMA on April 13 to evaluate its holdings, in an effort to make the museum responsible for the black and brown communities it served. See "Gist of April 3, 1969 letter from Tom Lloyd to Mr. Lowry," DCM III.25, MoMA Archives, NY.

21 "Manifesto for the Guerrilla Art Action Group," John B. Hightower Papers, III.1.11.b. Museum of Modern Art Archives, New York. Hereafter cited as JBH, MoMA Archives, NY.

22 "Abstraction or Essence," panel discussion, tape recording.

23 Jones, "To the Max," 15.

24 JBH, I.6.38. MoMA Archives, NY.

25 JBH, III.1.7. MoMA Archives, NY.

26 Valerie Smith, "Abundant Evidence: Black Women Artists of the 1960s and 1970s," in Cornelia Butler and Lisa Gabrielle Mark, eds., WACK! Art and the Feminist Revolution (Los Angeles: Museum of Contemporary Art; Cambridge, MA: MIT Press, 2007), 402–3.

27 Sally Banes, Greenwich Village 1963: Avant-Garde Performance and the Effervescent Body (Durham, NC: Duke University Press, 1993), 39.

28 Ibid., 106, 36.

29 Ibid., 111.

30 Pindell, Howardena Pindell: Paintings and Drawings, 13.

31 Kellie Jones, "Howardena Pindell," in James V. Hatch and Leo Hamalian, eds., Artist and Influence 1990, Vol. 9 (New York: Hatch-Billops Collection, 1990), 119.

32 "Abstraction or Essence," panel discussion, tape recording.

33 Jones, "To the Max," 20–21.

34 Kobena Mercer, "Tropes of the Grotesque in the Black Avant-Garde," in Kobena Mercer, ed., Pop Art and Vernacular Cultures (Cambridge, MA: MIT Press, 2007), 152.

35 Jones, "Howardena Pindell," 118.

36 AfriCobra stands for African Commune of Bad Relevant Artists. See Kellie Jones, "Black West: Thoughts on Art in Los Angeles," in EyeMinded, 428–30.

37 Jones, "To the Max," 15. The debate between abstraction versus figuration/realism was a historical one that was not strictly located in the black art world, spurred by art critic Clement Greenberg's touting of abstraction as high art in a 1939 essay in contrast to Marxist critic Walter Benjamin's more democratic move in his 1936 essay "The Work of Art in the Age of Mechanical Reproduction." For more discussion of this debate, see Lisa Farrington, Creating Their Own Image: The History of African-American Women Artists (New York: Oxford University Press, 2005), 117.

38 Hans Bhalla, "Introduction," in The Coordinated Art Program of the Atlanta University Center Present Paintings and Drawings by Howardena Pindell and Vincent Smith (Spelman College, November 7–23, 1971), exhibition materials. Museum of Modern Art Library, New York.

39 Darby English, How to See a Work of Art in Total Darkness (Cambridge: MIT Press, 2007), 7.

40 Lynn F. Miller and Sally S. Swenson, *Lives and Works: Talks with Women Artists* (Metuchen, NJ, and London: Scarecrow Press, 1981), 149–50. In fact, it appears that Pindell herself came up with the name A.I.R, not only to refer to "artist in residence," but as a pun on the Charlotte Brontë heroine Jane Eyre.

41 Martin Beck, "Alternative: Space," in Julie Ault, ed., *Alternative Art New York, 1965–1985* (Minneapolis: University of Minnesota Press, 2002), 257, 267.

42 According to the poster, the year was divided up into three-week blocks starting September 16, 1972; every third Saturday, two artists would begin their show. According to the poster, Pindell and Harmony Hammond's joint show was scheduled for January 3–13. Meanwhile, a group show of ten artists would begin the year, while the other ten would exhibit in a group show at the close of the year. Printed matter. Museum of Modern Art Archives, Long Island City, Queens.

43 Ibid.

44 Email correspondence with Daria Dorosh and A.I.R. Gallery, August 8, 2013. This photograph is in the A.I.R. Gallery Archives, ca. 1972–2008, MSS 184, Fales Library and Special Collections, New York University: box 18, folder 782.

45 Miller and Swenson, *Lives and Works*, 152.

46 Jones, "Howardena Pindell," 120.

47 Jones, "To the Max," 24.

48 Howardena Pindell, "Sticks and Stones," in *The Heart of the Question*, 30–31. "It is interesting," Kellie Jones remarks, "to think about the 'Nigger Drawings' in conjunction with contemporaneous 'investigations' of blackface by white artists, including early photographs by Cindy Sherman, Eleanor Antin's performances as Antinova, a black Russian ballerina, and the Wooster Group's theater piece *Route 1 & 9*." Jones, "To the Max," 34.

49 Pindell, *Howardena Pindell: Paintings and Drawings*, 22.

50 "Abstraction or Essence," panel discussion, tape recording; Pindell, "Free, White, and 21," 65, 66.

51 Jones, "Howardena Pindell," 120–21.

52 King-Hammond and Sims, "Reflections on *Art as a Verb*," 16.

53 Lucy Lippard, *Six Years: The Dematerialization of the Art Object from 1966 to 1972* (Berkeley: University of California Press, 1997); Shannon Jackson, *Social Works: Performing Art, Supporting Publics* (New York: Routledge, 2011), 39.

54 Pindell states in an interview that her mother was forty when she was born. Pindell was born on April 14, 1943, which means her mother was born in either 1902 or 1903. See Jones, "Howardena Pindell," 113.

55 Ann Cvetkovich, *An Archive of Feelings: Trauma, Sexuality, and Lesbian Public Cultures* (Durham, NC: Duke University Press, 2003), 6.

56 Ibid., 3–4.

57 See Elizabeth Alexander, "'Can You Be BLACK and Look at This?': Reading the Rodney King Video(s)," in her *The Black Interior* (New York: Greywolf Press, 2004). The risk of using a trauma framework within this book for understanding *Free, White, and 21* is that, when compared to Joice Heth, the abuses suffered by

Pindell pale in comparison and, hence, can make Pindell sound whiny. In particular, Heth's possible physical abuse at the hands of P. T. Barnum—such as the reported removal of her teeth to make her appear older—is especially gruesome, violent, and disturbing. That said, trauma is a useful rubric here, particularly since the articulation of trauma often finds a suitable partner in performance art. As Ann Cvetkovich notes, "the life stories of performance art are often structured around, if not traumatic experience, moments of intense affect that are transformative or revealing." Cvetkovich, *An Archive of Feelings*, 26. While Cvetkovich is specifically discussing queer subcultures, her insights can be stretched to accommodate Pindell's plaintive utterances and, in fact, offer a crucial vocabulary often missing in analyses of Pindell's underanalyzed work.

58 Jones, "To the Max," 23.

59 King-Hammond and Sims, "Reflections on *Art as a Verb*," 16.

60 Jackson, *Social Works*, 37.

61 Ibid.

62 Smith, *Enacting Others*, 102.

63 Diana Fuss, *Identification Papers* (New York: Routledge, 1995), 152.

64 Smith, *Enacting Others*, 157.

65 Ibid., 97.

66 The film, directed by Larry Buchannan, was based on the true story of a controversial trial in the 1960s of a black man in Dallas accused of raping a white woman. The film's trailer suggested the audience could act as the jury and decide the outcome of the case.

67 Hazel V. Carby, "White Woman Listen! Black Feminism and the Boundaries of Sisterhood," in Houston A. Baker, Manthia Diawara, and Ruth H. Lindeborg, eds., *Black British Cultural Studies: A Reader* (Chicago: University of Chicago Press, 1996), 73–74.

68 Pindell, "Free, White and 21," 65.

69 See Angela Y. Davis, *Women, Race, and Class* (New York: Random House, 1981); bell hooks, *Feminist Theory: From Margin to Center* (Boston: South End Press, 1984); Audre Lorde, *Zami: A New Spelling of My Name* (Berkeley, CA: Crossing Press, 1982); Audre Lorde, *Sister Outsider: Essays and Speeches* (Berkeley, CA: Crossing Press, 1984); Cherríe Moraga and Gloria Anzaldúa, eds., *This Bridge Called My Back: Writings by Radical Women of Color* (Watertown, MA: Peresphone Press, 1981).

70 See Audre Lorde, "Age, Race, Class, and Sex: Women Redefining Difference," in *Sister Outsider*, 114–23.

71 Audre Lorde, "The Uses of Anger: Women Responding to Racism," in *Sister Outsider*, 129. My positioning of Pindell alongside Lorde is also important, in light of the recent proliferation of work on affect, for reminding us how "women of color in the 1980s were also insisting on the theoretical relevance of engaging feeling and emotion." See Juana María Rodríguez, *Sexual Futures, Queer Gestures, and Other Latina Longings* (New York: New York University Press, 2014), 191.

72 Cvetkovich, *An Archive of Feelings*, 16.

73 Jones, "Howardena Pindell," 127.

74 José Esteban Muñoz, *Disidentifications: Queers of Color and the Performance of Politics* (Minneapolis: University of Minnesota Press, 1999), 146.

75 Michael Warner, *Publics and Counterpublics* (New York: Zone Books, 2002), 119; Combahee River Collective, "A Black Feminist Statement," in Patricia Bell Scott, Gloria T. Hull, and Barbara Smith, eds., *All the Women Are White, All the Blacks Are Men, But Some of Us Are Brave: Black Women's Studies* (Old Westbury, NY: Feminist Press, 1982), 13.

76 Cvetkovich, *An Archive of Feelings*, 7.

77 Jackson, *Social Works*, 5.

78 Anne Anlin Cheng, *The Melancholy of Race: Psychoanalysis, Assimilation, and Hidden Grief* (New York: Oxford University Press, 2000), x, xi.

79 Jones, "Howardena Pindell," 121.

80 Stuart Hall, "What Is This 'Black' in Black Popular Culture," in Gina Dent, ed., *Black Popular Culture* (New York: New Press, 1998), 27.

81 Anne Anlin Cheng, *Second Skin: Josephine Baker and the Modern Surface* (Oxford: Oxford University Press, 2011), 11.

82 Howardena Pindell, "The Aesthetics of Texture in African Adornment," in *The Heart of the Question*, 84, 86.

83 Cheng, *Second Skin*, 14.

84 The painting, owned by the Metropolitan Museum of Art, is not on display but viewable through the Met's website. This description of the painting's medium is taken from there. http://metmuseum.org/collections/search-the-collections/482050 (accessed July 26, 2013).

85 Email interview with artist, November 17, 2008.

86 Jackson, *Social Works*, 6.

87 The seven museums were the Brooklyn Museum, Guggenheim Museum, Metropolitan Museum of Art, Museum of Modern Art (MoMA), Whitney Museum, Queens Museum, and Snug Harbor Museum.

88 Julie Ault, "For the Record," in Julie Ault, ed., *Alternative Art New York, 1965–1985* (Minneapolis: University of Minnesota Press, 2002), 5.

89 The lecture was presented at the Agenda for Survival Conference, held June 27–28 at Hunter College, sponsored by the Association of Hispanic Arts. See Howardena Pindell, *Statistics, Testimony, and Supporting Documentation*. New York, photo-copied booklet, 1987. Museum of Modern Art Archives, New York.

90 For more on this incident, see Pindell, "Covenant of Silence," 39.

91 Howardena Pindell, "Art World Racism," in *The Heart of the Question*, 3–28. Unless otherwise noted, all quotations from this essay are from this source.

92 *The Law and Order Show* held exhibitions that were hosted by the Leo Castelli Gallery, Barbara Gladstone Gallery, and John Weber Gallery. The Paula Cooper Gallery hosted the "performance benefit." The ephemera advertising the show notes it was celebrating both the "200th anniversary of the United States

Constitution and the 20th anniversary of the Center for Constitutional Rights."
Print matter. "Howardena Pindell" file, HBC.

93 Transcription of handwritten letter, September 14, 1986. "Howardena Pindell"
file, HBC; Letter correspondence, October 22, 1986. Signed by Lippard and two
other members of Law and Order Organizing Committee. "Howardena
Pindell" file, HBC; Letter correspondence, November 21, 1986. "Howardena
Pindell" file, HBC.

94 Lowery Stokes Sims, "Introduction," in Howardena Pindell, *The Heart of the
Question: The Writings and Paintings of Howardena Pindell* (New York: Midmarch
Arts Press, 1997), vii.

95 Julie Ault, "A Chronology of Selected Alternative Structures, Spaces, Artists'
Groups, Organizations in New York City, 1965–85," in Ault, ed., *Alternative Art
New York*, 74.

96 Coco Fusco, "Passionate Irreverence: The Cultural Politics of Identity," in Brian
Wallis, Marianne Weems, and Phillip Yenawine, eds., *Art Matters: How the
Culture Wars Changed America* (New York: New York University Press, 1999), 68.

97 Jeffrey Tobin, "Girls Behaving Badly," *New Yorker*, May 30, 2005.

98 This ad is published in *New Observations* 70 (September 1989), guest edited by the
Guerrilla Girls. For access to this and other related materials, see Inventory of
Guerrilla Girls Records, 1979–2003, J. Paul Getty Museum, Los Angeles, California.

99 Pindell herself seems to suggest such a sentiment. In her words, "funding sources
that would possibly fund a Guerrilla Girls' action, because of their reputation for
dealing with white women's issues are reluctant to fund a group like PESTS which
deals with race." Pindell, "Sticks and Stones," 31.

100 Oral history interview with Guerrilla Girls Frida Kahlo and Kathe Kollwitz,
January 19–March 9, 2008, Archives of American Art, Smithsonian Institution,
Washington, DC. A transcript of this interview is in the public domain and is
available at http://www.aaa.si.edu/collections/interviews/oral-history-interview-
guerrilla-girls-frida-kahlo-and-kathe-kollwitz-15837#transcript (accessed October
23, 2012).

101 Ault, "For the Record," 3.

102 Pindell and I met informally in New York City, in the fall of 2008, to discuss her
work at the now-closed Balducci's in Chelsea.

103 Gill Saunders, "Street Art: Prints and Precedents," *Art in Print* 1, no. 3
(September–October 2011). See http://artinprint.org/index.php/articles/article/
street_art_prints_and_precedents#fn-ref-222-6 (accessed October 23, 2012).

104 The use of the phrase "art world apartheid" may be partly influenced by the
efforts of Art against Apartheid, a group founded in 1983 as an "independent,
multiracial, and politically diverse coalition of artists and arts organizations
working around the issue of apartheid." Quoted in Ault, "Chronology," 70. Pindell
also used the word "apartheid" to describe her own experience: "I had faced de
facto censorship issues throughout my life as part of the system of apartheid in
the United States." Pindell, "Free, White, and 21," 66.

105 Press release, PESTS. "Howardena Pindell" file, HBC. A copy is also available in Guerrilla Girls Records, 1979–2003, Getty Research Institute, Research Library, Accession no. 2008.M.14: box 7, folder 1.

106 The first issue of the PESTS newsletter is listed as Volume 1, Number 2. It remains unclear if there is (or ever was) a Volume 1, Number 1, and if it was distributed. Only two issues, this one and the next—Volume 1, Number 3 (Fall/Winter 1987)—are to be found in the archival records of the Getty and Pindell's file at the Hatch-Billops Collection. The seven-page newsletter also included a one-page addendum of four additional exhibitions. One can assume that, if the newsletter had already gone to print, Pindell added a Xerox of the addendum to each copy of the newsletter.

107 According to Pindell, one of these posters was hung in SoHo at Broome Street and Broadway, where someone had written on it, "Because you do poor work." Pindell, "Art World Racism," 18.

108 In an enlarged image of this poster I've seen elsewhere, presumably after it was printed and posted, someone had scrawled in "And Girls" next to the phrase "gifted white boys" while someone else (or maybe the same person) wrote "Sexist" underneath the two panels. In addition, three baseball-card-sized images of baseball players, again indexing "gifted white boys" we can assume, were interspersed in the poster.

109 Beck, "Alternative: Space," 267.

110 Ibid.

111 While I use José Esteban Muñoz and Michael Warner's scholarship on public-sphere theory and the possibility of a counterpublic sphere, both acknowledge a debt to the work of Nancy Fraser in thinking about the latter. See her "Rethinking the Public Sphere: A Contribution to a Critique of Actually Existing Democracy," in Craig Calhoun, ed., Habermas and the Public Sphere (Cambridge, MA: MIT Press, 1992), 109–42.

112 Muñoz, Disidentifications, 160, 143.

113 Warner, Publics and Counterpublics, 119, 114.

114 Pindell, "Art World Racism," 23.

115 Brian Wallis, "Public Funding and Alternative Spaces," in Ault, ed., Alternative Art New York, 1965–1985, 165, 167.

116 Margo Natalie Crawford, "Perform/Deform," in Elizabeth Gwinn and Lauren Haynes, eds., Re: Collection: Selected Works from the Studio Museum of Harlem (New York: Studio Museum of Harlem, 2010), 123.

117 Staged at The Kitchen in New York City, McCauley and fellow performer Jeannie Hutchins, a white woman, collaborated in this intense and highly personal performance, one that Pindell herself later credited for helping her "look further at some of the terrifying history of this country." Howardena Pindell, "Water/Ancestors/Middle Passage/Family Ghosts," in The Heart of the Question, 77. In the piece, McCauley attempted—like Pindell—to make sense of her family history, specifically her great-great-grandmother Sally, a slave who

had children by a white slave owner. Early on in the performance, McCauley indexed her own mixed-race ancestry and its ties to Sally's rape, remarking: "Almost everybody in my mother's family was half-white. But that wasn't nothing but some rape. These confessions are like a mourning for the lost connections." The key scene in *Sally's Rape* was also its most controversial. McCauley, stripped naked, stood on an auction block while Hutchins led the predominately white audience in the chant "Bid 'em in! Bid 'em in!" Hutchins attempted, then, to replicate the action by placing herself on the auction block, but stopped short of stripping herself or asking the audience to "bid" on her. Robbie McCauley and Jeannie Hutchins, *Sally's Rape: The Whole Story* (San Francisco: Bay Area Video Coalition, 1991). "The moment," William Sonnega remarks, "required little elaboration: Sally [. . .] had no choice; Hutchins did, and she refused to be degraded." In both the play and especially its post-show dialogues, spectators were asked to "confront, in personal terms" their complicity in (and possible resistance to) the "represented and actual histories" of Sally's rape. William Sonnega, "Beyond a Liberal Audience," in Harry J. Elam Jr. and David Krasner, eds., *African American Performance and Theater History: A Critical Reader* (New York: Oxford University Press, 2001), 93. The staged dialogue that occurred in *Free, White, and 21* is similar to the dialogical impulse in McCauley's post-performance rituals; in both, paralleling Joice Heth and the other fraudulent negresses in chapter 1, black women were staged as key actors in the grand tableaux of American history.

118 Elisa Turner, "Pindell's Bold and Bumpy Global Journey," *Miami Herald*, November 12, 1994, 5G.

119 The trope Cherise Smith describes of "rhetorical personae" is one starting place to understanding the personas we encounter in artists' writings. In her formulation, "rhetorical personae" are literary versions of the shape-shifting artists that are connected to an "artistic ideal" that is distinct from the "assumed persona" adopted during her own performances. And these texts do not simply document performances, but are performative themselves: "I understand their writings to be more than inextricably linked to their performances: their texts *are* performances. These speech-acts enabled the artists to act out and become the personae that they invented for themselves." Smith, *Enacting Others*, 22–23.

120 José Esteban Muñoz, *Cruising Utopia: The Then and There of Queer Futurity* (New York: New York University Press, 2009), 65, 71.

121 Pindell, "Covenant of Silence," 40.

CONCLUSION

1 The particular affective responses Ellen Craft's "white" appearance generated from white Garrisonians, while "no less emotional or physically graphic" than those evoked by other black women, was indicative of the "dynamics of race and sexuality inherent in white abolitionism" while also suggesting how former slaves risked being interpreted as little more than theatrical props for the broader

movement. See James Brewer Stewart, *Holy Warriors: The Abolitionists and American Slavery* (1976; New York: Hill and Wang, 1997), 141.

2 Amber Jamilla Musser, *Sensational Flesh: Race, Power, and Masochism* (New York: New York University Press, 2014), 154.

3 See Hortense J. Spillers, "Mama's Baby, Papa's Maybe: An American Grammar Book," *Diacritics* 17, no. 2 (Summer 1987): 65–81.

4 Alexander G. Weheliye, *Habeas Viscus: Racializing Assemblages, Biopolitics, And Black Feminist Theories of the Human* (Durham, NC: Duke University Press, 2014), 42.

5 Coco Fusco, "Performance and the Power of the Popular," in Catherine Ugwu, ed., *Let's Get It On: The Politics of Black Performance* (London: Institute of Contemporary Arts; Seattle: Bay Press, 1995), 174.

6 Paul Gilroy, "'. . . To Be Real': The Dissident Forms of Black Expressive Culture," in Catherine Ugwu, ed., *Let's Get It On: The Politics of Black Performance* (London: Institute of Contemporary Arts; Seattle: Bay Press, 1995), 15, 15–16.

7 Shannon Jackson, *Social Works: Performing Art, Supporting Publics* (New York: Routledge, 2011), 5. I purposely interpolate Jackson's language here, because both Leigh and Minaj exemplify in different ways the "experimental chiasmus across the arts" she describes in *Social Works*, a cross-disciplinary art practice in which artists continually break the traditions of one medium while welcoming the traditions of another. She uses the idiom of "social practice" to capture this "aesthetic conviviality" and its engagement with the social, whether artists seek to create social bonds or, conversely, aim to disrupt them. The end product, she notes, is a persistent challenge to the bounded integrity of the art object. Here, I ask us to consider Leigh and Minaj's artistic projects in a similar aesthetic register, the former a sculptor/visual artist collaborating with an opera singer to reimagine the theatrical event and Minaj, a rapper/pop star trained as an actress, deploying an often hyperfeminine brand of artifice and theatricality in a male-dominated genre—hip-hop—especially resistant to it.

8 Nicole R. Fleetwood, *Troubling Vision: Performance, Visuality, and Blackness* (Chicago: University of Chicago Press, 2011), 126.

9 Lisa Nakamura, *Digitizing Race: Visual Cultures of the Internet* (Minneapolis: University of Minnesota Press, 2008), 1–2, 29. Nakamura identifies 1995 as a turning point, since this is when Netscape Navigator, the first popular graphical Web browser, was launched, initiating wider public use of the Internet or what she calls "the massification of the Internet as a media and communicative form." This shift, she notes, has also led Internet usage away from the mostly white and male digital cognoscenti of the Internet's early days (and its reiteration in magazines like *Wired*) to a more spatialized distribution.

10 This is the fundamental point of B. Coleman's *Hello Avatar*, which proposes that the collapse between the real and virtual, a symptom of the generational shift toward intensified media stimulation, has resulted in us longer making judgments between the two. She coins "x-reality" to describe the constant slippage of exchanges across real and virtual spaces, and to more fully capture the

contemporary condition of hypermediation than such dated terms as "cyber-space" and "virtual reality." See B. Coleman, *Hello Avatar: Rise of the Networked Generation* (Cambridge, MA: MIT Press, 2011). Shaka McGlotten, meanwhile, traces how this hypermediation affects queer intimacies, especially the sociality of gay men, in the "range of contacts and encounters, from the ephemeral to the enduring, made possible by digital and networked means." See his *Virtual Intimacies: Media, Affect, and Queer Sociality* (Albany: SUNY Press, 2013), 7.

11 Nakamura, *Digitizing Race*, 14.

12 Coleman, *Hello Avatar*, 30.

13 Brent Staples, "Nicki Minaj Crashes Hip-Hop's Boys Club," *New York Times*, October 26, 2010. See http://www.nytimes.com/2012/07/08/opinion/sunday/nicki-minaj-crashes-hip-hops-boys-club.html?_r=1& (accessed August 7, 2014).

14 Kevin McGarry, "The New Queen Bee: Meet Nicki Minaj," *New York Times*, June 4, 2009. See http://tmagazine.blogs.nytimes.com/2009/06/04/the-new-queen-bee-meet-nicki-minaj/ (accessed November 4, 2012).

15 The former record is for her solo single "Anaconda" (number 1) and her collabo-ration "Bang Bang," with Ariana Grande and Jessie J (number 2); the latter record is for "Anaconda."

16 RoseLee Goldberg, "Public Performance: Private Memory," *Studio International* (July/August 1976), 19. Quoted in Jay Sanders, "Love Is an Object," in Jay Sanders and J. Hoberman, *Rituals of Rented Island: Object Theater, Loft Performance, and the New Psychodrama—Manhattan, 1970–1980* (New York: Whitney Museum of American Art; New Haven, CT: Yale University Press, 2013), 35.

17 For more on the use of artifice, and particularly black camp, in Minaj's perfor-mances, see Uri McMillan, "Nicki-Aesthetics: The Camp Performance of Nicki Minaj," *Women and Performance: A Journal of Feminist Theory* 24, no. 1 (March 2014): 79–87.

18 For more discussion of this, see Jennifer C. Nash, *The Black Body in Ecstasy: Reading Race, Reading Pornography* (Durham, NC: Duke University Press, 2014).

19 Kobena Mercer, *Welcome to the Jungle: New Positions in Black Cultural Studies* (New York: Routledge, 1994), 98.

20 Stuart Hall, "What Is This 'Black' in Black Popular Culture?" in David Morley and Kuan-Hsing Chen, eds., *Stuart Hall: Critical Dialogues in Cultural Studies* (New York: Routledge, 1996), 469.

21 Minaj's use of an iconic image of Malcolm X holding a rifle and peering out his window to promote her 2014 single "Lookin' Ass Nigga"—until public outcry forced her to withdraw it—is one particularly egregious choice that raises this question. Even this incident, however, was highly gendered, exposing uneven limits on who is allowed to appropriate historical icons and seamlessly integrate those narratives into standard hip-hop braggadocio (i.e., male rappers)—and who, it appears, is not. I thank Shanté Paradigm Smalls for this insight.

22 See the kerfuffle over the imagery used to promote the 2014 single "Anaconda," with a squatting Minaj posed prominently in a pink thong, looking directly at the viewer.

23 Hall, "What Is This 'Black' in Black Popular Culture?" 474.

24 Anne Anlin Cheng, *The Melancholy of Race: Psychoanalysis, Assimilation, and Hidden Grief* (Oxford: Oxford University Press, 2000), 27.

25 Julianne Escobedo Shepard, "Take Me to Your Leader: Nicki Minaj Is Rap's Queen Bee," *Fader* 66 (February/March 2010), 76.

26 Sianne Ngai, *Our Aesthetic Categories: Zany, Cute, Interesting* (Cambridge, MA: Harvard University Press, 2012), 184.

27 This is an example of what L. H. Stallings calls the "black ratchet imagination." See her "Hip Hop and the Black Ratchet Imagination," *Palimpsest: A Journal on Women, Gender, and the Black International* 2 (2014): 135–39.

28 Fred Moten, *In the Break: The Aesthetics of the Black Radical Tradition* (Minneapolis: University of Minnesota Press, 2003), 201.

29 Adrian Piper, "Some Reflective Surfaces," in her *Out of Order, Out of Sight*, Vol. 1: *Selected Writings in Meta-Art, 1968–1992* (Cambridge, MA: MIT Press, 1996), 154.

30 Brian Currid, "'We Are Family': House Music and Queer Performativity," in Sue-Ellen Case, Phillip Brett, and Susan Leigh Foster, eds., *Cruising the Performative: Interventions into the Representation of Ethnicity, Nationality, and Sexuality* (Bloomington: Indiana University Press, 1995), 179.

31 Kobena Mercer, "Tropes of the Grotesque in the Black Avant-Garde," in Kobena Mercer, ed., *Pop Art and Vernacular Cultures* (Cambridge, MA: MIT Press, 2007), 137, 138.

32 Leonard Cassuto, *The Inhuman Race: The Racial Grotesque in American Literature and Culture* (New York: Columbia University Press, 1996), 11.

33 See Weheliye, *Habeas Viscus*.

34 Aimé Césaire, *Discourse on Colonialism* (1955; New York: Monthly Review Press, 2000), 42.

35 Charles D. Martin, *The White African American Body: A Cultural and Literary Exploration* (New Brunswick, NJ: Rutgers University Press, 2002), 59.

36 See Joanne Martell, *Millie-Christine: Fearfully and Wonderfully Made* (Winston-Salem, NC: John F. Blair, 2000).

37 According to a video (made prior to the release of Minaj's first album) posted online on Wiki Minaj, the "Nicki Minaj Encyclopedia," "Harajuku Barbie" is a merging of two aesthetics that Minaj felt fit her personality. The persona was originally inspired by the visual style of young women in Tokyo's Harajuku district. In Minaj's words, "the way they dress is the way I am on the inside: like free-spirited, girls just want to have fun, kick-ass, like, you know, pop, rock-n-roll, whatever the fuck you want to do, hip-hop, um . . . that's how I feel." She decided to blend that style with Barbie, because "all girls are Barbies, we all want to play dress up, we all want to put on lipstick, and be cute and sexy." Female fans quickly adopted the style and nicknamed themselves "Harajuku Babiez," which eventually led to the current appellation, "Barbz." Wiki Minaj, moreover, distinguishes "Harajuku Barbie," an aesthetic style, from "The Harajuku Barbie," the avatar inspired by this style who "accentuates the qualities of an imaginative, fun,

coquettish girly-girl fashonista, that loves all things pink" and occasionally appears in the midst of Nicki Minaj's guest verses. Wiki Minaj is accessible at http://nickiminaj.wikia.com/wiki/Wiki_Minaj (accessed September 30, 2014).

Curiously, a separate wiki lists eleven steps on how to become a "Harajuku Black Barbie," including to "wear a lot of pink," to "be really cute and kind," and to "use a hot comb for your hair if you are keeping it natural. See: http://www. wikihow.com/Be-a-Harajuku-Black-Barbie (accessed September 30, 2014). The style practiced in the Harajuku neighborhood also inspired singer Gwen Stefani's use of four backup dancers (named the Harajuku Girls) for music videos and appearances connected with her 2004 album *Love.Angel.Music.Baby* and her 2005 North American tour, dubbed "The Harajuku Lovers Tour."

38 Michael Fried, "Art and Objecthood," in Gregory Battcock, ed., *Minimal Art: A Critical Anthology* (1968; Berkeley and Los Angeles: University of California Press, 1995), 127.

39 Uri McMillan, "Relics of the Future: The Aesthetic Wanderings of Simone Leigh," in *Evidence of Accumulation,* exhibition catalogue (New York: Studio Museum in Harlem, 2011), 6, 7. The essay can be downloaded from Simone Leigh's website at http://www.simoneleigh.com/index.php?/about/writings/ (accessed September 30, 2014).

40 *New Yorker,* February 27, 2012. The exhibition, *You Don't Know Where Her Mouth Has Been,* was curated by Rashida Bumbray and shown at The Kitchen, January 18–March 11, 2012.

41 A parody of a soap opera, *Mary Hartman, Mary Hartman* aired late at night in syndication for two seasons in 1976 and 1977. The show's titular character (played by Louise Lasser) suffered an infamous meltdown on national television. In the last episode of the first season, Mary Hartman appeared on *The David Susskind Show* as a prototypical American housewife interviewed by a panel of three people, including a feminist, media critic, and consumer advocate. Grilled by this critical trio, Hartman careens between topics (from her thyroid tumors to flight plans) before eventually unraveling in an incredibly touching and difficult-to-watch scene when she unconsciously reveals her husband's impotence. Stuttering in disbelief, Hartman's painful self-awareness is evident as she asks, "Please strike that . . . please don't look" and, making a wiping notion with her hand, "Erase." In an excellent essay, Claire Barliant historically locates *Mary Hartman, Mary Hartman,* describing it as symptomatic of a culture of 1970s breakdowns brought on by mass media and surveillance—it debuted three years after the Watergate hearings (and Richard Nixon's own eventual breakdown)—and the derailment of the Loud family on the first reality television show, *An American Family.* Decidedly of its time, Barliant argues, *Mary Hartman, Mary Hartman* captured a paranoid "awareness of the self as Audience" and a "target of advertising campaigns," while the characters' striking resemblance to real people helped lend the show a "surprising sincerity" and reinforced "its oddness." Fragile and volatile Mary Hartman, and her televisual decline, echoes loudly in the sonic descent

perceivable in *Breakdown*. In fact, Leigh acknowledges that Barliant's article, and its recuperation of *Mary Hartman, Mary Hartman*, partly inspired *Breakdown*. Telephone conversation with the artist, December 1, 2012. See Claire Barliant, "From a Waxy Buildup to a Nervous Breakdown: The Fleeting Existence of Mary Hartman, Mary Hartman," *East of Borneo*, http://www.eastofborneo.org/articles/from-a-waxy-yellow-buildup-to-a-nervous-breakdown-the-fleeting-existence-of-mary-hartman-mary-hartman (accessed November 28, 2012).

42 Jennifer Doyle, *Hold It Against Me: Difficulty and Emotion in Contemporary Art* (Durham, NC: Duke University Press, 2013), xi, xii.

43 "Ancient to Future: Sharifa Rhodes-Pitts and Simone Leigh," a conversation with Claire Barliant, New York Public Library, March 6, 2012.

44 José Esteban Muñoz, *Cruising Utopia: The Then and There of Queer Futurity* (New York: New York University Press, 2009), 178.

45 Ibid., 174.

46 I use this phrase purposely: Leigh noted that *Breakdown* was inspired by an "archive of hysteria" that includes motley sources such as the off-the-rails single mother in Belgian filmmaker Chantal Akerman's *Jeanne Dielman, 23 quai du Commerce, 1080 Bruxelles* (1975) and the television programs *Hoarders* and *Intervention*. Qtd. at Ancient to Future, New York Public Library.

47 Jayna Brown, *Babylon Girls: Black Women Performers and the Shaping of the Modern* (Durham, NC: Duke University Press, 2008), 39. Brown's scholarship is helpful in this discussion in thinking though black performances that seem to lack order due to their "contradictory, clashing elements" (39). She urges us to see these eccentric acts as a "skilled response in the guise of effortless spontaneity," emblematic of how perceptions of social alienation and dislocation by black performers living abroad were expressed through "the kinetic vocabularies of black dance" (38), and in *Breakdown*'s reincarnation, through the bravura trills of Alicia Hall Moran.

48 This filmic adaptation is also part of the "source material" for *Breakdown*.

49 In context, the line reads as: "If Bessie Smith had killed some white people, she wouldn't have needed that music. She could have talked very straight and plain about the world. No metaphors. No grunts. No wiggles in the darkness of her soul. Just straight two and two are four. Power. Luxury. Like that. All of them. Crazy niggers turning their backs on sanity. When all it needs is that simple act. Murder. Just murder! Would make us all sane." LeRoi Jones, *The Dutchman and The Slave: Two Plays* (1964; New York: Harper-Perennial, 2001), 35.

50 She refuses to reveal her real name, to emphasize how "Narcissister is separate from me," while allowing "Narcissister to claim who she is on her own terms." See Tim Murphy, "The Mannequin Also Speaks," *New York Times*, January 16, 2013, E5. Available at http://www.nytimes.com/2013/01/17/fashion/the-mannequin-also-speaks-up-close-with-narcissister.html?_r=0 (accessed August 17, 2013). According to curator Bradford Nordeen, she first developed the character in an ongoing residence at The Box, a Lower East Side performance burlesque, where

she still occasionally performs. See *Check Your Vernacular*, exhibition catalogue (New York: Dirty Looks NYC, 2014), 24. Nordeen positions her within a genealogy of experimental queer performance art and moving image media with a downtown New York sensibility that includes artists such as Jibz Cameron, Colin Self, and Chris E. Vargas.

51 See her collaborative film with A. L. Steiner, *Winter/Spring Collection*, which is viewable at http://anotherrighteoustransfer.wordpress.com/2013/05/12/adrienne-walser-reviews-winterspring-collection-a-collaborative-video-work-by-narcissister-and-a-l-steiner/ (accessed August 17, 2013).

52 Cesar Garcia, "Eroticized Corporealities," in *Fore*, exhibition catalog (New York: Studio Museum of Harlem, 2012), 70.

53 Biographical description taken from Johnson's Diaspora Hypertext, the Blog: History, Media, and Digital Humanities from an Afro-Atlantic Perspective, which is part of the Codex, a "social media triptych" that also includes two Tumblr accounts: #ADPhD (African Diaspora, Ph.D.) and Dark Matter. See http://diasporahypertext.com/ (accessed September 14, 2014).

54 Kismet Nuñez, "On Alter Egos and Infinite Literacies, Part 2 (An #AntiJemimas Imperative)," unpublished notes.

55 See http://iwannalive.wordpress.com/about-iwannalive-productions/ (accessed August 17, 2013).

56 For an example of this, see the WOC Survival Kit: http://wocsurvivalkit.tumblr.com/ (accessed August 18, 2013).

57 Kismet Nuñez, "On Alter Egos and Infinite Literacies, Part 2 (An #AntiJemimas Imperative)," paper presented at the annual American Studies Association convention, San Juan, Puerto Rico, November 2012.

58 Fiona M. Barnett, "The Brave Side of Digital Humanities," *differences* 25, no. 1 (2014): 70, 71.

59 Nakamura, *Digitizing Race*, 20.

60 Janelle Monáe, *Metropolis: The Chase Suite* (Special Edition) (Bad Boy Records, 2008).

61 Janelle Monáe, "Many Moons" (Bad Boy Records, 2008).

62 A.I.R. Gallery Archives, ca. 1972–2006, MSS 184, Fales Library and Special Collections, New York University, Box 21, Folder 971.

INDEX

abjection: already-abject, 49; black female bodies and, 26, 26–27, 32–33, 46, 49, 170, 210; blackness-as-abjection, 9, 9, 46, 49, 231n20; grotesque aesthetics and, 210; slave narratives and, 42, 76, 231n26; subjecthood and, 9, 170, 231n26, 232n27

actuant, 10–11, 232n31

Adams, Rachel, 44

aesthetic practices: aesthetic exchange, 232n28; antislavery aesthetics, 84–86; DIY aesthetics of, 127; grotesque aesthetics, 16, 20, 202–214, 210; objecthood and, 232n28; social practice and, 269n7; sonic of dissent and, 17–18, 57–62, 209

AfriCobra, 160, 215, 262n36

afro-alienation, 19, 103, 129, 138, 147

afrofuturism, 215, 220, 222, 224

agency: use of term, 231n21; abjection and, 9, 231n20; actuant, 10–11, 232n31; social dominance and, 231n20; sonic of dissent and, 17–18, 57–62, 209

agit-prop, 1–3, 70, 80–81, 227n1

A.I.R. Gallery, 154, 160, 162–166, 172, 225–226, 259n3

Akerman, Chantal, 272n46

Alexander, Elizabeth, 57, 170

alienation, 9, 19, 103, 129, 138, 147

alter-egos/personae, 103, 123, 171, 194, 227n4, 245n29, 268n119

alterity, 7, 12, 17, 44, 103, 205

Andre, Carl, 106, 166

Antin, Elizabeth, 133

Anzaldúa, Gloria, 175

Aretha Franklin Catalysis (Piper), 19, 104, 119–125, 121, 273n47

Art against Apartheid group, 185, 266n104

"Art and Objecthood" (Fried), 9–10

Art as a Verb exhibition (1988), 154, 155, 163, 181, 187, 259n3, 260n9, 260n12

Artists Space, 160, 166–167, 176, 183, 251n30

Art Workers' Coalition, 108, 116, 157–158, 180, 252n36

"Art World Racism" (Pindell), 180–183, 190–191, 194–195, 260n12

audience: afro-alienation and, 19, 103, 129, 138, 147; identification and, 19

autobiographical expression, 6, 97, 153–155, 167–180

avant-garde, the, 6–7, 20, 230n15, 255n69

avatar production: use of term, 11–14, 232n32; agency and, 11, 12, 269n10; avatar-play, 20–21; avatar production, 12–13; cross-racial embodiment and, 19–20; digital media and, 12–13, 269n10; dramatis personae, 91, 103, 171; personae, 103, 123, 171, 194, 227n4, 245n29, 268n119; racial formation and, 19; subterfuge and, 4, 40, 75; temporal ambiguity and, 13–14; temporality and, 13–14

Baartman, Sarah, 25, 27, 235n6

Baer, Jo, 251n33

Bakare-Yusuf, Bibi, 5

Bambara, Toni Cade, 5

Banes, Sally, 121, 158–159, 230n16, 255n69

Barliant, Claire, 272n41

Barnett, Fiona M., 222

Barnum, Phineas T.: abolition narrative and, 40–42; abuse of Heth, 263n57; autobiographies of, 43–44, 53–55; automatons and, 47–57; Bateman Show and, 32–33; blackface and, 240n83; Craft and, 5; finances of, 239n51, 239n55; freak showmanship of, 24, 35–40, 45–46, 58–59, 61–62, 211, 225, 234n1, 237n41m 238n44; "Joice Heth's Grandmother," 17, 30–31, 32, 34; Judy Heath avatar, 54–55, 56; narration vs. performance of history and, 14; racial animatedness and, 17, 49–50, 55–56. *See also* Heth, Joice

Barret, Lindon, 66

Barthes, Roland, 54, 86, 88

Bateman, Josiah, 32–33

Benglis, Lynda, 115, 132

Benjamin, Walter, 262n37

Bennett, Jane, 231n21

Berger, Maurice, 105

Berlant, Lauren, 60

Bernstein, Robin, 27, 42–43, 79

Bhalla, Hans, 160–161

Billops, Camille, 158

black: use of term, 228n7

black artist movements, 115–119, 144, 156–157, 156–167, 160, 254n56

Black Arts Movement, 116–117, 144, 160

Black Emergency Cultural Coalition (BECC), 116, 157, 180, 261nn17–18

Blackett, R.J.M, 67–68, 243n7

blackface minstrelsy, 48–49, 235n8, 240n83, 263n48

black female bodies: abjection and, 26, 27, 32–33, 46, 49; as medical curio, 25–26, 36–39, 57–58, 61, 199; medical experimentation and, 25–26; private as public and, 25–26

black female performance art: use of term, 3–7; alterity and, 7, 12, 17, 44, 103, 205; autobiographical expression and, 6, 97, 153–155, 167–180; as avant-garde, 3–4; as black feminist counterpublics, 19–20, 176, 191–192, 267n111; cross-racial embodiment and, 19–20; historic erasure of, 61, 225–226; white female subjectivity and, 3–5

blackness: abjection and, 9, 231n20; afro-alienation and, 19, 103, 129, 138, 147; artistic/political communities and, 20; performing blackness, 231n20

black performance art: afro-alienation, 19, 103, 129, 138, 147; agency and, 8, 60; histories of, 3–4, 10, 199–202, 206, 229n7; performance studies and, 15–17, 234n50, 234n53; performing blackness, 231n20; risk taking of, 229n7

black women performers: alterity and, 7, 12, 17, 44, 103, 205; artistic/political communities and, 20; elderly black women archetype, 14, 29–34, 238n43, 242n115; failure and, 20–21; objecthood and, 8–10

Bland, Sterling Lecater, Jr., 86–87

Bowles, John P., 105, 106, 107, 114, 115, 118, 257n134

Brody, Jennifer, 83, 247n66, 255n81

Brooks, Daphne A., 19, 61, 62, 85, 91, 103, 146, 244n10

Brown, Bill, 10

Brown, Henry Box, 84, 103, 243n5, 244n10

Brown, Jayna, 217, 272n47, 273n47

Brown, William Wells, 67–68, 69, 80, 81, 83, 84, 102

Bryant, Linda Goode, 227n2

Buchannan, Larry, 263n66

Bullman, Hans, 48

Bumbray, Rashida, 272n40

Butler, Judith, 88, 249n81

Carby, Hazel V., 5, 12, 90, 91, 174–175

Cassuto, Leonard, 210

Cervenak, Sarah Jane, 135

Rogers, David L., 24
Rorimer, Anne, 133
Rose, Peter, 227n2
Roth, Moira, 245n29
Running a Thousand Miles to Freedom
(Craft and Craft), 18, 39, 68, 70–73, 85,
87, 89, 168, 243n1, 246n54, 247n68

Saar, Bettye, 161
Sally's Rape (McCauley), 194, 267n117
Samuels, Ellen, 76, 86–87, 241n102, 248n77
Schneemann, Carolee, 15, 124
Schneider, Rebecca, 63, 89, 249n85
Scott, Darieck, 9
Sedgwick, Eve Kosofsky, 93
self-estrangement, 19, 103, 129, 138, 147
Sherman, Cindy, 133, 182
Simone, Nina, 242n115
Sims, J. Marion, 25, 235n6
Sims, Lowery Stokes, 6, 259n1, 260n9
slavery: antislavery aesthetics, 84–86,
243n7; Fugitive Slave Law, 68, 92,
244n9; idealized sculptures of, 247n66;
objecthood and, 10; passing perfor-
mances, 18, 69–70, 70–75, 245n23;
Sally's Rape (McCauley), 194, 267n117;
slave narratives, 42, 76, 231n26,
242n112. *See also* mammy memory
Slavery in New York (2005 and 2011), 23,
225
Smalls, Shanté Paradigm, 270n21
Smith, Cherise, 101, 105, 123, 132, 136, 138,
172, 173, 194, 267n119
Solomon-Godeau, Abigail, 133
Sonnega, William, 267n117
Sontag, Susan, 139
The Spectator Series (Piper), 19
Spillers, Hortense J., 8–9, 199, 231n23
Stallings, L. H., 271n27
Stefani, Gwen, 272n38
Sterling, Dorothy, 67, 244n9
Studio Museum of Harlem, 115, 150, 155–
156, 181, 183, 201, 220, 229n7

Taylor, Diane, 235n7
temporality, 13–14, 15, 27, 40–44, 78,
235nn8–9, 239n50, 249n85. *See also*
Heth, Joice; mammy memory
Thomson, Rosemarie Garland, 36, 37

Vazquez, Alexandra, 58

WACK! Art and the Feminist Revolution
exhibition (2007), 154, 228n6
Ward, Frazer, 233n48, 254n59
Warhol, Andy, 133
Warner, Michael, 26n7111
Washington, George, 14, 17, 24, 26–28, 34–
35, 39, 46–47, 198, 211, 238n44
Washington, Harriet, 36, 235n6
Weheliye, Alexander G., 199, 210
Weinauer, Ellen M., 86–87
Weiner, Lawrence, 227n2
West, Kanye, 20, 201, 207, 211–212, 213
Wexler, Laura, 29
Whalen, Terence, 43
Wheatley, Phyllis, 84, 247n69
"Where We At" Black Women Artists
(WWA) collective, 116, 158
Whitney Museum of American Art, 114,
157 181, 251n33, 253n50, 254n56, 261n17,
261n19, 265n87
Williams, Carla, 87, 248n74
Williams, Raymond, 27, 235n8,
235nn8–9
Wilson, August, 242n115
Women Artists in Revolution (W.A.R.),
158
Women Art Revolutionaries (WAR), 116
world-making, 21, 192, 234n55

*You Don't Know Where Her Mouth Has
Been* (2012), 272n40
Young, Hershini Bhana, 241n102
Young, Kevin, 69

Zealy, Joseph T., 86, 90, 248n74

ABOUT THE AUTHOR

Uri McMillan is Assistant Professor of English, African American Studies, and Gender Studies at the University of California, Los Angeles.

CPSIA information can be obtained at www.ICGtesting.com
Printed in the USA
BVOW05s0905100116

432065BV00004B/2/P